MISSION ALPHA

The WISE & PASSIONATE YOU

EUGENIA OGANOVA

MISSION ALPHA

The WISE & PASSIONATE YOU

EUGENIA OGANOVA

ZAHIRA, INC.
Las Vegas, Nevada

Library of Congress Cataloging-in-Publication Data

ISBN-13: 978-0-9793817-0-6
ISBN-10: 0-9793817-0-3

Acknowledgments

With enormous gratitude to Adam for not divorcing me, even though for a year I was married to my laptop most nights after work; to my soul-friend Isabelle Lambert without whom this book would not be possible, since most of the material came from our teaching together; to Dasha Petrov for being a stable, loving friend; to Jackie Knight for dealing with my formatting freak outs; to all the energy guides for being there and to my dear grandparents for watching over me.

PROLOGUE
Spirals of Consciousness

PROLOGUE

H ave you felt curious about the Soul, the Universe, balance, evolution and your own place in all of this, but each time you found answers, you realized that in some deep place inside yourself you already knew them? I myself run into this all the time! That is because consciousness is cyclical. Knowledge exists kind of 'by itself'; it is there for anyone to 'tune into' and 'know' all the time, but we remember or forget the knowledge in accordance with the cycles of our consciousness. Our wisdom and passion come from the proper access to the cycling consciousness, leading to fulfillment of the Mission Alpha, or the 'main objective', for human beings. The understanding of the cycles of conscious evolution results in self-empowerment. The last major Fall of Consciousness, about 12,000 years ago, plays an important role in our current development. We are still recovering from forgetting who we are. This whole book is about remembering and 'waking up'.

The Source of all existence is the consciousness that is often referred to as God. (We are talking about the origins of consciousness here, not necessarily the origins of humans.) The Source is not a man, a woman or a being of any sort, but a composite of energies. Originally, contrary to mainstream belief, Source or God was not conscious, not aware of a Self in the same way that It is today. It was only conscious of what we can call a 'dream state', sensing possibilities without a centered Self to experience them consciously. But It became aware of Itself through witnessing the push-pull dynamics of expansion and contraction (like a beating heart of consciousness). These two forces are the main driving mechanisms of the Universe. The Source's awareness traveled outward and inward in continuous motion. This internal movement, which resembles the infinity symbol, caused an origination point to occur, like an intersection in the infinity sign. This continuous movement through the same point again and again created a self-memory, a form of self-awareness, which allowed the Source to explode. This explosion of splitting awareness resulted in the creation of the Universe. Our science refers to this phenomenon as the Big Bang.

You think this is complicated? Just look at the same creation story without linear time! Yes, that's right, no linear time! Linear time is a third-dimensional perception, not a universal one. Universal time is 'spherical', or simultaneous. This means that the Source was not aware and aware all at the same time, and that everything that happened through the explosion, that is, the creation of the Universe, already existed, parallel to the 'dreaming' state of the Source!

How does all of this 'abstract stuff' affect us humans? Through a phenomenon called the Spirals of Consciousness. Everything in the entire Universe is cyclical. Our human perception is often too short-lived to see the larger cycle. Consciousness itself travels on an upward spiral, which is what we call 'waking up', and a downward spiral that is referred to as 'falling asleep'. This is how the Source evolves.

The word 'mission' implies a linear development of events, a goal of sorts, but since universal time is spherical, there cannot be a mission. On the other hand, for us humans down here in density, things have to be put into linear perspective or we cease to understand them. So from the human perspective, yes, Source does have a 'mission': it is self exploration and comprehension, and through moving Its awareness up and down with the Spirals of Its consciousness, It evolves Self.

The downward spiral takes us further into the atomic structure of matter, while the upward spiral brings us into the spiritual structure of the Source. As we descend, we 'fall asleep' or lose memory of Self as the Soul, and the Source, and we begin to blame matter as a causative reason for our pain of separation. Since in 'falling asleep' we lose our perspective on the entire journey, or the 'mission alpha' of our Soul, we see only what is in front of us. The separation from the Source is perceived as pain and the cause of that pain is obscured by a loss of perspective, and so we project the origin of that pain outside of the Self. In the human condition this pain is projected onto matter.

Every time we move on the downward spiral, we become less and less able to hold all of our consciousness. Sound strange? Imagine yourself as a very big house, able to hold an incredible amount of unique furniture and lots of other stuff. Then one day you forget that you have a second floor, now all that is accessible to you is on the first floor. Suddenly at least half of the furniture is left out on the lawn, unable to fit. We human beings are like a large house, but we only remember one small room, and that is where we live, while accumulating furniture in amounts for a whole house. Because of this, more and more of the experiences that we go through we are unable to process completely. We leave this uncompleted energy unintegrated in our system, but it follows us all the way down the downward spiral, until we can find enough courage, curiosity and self-love to look at these unintegrated experiences. These experiences are not following us in revenge or punishment; they do not have identities of their own, but are part of us. Since the energy trapped in them is ours, it has no place to go but into us. Every experience we have has to integrate and become part of our identity at some point.

These unintegrated energies are often referred to as 'karma'. Karma is not some scary thing we 'have to pay back for our sins'. It is simply the lessons which were not learned, like going through college again and again but never bothering to graduate. We become a perpetual student, gathering information, but not applying it to our life due to the absence of completion. The concept of 'paying back karma' (i.e., I harmed you, now you harm me) comes from the degrees of separation from the Source. The further we are, the stronger this misconception, which also shows up in the belief that one has to appease God in order to receive God's blessing.

We all are components of the Source, with the innate memory of the knowledge It has. Continuing the metaphor, we are always a large house, even if we only remember one small room in it. When we are in the fully enlightened state of consciousness, on top of the upward spiral, we know and feel all that is. When we begin the downfall, we lose the memory of the knowledge we had. We do not lose the knowledge itself, just the memory of it. Because we, humans, associate ourselves much closer with matter (hence the downward spiral) we believe that we 'forgot' what we knew, and so we feel diminished by the experience. This causes a lack of safety, which results in the experience of fear that manifests as shame and guilt for having lost the knowledge. The identity (the human's main functioning Self) tends to associate knowledge with safety and when the knowledge disappears, the feeling of safety diminishes. Fear is a consequence of this diminishment, further splitting into shame and guilt in our energy system. The energy of shame is about us feeling bad about who we are ('I am not good enough because I do have the knowledge' or 'I feel so ashamed about being such a little Self!') and guilt energy is about feeling bad about what we did or didn't do ('I didn't do enough and I lost the knowledge' or 'I feel so guilty for not doing more about holding on to the knowledge'). Nevertheless, this was part of the Plan of universal evolution.

As a result of this evolutionary flow, we carry the shame/guilt archetype as a punishment imbedded in the human psyche. This means that we further forget what actually happened and project the feeling of shame or guilt on the circumstances of our life. We feel shameful about not measuring up to our ideals and guilty for not accomplishing more. The shame about 'not being a good mother' or guilt about 'going to the game instead of having dinner with a sick friend' are the split-off projections of the original consciousness of shame and guilt. Shame and guilt are not just concepts. They, as energy distortions, have an actual location in the human energy system. In reference to the physical body they are usually present in the area of the belly; the lower part (corresponding to the second chakra) is where we feel guilt, higher (the third chakra) relates to feeling shame. Both limit our capacity to be free. Lack of freedom further limits our perception, locking us into the narrow view of perpetual self-punishment. It is like being stuck driving in a circular tunnel and yelling in punishment at yourself for being stuck there, as you complete yet another circle. We believe our shame and guilt to be real, which limits our freedom, and which then amplifies shame and guilt more, creating even less freedom.

The feeling of being punished is self-inflicted because of the inability to remember the complete cycle of consciousness. We blame ourselves for the 'wrongness' of 'falling asleep'. The longer we are in the lower consciousness, the more we project this onto our life circumstances, forgetting the origin of the self-punishment. Projections become either 'I hate myself for being fat', 'I am an idiot!' 'I don't deserve anything good', or 'Life will always screw me', 'They used me', 'Of course something bad will happen to my investment, if not the company itself, then the market will crash!' or 'No matter what I do, it is wrong' and more like it.

We are always loved by the Source but as our perception becomes more limited, so does the ability to feel this love. Self-love is always equal to the amount of the love from the Source we are able to feel: it is like a mirror. In other words, if we open our awareness to perception of Self as a part of the Universe, we end up actually opening our crown chakra and the Source energy of unconditional love flows through our system. This energy inside our system is perceived as us loving ourselves.

Self-love is the necessary component for healing the emotions of shame and guilt. During the previous states of 'sleep', in our attempts to connect to God we saw self-love as selfishness. Due to the 'sleep' state, God was perceived to be separate from the Self and value was placed not on the uniqueness and preciousness of each person, but on the image of God in the societal hierarchy structure. Paying attention to the Self, treating the Self with kindness and support was judged as 'bad' to the point that the opposite became judged as 'good'. This is how self-punishment became glorified. We, humans, drew negative pleasure from squishing our Selves with unimaginably cruel rules; denying Self the love of the Source became a 'good thing'.

Seeing self-love as selfishness works against our evolution, further 'cutting off' our return to full awareness. The 'falling asleep' process is the necessary condition for our comprehension of self-love. Just like with anything, if you never had it, or never lost it, how will you know its value? We all originally feel love, then we perceive the separation and experience of love becomes limited, diminishing further to almost nothing. This is when we 'hit bottom'. Our being cannot exist without love, but it cannot not exist either, so we have to re-learn the value of love, slowly reconnecting ourselves to the Universal 'big picture' and again expanding our experience of self-love. This is how self-love is comprehended through movement on the Spiral of Consciousness.

Right now, in this galaxy on the planet earth, we, humans, have just switched from the downward spiral to an upward one and are beginning to 'wake up'. In this awakening we reframe punishment into an opportunity to integrate the uncompleted experiences. We are returning to the 'big picture', the big family we belong to. Learning to dismantle our erroneous beliefs that we will be rescued from the dreadful existence of third-dimensional physicality by some wonderful beings (or aliens) from an angelic realm, or that we will leave painful duality and return to some faraway utopian balance of 'home', we grow up. Home is right here, right now! It is opening our perception to encompass more of the reality of this Universe. Universal consciousness is our 'family'. What we perceive as reality is a tiny component of the Universal energy/consciousness, on which our intention has focused. In any moment we can shift our intention and focus on something else, changing our perception of the Universe; that is, changing our reality. The further we are in the upward Spiral of Consciousness, the larger amount of energy we can hold in our focus. Discover how big your house really is!

In our life today we can travel on the path of mystery, becoming wizards, magi, sorcerers, witches and shamans of the modern world, and embodying the joy of the Universe we can bring magic into our everyday lives. This magic is not about putting on a witch's cloak or wizard's hat, it is not about dressing up to look the part. That is a human illusion. Magic does not look like a candle and a potion bottle; the magic of life is not about ritual but reality bleeding through the illusion. In the world of magic a middle school teacher becomes today's shaman, a scientist becomes a sorcerer, a business manager a witch, a computer architect becomes a wizard, there are no limitations... The alignment with the Source, the power of our identity, the balance of our energy system and health of our physical body all become enhanced by the expansion of conscious focus. This is the Mission Alpha of every spark of God.

CHAPTER 1

A Human Being as an Energy System

CHAPTER 1

Human Energy Field Anatomy,
Part 1: Levels of the Aura

Interested in experiencing more love and fulfillment in your life? In feeling more excitement and exhilaration flowing through you, guiding and supporting you? If we want this elusive feeling of power, of alignment with the Source, we need to be able to recognize when we are not in alignment and know our own unique ways of restoring it. In other words, we need to know about our energy system. What often happens when we incarnate on Earth in our somewhat asleep state of consciousness is that, instead of growing from the time of birth awareness of the energy system diminishes because of the absence of curiosity and focus. That doesn't mean that we 'lose' our energy field, we still have it and use it, but unconsciously. Imagine purchasing a top-of-the-line sound system for your home. It is the latest technology, plays all types of formats, programs many CDs, can record, rewrite, change, adjust, make sound appropriate to the type of music, connect to everything wirelessly from a home theater DVD player to your computer and an electric piano, et cetera. You place this system in your living room and make sure it looks nice there. You play one CD at a time on it, and take care of the stereo by dusting it regularly. But you never read the manual to even find out what this system is capable of, and you never learn to program it or do anything on it but play one CD at a time. Sound like an inefficient way to use your investment?

We are like this very expensive new stereo system, but we never read our manual and only use one basic option. Yet we dream of being a 'new stereo, capable of anything!', unaware that we already are that stereo. Does a high-tech sound system stop being a high-tech sound system just because we do not use it to its full capacity? Of course not! We look for some grand 'purpose' for our life, some amazing 'magical power', get bored with everyday things, feel insufficient and lost, forgetting that we already have the purpose and the power, the excitement, the worth and direction in our lives. 'Reading the manual' applies to consciously understanding our internal workings, beginning with our energy system and looking into our physical, psychological and spiritual components. In this book we will look at all these pieces of the Self, diving into the mystery of life. Looking at these things leads to purposeful living and satisfaction. Each one of us already has all the 'equipment', we just need to learn to 'read the manual' and use it correctly.

The first page of each person's 'manual' for evolution is the energy system itself. Without the energy system surrounding and interpenetrating us, our physical body would not be able to exist. The energy field is a pathway of consciousness from the Soul to the physical body. The energy field is the cause for the physical body, not an effect of it. What we usually call 'the mind' is the consciousness of the energy field (not to be confused with the intellect, or the physical brain). The human energy field, just like the Universal one, is aware, intelligent and alive. Our emotions, feelings and thoughts are all part of the energy field consciousness. The physical brain, nervous system, blood and other physical systems are the hardware, while the energy field is the software. The levels of the energy field are a system of *interconnected genius*—that is, *unlimited creative power* (the understanding of genius became limited to 'mental ability' as a consequence of the Fall of Consciousness). The genius contained in the human energy field interacts with the Universal energy field (the entire Universe with its higher and lower frequencies).

A human being is a composite of many systems, not just the physical body. The Soul is the genius behind the creation of the form; the energy field is the operating system with all our feelings, emotions, thoughts and beliefs, while the physical body is the anchoring point. The Soul is a spark of God, an individuated component of the Source. Each Soul has a journey, a particular path of learning. All Souls are the same because they come from the Source, and different because each Soul's journey is unique. During its journey the Soul builds its identity by creating forms, structural mini-environments in which it plays. We call these environments of the Soul the lifetimes. The Soul incarnates into a form by first creating an energy system appropriate for this future form. Into the construction of this energy system goes all previously acquired knowledge and all unintegrated experiences (karma), plus the encodement for the particular lesson of the lifetime. And so the Soul's consciousness rides through the energy field into form, anchoring there. Here on Earth we call this anchor a physical body.

Surrounding the physical body is the energy field of consciousness. There are many levels differentiated by frequency of vibration, each responsible for a particular territory of our psyche (interpretation of the Self). These are often called 'subtle energy bodies', and are named the etheric, emotional, mental, astral, truth, and conceptual or higher spiritual bodies. The entire energy field is egg shaped when balanced. The levels are not separate, yet are clearly defined by their vibratory diapason. The human energy field, or aura, has seven levels. They all interpenetrate each other; closer to the area occupied by the physical body they exist all in the same place, farther away from the body each higher level extends a little farther than the other. Universal energy pulsates, like a beating heart, at different rates. The human energy field mimics this pulsation when balanced and aligned with the Source.

The closest level in vibration to the physical body is the **etheric energy level**. It is filled with micro-circuitry and is a bright blue color when charged. It is like a super-complex architectural blueprint not just for the shape of the body and its organs, but for every cell and every component inside it. In this blueprint are many small grids inside large grids, with the energy speeding through some and moving slowly through others. It is not dissimilar to highways with fast-flowing traffic and small roads with lower speed limits (acupuncture meridians, for example, are the 'highways' of the etheric level). Before there is a physical change, there is an etheric change (during spring I can see a tree's etheric level growing on the ends of branches, showing me the future 'plan' for elongating the branches and growing leaves). Etheric level architecture is what holds atomic structure together, binding one atom to another and preventing us from disintegrating into space. The electric and magnetic charge then further enables atomic structure to function, anchoring our physicality. Etheric level architecture is extremely complex, even more so than the physical body. It outlines the internal boundaries of cells, organs and systems with bright cobalt blue lines, but then interpenetrates everything with lighter and darker thin webbing, filling the spaces between the obvious boundaries down to the micro-cellular level. It looks like a blue glow of the physical body—the outer edge of the etheric level extends only about a quarter to two inches from the skin. Imagine yourself swimming underwater through luminous sapphire threads, light and movable, clear and vibrant—that is what it would look like inside the etheric level.

The etheric level represents safety, security, vitality, stability and physical health (autonomic functioning of the body). If this level is strong our physical body has the structural blueprints necessary for health. Any other energy level can affect the etheric one. If we feel stress for long periods of time (this will show up on the other energy levels), we can decrease the flow of energy into the etheric level, making it change its potency, which shows up as a much lighter, diluted blue. This in turn will affect the physical body by making you exhausted, as if you ran out of fuel. If we have a particular belief, let's say that we are never supposed to be angry (again this will show up on another energy level), we then suppress the anger any time we feel it, but the energy of anger has to go somewhere, so it accumulates in the area of the liver, even though much farther from the physical organ on the energy levels that hold emotions and feelings. So far this has nothing to do with the body, right? Aren't these feelings we are talking about? But if this situation continues, the etheric level's blueprint for the liver becomes affected, it gets clogged and cannot receive the necessary amounts of energy anymore to 'feed' the liver and becomes washed out in color, which affects the physical liver, making it feel the imbalance. Now the physical liver can get sick because its blueprint is weakened, and it might stop processing toxins or create cancer cells in an attempt to 'fix' the situation. Another example: you think negatively all the time about life, waiting for it to come crashing in on you. This makes you feel unsafe, right? Actually, it is the other way around: you on the mental level decided life is unsafe, and in doing so you cut off your access to the etheric level (this is like self choking). The etheric level (responsible for safety) doesn't receive all of 'you' continuously and becomes weak, as if it is uninhabited. This is what makes us feel unsafe in life, our own non-presence in the etheric level!

But all these situations are reversible if we choose to participate in self correction through conscious awareness and an understanding of how our etheric level works. If, let's say, your liver is having physical challenges and is not healthy, you can increase the flow of energy to the blueprint of the liver on the etheric level and amplify its structural integrity, making the physical liver feel better. This is done through intention; that is, you set up the intention for a stronger etheric template of the liver and over time it will become stronger. (Intention is not the same as 'wishing' or 'wanting' to get better, it is a trust-based connection to a state where 'better' has already happened; you are building a bridge between the 'now not well' and the 'already better' point.) The physical liver will feel better because the energy field responds to our focused intentions. (We will talk about this more in later chapters). The same technique works not only for individual, separate organs (although nothing is ever separate in us), but also for whole systems, like the endocrine or circulatory, for example. How do you 'set up an intention'? Take a deep breath and center yourself in the moment (focus on the chair you are sitting in, or the pose of your body, make sure you are relaxed). Then envision or think about a snapshot of yourself (or an organ, a system) on the blue etheric level in its perfect, healthy state. Do not follow it like a movie, but instead make it like a still picture of balance (let's say, a balanced liver)—remember, it can be a visual image or a thought (like 'my liver is healthy on the etheric level'). And just take a couple of relaxed, deep breaths as you hold this picture or thought without wobbling for a minute or so. This encodes your intention into the etheric level. Now the etheric level can start weaving energy back and forth between the actual state of the blueprint of the liver and the balanced one you were intending. The old one doesn't get erased; instead it is like making a bridge between the two. If your intention is clear, eventually the liver template will fully return to balance (i.e., the physical liver will get better). Of course, this has to be done in relationship to processing the blocks in the other energy levels that were affecting the etheric in the first place, so the issue that sickened the liver is not recreated.

No physical illness ever starts in the physical body; the etheric level has to have an imbalance first for the physical to react. What about when you get a bruise, or a scar after an operation, that had to be physical first, right? No, actually, to get a bruise or in any way physically bump into anything and hurt yourself, you would have to have first had a weakness in that area on the etheric level. You are walking down the stairs and suddenly twist your ankle, or hit the lower part of your leg on the curving rail. Were you just 'not careful'? Chances are that on the etheric level the lower part of your leg was weakened, it was light blue and not a deep, potently charged cobalt blue, so it drew the physical accident to that area to draw your conscious attention there. Probably your etheric level was trying to tell you that you were not grounded, not quite in your body. To prevent such 'accidents' in the future, pay more attention to being in the moment (instead of talking on the cell phone while walking, or thinking about something a million miles away from your body). If you had an operation and the recovery is slow, it is also because the etheric level isn't charged or repaired. The etheric level is designed by the Soul in such a way that it is capable of repairing self, but only if it is given the energy for it. If the etheric level is charged after an operation, it will realign the internal architectural lines fast, helping the physical body to recover. If an organ was removed (a kidney, or a uterus), it still exists on the etheric level. If there is enough charge, the physical body will have a much easier time adjusting to the absence of the organ, because the etheric level will run the energy as if the organ is there and healthy. For example, after hysterectomy hormone levels can rebalance themselves with a little help from a correct diet, if the etheric level's uterus receives enough charge. If not, a woman will suffer many hormonal changes and try to rebalance using artificial hormones. Scar tissue, internal or external, shows up on the etheric level as a pull in its structure, like a pulled thread on a sweater, and there may not be enough energy to detangle it. Again, intention can be very useful here: hold in your consciousness a visual snapshot or a clear thought of clear skin (or healthy internal tissue) on the cobalt blue etheric level. Try doing this every night for a minute before going to sleep and watch your physical body get better! To recharge your etheric level and make it bright blue, you can do any physical exercise, from stretching to weight lifting, or (if you are not able to move much) visualize your physical body becoming deep cobalt blue, shiny and bright, as if you are painting every cell that color, not just the skin or the outer surface. And of course make sure you are in the present moment when you are exercising or 'becoming cobalt blue'. Your body can only respond to your intention if you are in it.

The **emotional level** extends two to three inches from the physical body and interpenetrates the etheric one. It is filled with beautiful multicolored light and if it is healthy, the colors are bright and flowing. Each emotion looks like an energy cloud of a particular color inside the larger cloud of the whole egg-shaped emotional field. Emotional level energy, like multicolored smoke, flows through the etheric level architectural lines, but it is faster in vibration. Both the etheric and emotional levels pulsate, but at different rates. Also, while the etheric level is structural and mostly non-movable, the emotional level is the exact opposite—it is fluid, flowing and ever-changing. The emotional energy level is the home of our personal emotions and is responsible for emotional wellbeing. In this level, usually numbered the second counting away from the body, there should only be personal emotions. In other words only your energy, not the energy of friends, partners, children, pets, et cetera, which we tend to suck into our emotional level when we are not balanced. Imbalances of Self such as the need for approval; need for drama; need for connection (not to be mistaken with a true, balanced desire to connect your Self with another Self); need for validation and so on are reasons for the sucking in of other people's/creature's emotional energy. The sucking in temporarily fulfills our imbalanced needs, but only pollutes our emotional level. Energy on the second level is experienced by us as emotions. When for some reason someone else's energy gets trapped there, it is not really the other person's/being's emotion, but their energy that, because it is on *our* second level, is experienced by us as emotion (another person might experience the same energy as a thought or even a physical sensation, if their consciousness is on another level of their aura at that moment). By rebalancing your Self (becoming a Soul-sufficient Self) you make your field uninhabitable for other people's/creature's energy and it clears out automatically.

Energies like joy, pleasure, self love, excitement and creativity are experienced through the second level. Just like water (a physical fluid) there are three states the emotional level can experience: flowing, frozen or gaseous. Flowing and gaseous are usually much better states than the frozen one. When a person is depressed, this level looks grey and dull, as if it is devoid of life, with almost no movement. But it is not frozen, instead it is heavy, like a thick liquid, and stagnant like a swamp. When we get scared, the energy in the emotional level can freeze up and look white. Any emotional shock also looks frozen—the emotional level stops flowing completely, but usually this lasts for only a short time. If we live in constant fear or experience shock often, the emotional level begins to fragment, and the flowing, colorful energy (liquid or gaseous) becomes frozen in small portions or fragments. These fragments are unable to communicate with each other because they are 'unplugged' from the life flow. A person with an emotional level like this becomes mechanical/withdrawn or hyperactive/nervous, while the experience of fear is a constant undercurrent. 'Negative' feelings like guilt, shame, self judgment, jealousy or grief, have much darker, muddy colors. Like a thunderous cloud ready to rain, they change the flow of energy, making it slower and less healthy, minimizing our capacity for joy and pleasure.

When we experience any emotion, the energy on the second level changes and a particular cloud of color becomes more noticeable. Strong emotions like joy, love, excitement, desire and anger have bright, potent colors, while others are lighter or darker, less charged and focused. You are standing in front of a bakery looking at the multitude of wonderful cakes and pastries on display. You focus on one in particular and... no matter what you tell yourself ('I will get fat if I eat this', 'I promised myself I wouldn't'), the desire is so strong that it is almost painful not to taste it! At that moment the energy of desire in your emotional level grew very potent, expanded from a small charged cloud and momentarily took over the whole field.

How do we clear heavy, painful or scary emotions? It is similar to what we just looked at in desire energy—we amplify it, then clear it. If you believe the emotion, you will be trapped by its charge, its power over you. If you become a witness to the emotion, separate a little your Self from the experience (part of you is feeling the emotion and a part is witnessing it), it loses its hold and can be cleared by breathing energy through it. Why does this work? Any negative emotion is already 'wounded' somehow, it is not in its healthy state of flow and brightness, but is usually compressed, muddy or even frozen. If we breathe energy into it correctly, we can rebalance it, so the darker, muddy colors become brighter and healthy. If you are feeling bad about something, you will have a darker color cloud in your emotional level. If you stay focused on it, you will amplify it. At this point if you breathe through it, or 'process it' through your system, while being a witness to it at the same time, it can be completely cleared (not 'out of your field', but into a brighter, lighter color). If you stay focused on it and 'believe' it instead, it will keep getting bigger until it takes over the whole field (just like with the cake—a person 'believed' the need to have the cake instead of noticing 'oh, I seem to feel incomplete without this cake, how interesting?!'). How does one breathe into her/his emotion? Three components of consciousness are necessary: presence, focus and curiosity. Presence on the emotional level (we can't do it by 'thinking' about it from the mental level), focus on the emotion itself means experiencing it without resistance (no judgment) and curiosity allows us to become a witness to the experience, opening the door for charging the blocked emotional energy.

Why is it not beneficial to suppress our 'negative' emotions? Because these emotions are made of our own energy, they can't go anywhere outside of ourselves, they stay compressed, become blocks, and create imbalance. If we take our energy on the emotional level and compress it to a very small, condensed speck, the consciousness of that emotion is still inside the speck. Let's say you experienced something painful as a child: you made a great drawing and were very proud of yourself, but your parents yelled at you for it and punished you (you didn't realize that drawing on the wall was against the rules). Now there are two emotions, the self honoring ('I did great!', 'I am great!') and the shame ('I am horrible!'). They are conflicting, and we usually have trouble holding conflicting emotions in our consciousness. So the child suppresses both emotions, they become tiny specks of compressed energy on the emotional level. Usually the emotion which was least supported by authority/majority is suppressed first and the other one is layered 'on top' of the first in the compressed block. In this case the 'feeling bad about Self', the shame emotion, was supported and so becomes the dominant outer layer of the block. The child grows into an adult who is afraid to take any initiative and who has a haunting feeling that 'there is something wrong with me'. This person will feel the shame, since it was a dominant suppressed emotion, and will not be aware of her/his own greatness, because that emotion is underneath the shame.

How do we clear that? First of all, we have to not be afraid to go right into the uncomfortable emotion; in this situation, the shame. Amplify it by breathing into it (be present), do not judge it and do not believe it to be the reality (be a witness to it), and have curiosity about what is under it. If you sit in this state for a while, the blocked energy will open up and the shame emotion from the outer layer of the block will 'defreeze' and become smoke-like, eventually dissipating and clearing. This opens up the internal part of the block, freeing up the suppressed 'honoring' emotion and amplifying personal greatness.

The next level of the energy field, the third, is the **mental level.** It is a structural level, and it is here that our thoughts exist. That's right: your thoughts are not in our head, but in the energy level throughout and around your entire body. Our physical brain receives the energy impulses from the mental level and we interpret them as thoughts. You can have a thought on the mental level in the area of your feet or your belly! The mental level is like a large computer. It is not smart by itself, but acquires information—the more it 'knows', the better it can 'think'. It develops connections, mental pathways that energy habitually travels on. These are repetitive thought patterns. When we are not aware of our habitual thoughts, they become automatic pathways, like a main operating program. Before long we don't even realize that we are basing our entire perception of reality on some not-too-beneficial thought! There are no concepts or higher reasoning on the mental level, just your basic linear thinking. Again, imagine how a computer operates—it can't reason, but can compare and come up with the most logical solution. This linear logic is connected to physical-based perception, and the entire mental level is more connected to the body in its consciousness than to the Soul.

The mental level is filled with fine structural lines and webbing that look like the physical body, but extends up to eight inches farther. The more time we spend thinking, the more elaborate the structures get. When the mental level is healthy, it looks bright yellow, which represents clarity. If we feel confused and unable to focus, the mental level is undercharged and looks washed out. The health of this level is a reason why education in the early years is so important. When we are little, our mental level is usually very basic, barely there. If we are clear about life and have a good support system, our mental level is bright yellow. If we are confused a lot and do not get clear directions about life, our mental level is cloudy and weak. If we study, we receive a lot of new information, which allows our mental level to grow many new pathways, creating very complex webbing. We might never need the information itself later on in our lives, but simple interfacing with this information allowed the mental level to grow. It is just like exercising a muscle, it takes effort but it is better in the end. If a child doesn't study, she won't grow new pathways in the mental level. When she is older, it will be much harder to study, because her mental level already formed a habitual path for energy to follow and any new information will disrupt this path. In other words, if we study when we are little, there is nothing to resist the information and the mental level develops in a healthy way. If we didn't practice studying early in life, but only much later, there is a resistance from the old patterns which first has to be processed and cleared before new pathways can be developed. This takes much more effort on our part but, of course, it is still possible.

The mental level is not separate from the rest of the aura. Emotional fluid energy of many colors travels through the structures of the yellow mental level the same way that it does through the structures of the etheric level. They are all connected, yet separate. The thought forms look like bubbles or blobs of yellow on the mental level, but on the emotional level the same 'blob' is supported by some other color of the emotion in connection with that thought. There are also very fast flowing charges of energy on the mental level traveling through the yellow webbing. Not all the yellow webbing has these charges speeding through (like bubbles of air traveling fast in narrow tubing); the webs that do are the habitual pathways.

How do we clear 'negative' thoughts? First of all, they are only 'negative' because we find them uncomfortable. Second, they are made of our own energy, so we cannot take them out of the aura (just as with the emotions). What we can do is balance them with the opposite, or the 'positive', thought. Let's say you are thinking about your new idea at work, how this would be a great thing to implement, how it could make your co-workers' lives easier and bring more business to the company. But then the 'negative' thoughts arrive: 'This will never work', 'This is a stupid idea', 'My boss will laugh at me', and so on. These thoughts are uncomfortable and definitely not productive; they are in the way. What we can do in this situation is to look at the opposites, like 'This can work', 'This is a creative idea', 'My boss might need to be convinced about implementing it, but s/he will see it is a great idea'. That way we do not waste our energy fighting the 'negative' thoughts, but neutralize them with 'positive' counterparts. One does not need to agree with the 'positive' counterpart thought, only truly allow it without judgment. It is done from the place of 'everything is possible' (a form of believing): the bad thing might seem more likely, but since 'everything is possible' the good thing might exist too. The uncomfortable thought does not disappear, but (like a deflated balloon) it does lose its charge on the mental level, and that allows us to follow a more beneficial mental pathway. Of course, this shift will affect the other energy levels involved in supporting the 'negative' thought (by allocating energy for the new thought), triggering the unraveling of this issue further until completion/clearing.

The fourth level of the aura is the **feeling level,** or **astral.** The astral level is a magic domain of dream-like, potent mini-universes. This potency in the balanced state is the intensity of our experiences, the passion and exhilaration. The imbalance becomes drama, huge swings of mood in opposite directions. The astral level is fluid, like the emotional one, and also has many colors. When it is healthy and charged, the colors are bright and flowing one into the other, not separate. Feelings of love, compassion and peace flow smoothly. Anger and hatred are also felt intensely through this level, but they clog it, making it harder for us to feel love. In its consciousness the astral level connects much more to Soul reality than human perception. On the astral level many 'realities' can exist at the same time, it is completely unreasonable and illogical; though often making no sense at all to our mental level, astral level feelings can be extremely fascinating, from the experience of pain to fulfillment. When an artist makes a masterpiece, the 'reality' of that painting or sculpture gets its potency from the astral level. When an actor plays a role, he enters into the 'reality' of that character on the astral level, *becoming* him for the duration of the experience. When a child daydreams, telling us about this amazing adventure she just came from, she is relating the experience of one of her mini-universes on the astral level of her aura.

The astral level is the level of feeling interaction with others. While on the emotional level only personal emotions (about you) have a place, on the astral level there are feelings about the Self in relationship to something else (this is the difference between the 'emotions' and 'feelings' in general: feelings are interconnected with others while emotions are always related to you only). 'I feel good' is the emotional level energy, while 'I feel good about this idea' or 'I feel good because of what you said' are astral energies. When we feel something about another person, about a plant or a pet, or even a car, house, or clothes, we interact with it on the astral level. We might astrally feel pleasure, guilt, love, disgust, attraction or excitement, because someone has said something to us. Have you ever felt that in a crowded room someone was checking you out sexually, but when you found out who that person was, s/he wasn't even looking in your direction? You probably felt the astral level charge from him/her, their astral energy interacted with yours, and it might or might not have been conscious. Or when two people pretend they have nothing between them (like ex-lovers or co-workers), but actually lots of energy is exchanged astrally—there could be astral 'arrows' of hatred or jealousy, or fluffy clouds of attraction and curiosity. We are never separate on the astral level. We can keep our astral level clear of other people's energy and still interact with the world around us. When this interaction becomes conscious, we discover a whole universe of intricate exchanges and sharing, giving depth to our lives.

The astral level is penetrated by all the structures of mental and etheric levels, and can flow in harmony or with resistance to the emotional fluid energy from the second level. A dis-harmony between the astral and emotional levels might look like experiencing emotional hurt but suppressing it for the sake of 'pleasant' social interaction, or emotionally hating while submitting to the astral charge of the one you hate (overriding your emotion with your astral energy). The mental level is often at odds with the astral, since their interface with the external world is so different. The astral level generally has more charge since it has a faster vibration than the mental, so it can override thoughts. That's why sometimes we take action following an impulsive feeling, even though we 'know better'. It takes clear mental focus to organize astral level feelings and control their effect on the personality. This is what we usually call discipline.

Have you heard of astral travel? In its literal sense it means that our consciousness on the astral level separates from the lower three levels and the physical body, and 'travels' somewhere else. But what actually happens is that when we let go of the mental level demand that reality make sense linearly and of the emotional, etheric and physical fear of losing the Self, we are able to perceive our own astral level without obstructions. It is like opening the docking clamps and letting the ship free. This ship can stay at the dock, even though it is not attached to it anymore, or it can sail away. Obviously, we cannot 'lose' our astral body, but it can lose us, so this type of extreme astral travel, when you leave the body behind, can be dangerous for the physical body and should be attempted only when you know what you are doing.

This doesn't mean you cannot 'travel' through your astral level! Make your space by disconnecting the phone and preventing any other distractions, lie down, relax and tune into where you would like to travel. It can be a physical location on Earth, or another planet, or the center of the galaxy, or the past/future, or your other life, anything. Tune into that direction and let go of any preconceived ideas about how this destination is supposed to look (letting go of the 'docking clamps' of the mental level). As you do that you might feel slight fear because of 'not knowing' (we often use mental level 'knowing' for safety). Just breathe through it, you are perfectly safe. Stay focused on the destination and let go. Now you are in your astral level and you might get visual images, or feelings, smells, sounds, or just a sensation of the destination. Your astral level actually is right where you are and at the same time it is connected to the destination of your travel, bridging the two, allowing you, the consciousness, to experience it. Some people have a very particular ability in connection with astral travel and can receive information such as a readout on the space satellite in orbit, or about the clothes and other information about the life of particular people from the past, and so on. Being in your astral level without the 'docking clamps' feels similar to being weightless, or as if you are floating 'above' your body (even though you are still right there in it).

The next frequency level, the fifth, represents the patterns of truth and its expression. It is structural and looks like the negative of a photograph. The background or the space in this energy range is cobalt blue, but all the structural lines are transparent, as if they are empty space, while the blue is 'solid' space. The **truth level** contains all the lower four energy levels and is the blueprint for the etheric level's structures. In other words, the architectural guidelines for the physical form exist on the truth level as empty space, and this space in turn allows the existence of the etheric level, which mimics the truth level. Where there is an empty tube-like space in the truth level, there is a line and energy channel on the etheric level.

If we get seriously sick physically, our etheric level blueprint gets distorted and it requires connection to the truth level to receive a clear virus-free 'file' again. How do you make this connection? We already know how to connect to the etheric level, right? Center yourself in your body and intend to connect to the etheric level (blue lines, as in a Spider Man-like computer simulation of your body). Then focus on your personal truth in that moment. This doesn't have to be some huge thing, just a true statement about your reality in that moment ('I feel lousy', 'I am breathing', 'I feel fear/pain', 'I am lying down'). It *has* to be the truth. As you focus on that truth, keep your awareness with the Spider Man-like blue structures of the etheric level. You are now connected in a very basic way to the etheric and truth energy levels simultaneously. This allows energy to flow from one to the other. Notice that your truth might change as you are doing this exercise, from 'I feel lousy' to 'I feel relaxed', to 'I feel safe', et cetera. Allow yourself to keep changing the personal truth of the moment, adjusting the interface between the two levels. This supports the energy flow from the truth level to the etheric, maximizing the healing energy for your physical body. This is useful in any serious or chronic illness and, of course, in meditation for building self awareness.

The truth of the Soul is the composite of all the Soul's experiences and learned lessons. The fifth level also has the truth of our present life, the personality perceptions about the Self, which resonate with our beliefs about life. The fifth level records everything that is happening inside us in any moment. We operate on these assumptions about life, constantly adjusting them in accordance with new information entering our field. If you know your personal truth, you feel strong, clear and present. Through this level we also know if something 'rings true' to us or not (the idea will either vibrate with our fifth level or not).

Each of us has active and dormant energy patterns on the fifth level. Usually the dormant ones are the patterns of the Soul truth that we have not yet expanded to encompass. You have a brother and he is an alcoholic. You get very angry with him every time you see him, because you find that his promises are empty and he is still drinking. You are running the truth pattern in your aura about helping/supporting and are being adamant that he should not drink. Then one day something changes and you are not angry with your brother anymore. You still care about him and still take action to help him, but you are not angry. It is because on the fifth level you have activated a dormant truth pattern for unconditional love, realizing that the reason he triggers you into so much anger is because you love him so much.

Our personal truth reflects our perceptions about the Self, and they resonate with the beliefs about life/Soul/Self/God, et cetera. One has to be brave to allow conscious awareness of these Self perceptions (even if the personality does not like them), and to stand in personal truth. When personal truth is ignored, we tend to borrow someone else's patterns to operate on. Our fifth level obviously still exists in our energy system, but now runs someone else's patterns, which creates a discrepancy in our alignment with the Soul. This blocks the Soul truth, forcing it to become dormant. The result is that we feel lost, unsure of who we are and why we are here. Eventually we still have to face our personal truth and let go of outside conditioning. Standing in personal truth (this incarnation's perception) opens options for accessing the Soul truth (lessons from all incarnations).

You felt different from other children somehow and that was curious to you. But you were conditioned by your parents that 'being different' is bad. Their pattern begins to run on your fifth level. You still often feel different, but instead of curiosity it brings you pain and shame. The parent's pattern is unconscious yet active, while your own is dormant.

This is why humans have mid-life crisis! We end up with the parents patterns on our truth level, we go to school, choose a profession based on their expectations of us, try to please them to the best of our ability in exchange for love and support. Then at about forty our Soul hits the brakes. It figures that almost half the lifespan has already been spent not on the path and it's time to get on it. Some of the dormant Soul patterns suddenly activate on the fifth level, and a person has a reality check. He lets go of pleasing his parents and following someone else's path, but is unsure about what his own path looks like since for forty years he was not on it. And so he begins to build it from scratch, usually acting like a kid or a teenager, embarking on his journey. Unfortunately this often ends in him calming down and listening to everyone's advice, becoming 'normal' again, and this closes Soul patterns. But what could happen is that that person really changes who he was into someone more in line with his own ideas and truths, embarking on his journey and keeping Soul patterns active.

Another most remarkable thing about the truth level is that it has conscious sound! What does that mean? Well, every frequency has sound. But the consciousness of sound exists here. The 'soul of sound' lives on the fifth energy level. This is where, if used with clear intention, sound creates matter. Our Soul has a clear intention about what form it wants to create/embody, and this intention creates a blueprint on the fifth level, with 'empty' lines that get filled with charge on the etheric level (in support of the physical body). But these 'empty' lines are not really empty, they have sound. This is the sound of intention, anchored in the clarity of structure on the fifth level. Have you heard of sound healing? This is when a person tones (makes a sound) into another, helping them heal. What really happens is that a healer using her/his intuition chooses the sound of a balanced organ (or of the entire body) that is higher and clearer than the one present. This sound as a focused intention vibrates into the truth level of the aura, adjusting and amplifying the balanced pattern for the organ (or body). Then the etheric level picks it up and the physical body responds. The same principle is used in prayer. The sound of the chanting or prayer goes into the fifth level, rebalancing it. In ancient times we used to be much more aware of fifth energy level and used it daily. We used to know how to sound into an ocean or a volcano to divert its destructive powers from our villages, how to heal imbalanced relationships by having couples sound together, help birth babies in peace and love by having the entire community chanting during the birthing process. We knew how to move heavy logs and rocks by using sound in alignment with our truth and the truth of the log or rock. We used to know how to follow sound patterns on the fifth level of the planet, like birds and whales do, helping us find a way home. The more we uncover our own truth underneath parental and societal patterns, the stronger we feel, journeying through a magical life in alignment with the sound of truth.

The next larger vibrational step is the **unconditional level.** It looks like an opalescent, light cloud of energy. It is similar in appearance to the emotional and astral levels, which are both without structure, but the unconditional level is luminescent, with a potent internal glow (similar to a candle). When it is charged, there are also visible beams of light coming from the center of it. Like the other fluid levels, the unconditional level has many colors, but they are pastel and soft. It doesn't have a clear shape; its boundary fits into the other structural levels. The unconditional level can expand a lot, many times our size, but in its usual form its outer boundary is about four or five feet from the body.

The energy of interconnectedness and unconditional love from the Source flows through this level. The human ability to look at the internal and external world unconditionally comes from this level. There is no judgment, everything is equally valued.

You organize your daughter's birthday party. You are determined to make it the best in the neighborhood. Your five-year-old daughter looks phenomenal in the outfit you made for her for the occasion. Kids arrive and... their outfits are prettier, professionally made. You begin to feel bad that your daughter's outfit isn't as good, is 'home made'. The party begins. Nothing goes according to plan: your daughter is outside playing in the garden with other kids, making her outfit dirty, while the hired entertainer is sitting bored to death in the empty living room. The night comes, parents pick up their kids. You feel like a failure, since all the children are dirty and the party was a disaster. Your unconditional level is deflated and undercharged. If you move more conscious awareness there, you will feel love for yourself in this difficult situation, not based on your external circumstances matching your expectations, but unconditionally. Feelings of failure will dissipate and you will feel supported in your being-ness. Then you might hear your daughter telling her older sister upstairs that she had the best birthday party ever!

Our self judgments are based on our expectations and competition with the images we consider perfection. If the sixth level is undercharged, we feel alone and unloved, as if our lives are meaningless. The images of 'perfection' become our guide for self love, making it conditional (I did well, I get love; I didn't match my image of perfection, I don't get love). The unconditional level is the antidote to self judgment and punishment for not matching up. When we feel the love of God, that we are taken care of and loved, we have a balanced sixth level of our aura. The feeling of being guided is a result of this balance. The Soul, the Source and balanced energy beings can communicate with us through this level. Ever felt like you were in the flow of life, with everything happening the way it is supposed to, not necessarily perfect, but you feel moved into a certain path, as if the doors open for you even before you arrive in front of them? That's when we have a charged, healthy unconditional level with brilliant multicolored rays of light shining through it.

Because of our conditionality we tend to block off Universal support, which is unconditional, assuming that we have to be a certain way in order to receive it. The sixth level then turns gray with droopy smears; it is out of balance. How do we bring balance back? Breathe deeply and relax your physical body and your mental level, and allow your emotions and feelings to flow without monitoring them. Focus on your body first, then expand your awareness to include the whole room (do it spherically, expanding your field in all directions like a big bubble). Keep expanding to include your town, then larger, until you become the size of the planet. Do it slowly. Try to feel your body at the same time as the whole planet. As you hold both in your awareness, you are expanding your personal idea of the Self, allowing the unconditional level to recharge and balance. Practice this when you have at least half an hour of time. This exercise is very useful when you are in self judgment. Once your energy field gets the hang of it, you can do a small version of it in 'emergencies'. Quickly focus on your Self and breathe into your field as if blowing up a balloon, until you reach the size of a planet. This will rebalance the sixth level and the self judgment will dissipate, allowing the love from the Source to enter.

The outermost level of the energy field is the **conceptual level,** often also referred to as spiritual. It is structural, golden and bright when healthy. Its structure consists of trillions of architectural lines, a web-like suit for the entire aura. It holds the conceptual system for every cell in our physical body, for the outer boundary of the egg-shaped field and everything in between. All the other levels of our aura fit into this one. The seventh level can extend as much as six or seven feet from the physical body in its balanced state. Bright golden light pulsates in its architectural lines, creating a shimmering glow, similar to the unconditional level, but brighter (like a 100 watt light bulb vs. a candle). When it is imbalanced, the golden lines are depleted, looking whitish and washed out; some can be torn, creating energy leaks and disruptions in the programming. The outer edge of the conceptual level is very resilient when healthy. It is filled with a tight webbing of golden lines, creating a boundary about a quarter of an inch thick. It contains 'us', what our Soul determined is necessary for this incarnation, it defines us without creating separation.

This level represents our belief systems and the concepts from which our lives assume significance. The conceptual level is also similar to a computer, like the mental one, but much more sophisticated, with intelligence. The difference is like a tabletop computer versus an android: one just executes decisions made by someone else, the other is an independent consciousness, able to make decisions itself. The conceptual level is 'the mind' with intelligence. The programs for our significance that the conceptual level holds are what we consider the Self. There are Soul, other lives, parental and societal programs and more. We usually call these programs belief systems. What we believe determines our perception of life, Self, Soul and the Universe/Source/God. Higher reasoning and logic is the operational system on the conceptual level. Remember, our mental level has linear logic and reasoning, so what is the difference? You are stuck in traffic and upset about being late for a meeting. You are trying to figure out why you are stuck. If you think you are in the jam because there is construction on the road and it creates delays, you are using your mental level linear logic. If you figure out that you had an issue in connection with the meeting you are late for (you were afraid that you were unprepared, or you felt you would have to lie about something, or you really didn't want to have the conversation in the first place) and your own intentions 'created' a traffic jam so you can work with that issue, then you are using your conceptual level higher reasoning. When balanced, our conceptual level allows us to make connections between the facts, which linearly might not look connected. These connections create a webbing of conscious awareness, teaching us to have consensus in the aura. If we do not fracture and compartmentalize this webbing, our Soul connects directly to the conceptual level, opening up the vision (higher 'plan' or path) of the Soul to our human consciousness. When our consciousness extends to the seventh level, we know we are one with the Source/God.

There are more energy levels in this dimension, twelve all together. But frequencies after the conceptual level are more universal- versus self-oriented, so they are not contained in our field. We can connect to them by expanding our vibrational range (we will talk about some of them in the next chapters). The eighth level is the timeline level, the ninth is the crystalline, the tenth, eleventh and twelfth are celestial or spiritual. As you have probably already noticed, the levels are alternating in type: all the even numbered ones are fluid, cloud-like, and they are contained inside the structures of the odd numbered levels.

Human Energy Field Anatomy, Part 2: Chakras

All of these levels/energy bodies interact with each other through pathways that look like vortexes. In the Indian tradition these vortexes are called the chakras. We can call them by some other name, but this will probably only add confusion, so let's stick to the usual name. There are many chakras in the human energy field with the number depending on our evolutionary step, but we all have at least seven main ones. Each level has all seven chakras and more, even though a particular chakra could be used as an entry way into that level. Imagine an energy swirling in a large vortex, inside which is another vortex, and inside that one is one more vortex, and so on. The conceptual level chakra contains the unconditional level chakra; they are located in the same space, but on a different frequency. It in turn contains the truth level chakra, and inside it is the astral level one, and so on. On the structural levels (etheric, mental, truth and conceptual) chakras are all the same color because they take the main color of the entire level. On the fluid levels chakras have many different colors, some are healthy and others are not. The energy flows through a chakra on one level, changes frequency by the rotation of the vortex (either faster or slower) and enters the next level, allowing for communication between them. Inside each chakra are mini-vortexes, depending on the type of consciousness. The root chakra has four internal mini-vortexes, while the crown has 972.

All chakras rotate clockwise when balanced. They take Universal energy in and translate it for our consciousness. When we have imbalances in the aura, our chakras begin to turn counterclockwise, pushing energy out instead of taking it in. This means we project our energy (beliefs, thoughts, feelings, emotions) into the world, then sense that energy and believe it to be the world. If you have self hatred in your energy field, some of your chakras eventually will spin counterclockwise and before long your external reality will reflect this emotion to you, and all you will see in the world is hatred. Or you think women/men are cruel. Your chakras will spin counterclockwise, providing you with external circumstances of people's cold-heartedness, which might lead to an inability to have a balanced relationship. The misconception about the external world always begins inside first.

A vertical flow of energy feeds all the chakras and connects them to each other. It looks like a hollow tube filled with light. (You might be familiar with the Indian traditional name for this vertical tube—the 'prana tube'—and the Universal energy flowing through it, 'prana'). The tube shape exists on each level of the aura, one inside the other from the etheric level up to the conceptual, just like all the chakras (similar to the Russian matreshka dolls). Energy pumps up and down inside the tube. It is like an internal engine without which we cannot exist; it is the 'warp core' of our being. Energy charge moves in multi-spiral motion in both directions. The top and bottom of the tube are open vortexes, known as the crown and the root chakras. The narrow tips of the other chakras connect to the vertical tube perpendicularly (at ninety degree angles) from the front and the back of the body. All the chakras have to be open for the vertical flow to work well. If our chakras are clogged and not functioning, the vertical flow is disrupted, limiting our ability to fully exist here on Earth. The body becomes weak or ill, the energy levels cannot communicate with each other creating fracturing of the personality, making us feel alone, lost, stuck, trapped and not worthy of love. Pretty much a fragmented vertical flow locks us in our personal hell. Knowing about the chakra system gives you an ability to correct the imbalances, modifying the vertical flow. You can bring then health, fulfillment and the excitement of meaning into your life.

The lower end of the vertical tube brings energy into the **root chakra,** the one that connects us with the planet. The function of the root chakra is the consciousness of survival, the association with the tribal energies and belonging, stamina and physical health. It looks like an energy funnel with four mini-vortexes inside. On the fluid multi-colored levels the root chakra is red or red-orange when healthy and strong. The color generally becomes lighter as the frequency range rises (red on the emotional level, rosy red on the astral, pastel red on the unconditional). In relationship to the physical body, the root chakra occupies the area between the legs, and its energy is supported by the coccyx, through the anus, perineum, vagina/scrotum and clitoris/penis. The flow then moves down through the legs and the area between the legs, like a red skirt, expanding downwards. The root chakra is the main entry center for the etheric level, so if we tune into the base consciousness of the root, we will also end up in the etheric level range.

The will to live is the consciousness of the root chakra. If that chakra is closed, we will have no will to live and the physical body can literally die without having any particular illness ('she lost the will to live after her husband died and slowly withered away'). The amount of energy available to the physical body is determined by the root chakra. Even if the other chakras have a lot of energy, but the root is blocked, the physical body will be in trouble, unable to get the supply of energy 'food' necessary for health.

Root chakra energies are expressed when a person chooses to go exercise. If you just hate to work out, your root chakra is limp. This limp configuration looks like a dog's tail between its legs instead of the funnel perpendicular to the ground. It is not possible to be motivated about exercise, no matter how strong your active will is, if your root chakra is limp. To pump it up, focus on stamping your feet or rocking the hips while squatting. This simple movement will bring more charge to the root chakra and you will feel a natural motivation for physical activity, instead of willful forcing.

Each chakra has a particular sense connected to it. The root chakra is responsible for kinesthetic perception. Physical pleasure or pain, the sense of balance, movements of energy through the body, shivers and temperature changes, all of these are perceived through the root chakra. When we use the root chakra for energy perception, we tune into the energy movements inside the body. If you are stretching slowly and focusing on your leg, you might feel that there is a blockage in the knee area so that energy can't go easily though it when you stretch your leg, making it harder to physically stretch. If energy of a different frequency (an energy cloud or a being of some sort) has passed through your field, you might have a shiver. If you walked into a situation where your root chakra senses danger, you might have the sensation of your hair standing on end.

The root chakra always exists in the present moment. This is the only time it knows. So one of the ways to tune into it and amplify the energy there is to be present in the moment. If you look at this in relationship to your whole life, if you are present moment to moment, you are 'in your body' and you have a physical presence in your life and can make a mark in the physical world. If you are not present, not in your root chakra, you are 'not here', and cannot 'make a mark', cannot accomplish things physically (they stay as ideas or intellectual pursuits). (It is easy to know if someone is in their root chakra or not, just look into their eyes. If a person is pretending to listen to the conversation, but is spacey and vacant or distracted, in his own world, he is not present in the root chakra.) Other ways to improve your root chakra are focused physical touching, walking meditation and deep relaxation. Physical touching works by bringing your awareness in relationship to the physical body presence. Walking meditation is a brisk walk while focusing on your heart beat, breathing and movement of your body in space. Deep relaxation is a step-by-step muscle-tension release that can be done through massage, yoga, many forms of slow stretching, or by lying still and relaxing. This last type takes a longer time, you need to have at least thirty minutes, or better, an hour, for that type of relaxation.

The **second chakra** has two aspects, the front and the back. The front aspect is located at the belly, the back one in the lower back sacrum bone area. They have different purposes, even though they work as a unit. They connect to each other through the vertical tube in the center of the body. Both aspects relate to the consciousness of pleasure, passion, abundance, joy, creativity, sexual potency and self love in their balanced state, and shame, guilt and scarcity in their imbalanced state.

You are calling to order a pizza, here it comes to your door and you are paying for it, no problem so far, you are placing it on the table and opening the box, here it is... and you gobble it up in the next thirty seconds! You have just flunked second chakra pleasure. Why did you eat it so fast? This is not about physical hunger, this is reacting to our feeling that pleasure is dangerous. Now, what could have happened? You are ordering the pizza, it comes to your door, you are paying for it, placing it on the table, opening the box and... you inhale the aroma of the pizza, you enjoy the sight of it, you are placing a small piece into your mouth and oooing as your sensual nature is being fed. Congratulations on an A in second chakra pleasure!

The front of the second chakra deals with abundance and receiving and giving pleasure/creative/sexual energies, the back with the amount of charge available. If the front aspect is closed, you do not feel the abundance of the universe, you feel that there is never enough for you (or 'for everyone'), and feel unable to receive nourishment from external reality, which separates you from it. There is no joy in your life and everything seems to make it worse, as if the world is determined to punish you, to hurt you somehow; you feel a victim of life, in self pity, your resources are scarce. There is also no satisfaction, you accomplish things that are supposed to make you happy, but feel no fulfillment. In connection with sexual energy a woman will have difficulty achieving an orgasm because she will be afraid to give, she will want to be in control in sex or not trust the partner's ability to pleasure her. A man will either have a premature ejaculation or be impotent, both because he fears giving his energy out; hence, he holds it back. In relationship to pleasure, a clogged second chakra on the front will mean a twisted perception of pleasure—it will feel unattainable, incomprehensible, even dangerous. If the front aspect spins strongly but in the counterclockwise direction, a person will feel entitlement for his needs to be met, a demand for pleasure to be given to him, but be unable to commit to anything or anyone. Obviously there are gradations of how closed the chakra is. It can be completely clogged or damaged, or only partially, distorting energy to some degree but not shutting it off completely.

The back aspect is responsible for curiosity, the drive to explore and to have new experiences. It is like a propeller at the lower back, a generator for excitement and an accelerator for curiosity.

The absence of energy in the back aspect makes life feel boring, devoid of magic, direction and passion. If the back aspect is closed, you feel weak. Pleasure seems unimportant and there are no desires of any kind. You feel powerless. If some other chakra in the aura is very strong and compensates for the second chakra's back aspect not working, you might not feel the powerlessness (even though it is still there), but your life will feel joyless and devoid of support and meaning; it becomes mechanical and predictably boring. In connection with sexual energy there is no sex drive—it is as if you ran out of steam before you even started. Sex becomes too much work to bother with. If, on the other hand, the back aspect is strong, but spins counterclockwise, a person will have destructiveness and recklessness connected to excitement and curiosity. He will have a strong sex drive with aggressive tendencies, perhaps even violent sexual fantasies, and an inability to commit.

We humans often have difficulty feeling the potency of our sexual power and openness at the same time, so we close one of the aspects, which leads to imbalance. If the front aspect is open, we can receive energy from the external world, feel pleasure in our existence and deep sexual intimacy with ourselves and our partners. But if at the same time the back aspect is closed, we won't have much energy for exchange with the world/self/partner.

If the back aspect is open, we will have a clear will to interact with reality, lots of charge for the experience of pleasure and a strong sex drive. But if at the same time the front aspect is closed, we won't have a way to satisfy our very strong desire for pleasure and sexual love, because of the inability to give and receive energy. This will lead to disappointments, pain and frustration.

The sense connected to the second chakra is emotional feeling. You can feel joy, anger, fear, pleasure—these are the emotional energies inside your field. You also might feel that your pet is sad and missing its playmate, or that even though your friend is telling you about how he is just fine about the conversation he had earlier with his sister, he is really emotionally angry with her. You are sensing others' emotions.

How do you open both aspects of the second chakra? You can do physical exercises that support the energy flow there, such as rocking your pelvis forward and backwards (like during sex) or doing scissor kicks with your legs when sitting. But the easiest way to open the second chakra is to go into pleasure. Any pleasure will do: watching the sun light beautifully stream through the trees, touching the velvet sweater you are wearing, tasting amazing tea from a faraway land or smelling an essential oil. When you feel 'not enough', or feel scarcity or boredom, focus on something that can bring an experience of basic pleasure immediately. By doing that you recode your energy and jump-start your second chakra.

The **third chakra** also has two aspects: the front one is located at the solar plexus, the back one in the middle of the spine. The front of the third chakra represents identity power; it is a statement about who you are in the world. This chakra is filled with energy patterns called personal codes, which are operational programs for your identity. When the third chakra on the front is balanced, we respect ourselves and have high self esteem. The potency of this chakra relates to mental clarity, the more charge we have there, the more sure we are about ourselves. We cannot respect ourselves if we do not have a clear idea about who we are; that is, if this chakra is clogged, we disrespect the Self and others. When we do not like something about ourselves, we tend to twist and turn our third chakra, making it 'look' down or to the side, instead of right in front of us.

If your third chakra on the front is clogged, you won't feel sure about yourself and your actions; you will have low self esteem and rely on the external world to support your identity. Your personal power will be unclear to you, or you might feel like you have no power at all. You would not feel secure remaining yourself at all times; instead you will mimic the patterns of others, trying to fulfill their expectations of you.

You just got a promotion and a raise at work, you are so proud of yourself, and tonight happens to be your usual monthly dinner with you father. You describe your accomplishments to him and he says 'pass the salt'... you are devastated, crushed, invalidated. Your third chakra is sweeping the floor. In order to recover you will need to focus on mental thoughts like 'my promotion is *my* accomplishment' and 'it brings *me* power'. That will lift the third chakra back up and bring more clarity for self validation.

If your third chakra on the front spins counterclockwise, it generates a strong charge of projection. A person with that kind of charge will be selfish and interested only in gaining more power in the external world. He will be obsessed with others noticing his powerful position in life and will ignore his feelings and reason in order to prove his strength.

The third chakra on the back is the will to be whole. It represents our capacity to unify the Self, like a defragmenting program installed by the Soul. If this chakra is open, you feel together, your emotions, thoughts, beliefs, senses all are in synch. Since no one is perfect in this physical world, we are all fragmented to some extent. In other words, your energy levels might not be in communication with each other, so sometimes you feel like a rabbit, and at other times a lion comes out. The key is to unite them. Not to moosh them into some bizarre rabbit-lion creature, but to allow a safe space for them to talk to each other and respect each other's needs. The third chakra on the back is responsible for making sure this communication happens. Remember we talked about how energy can flow through a chakra from one level to the other by changing the speed of its vibration? Well, it takes active willing to make the process happen. Imagine a large company, many departments, everyone is running around doing their business. Employees are supposed to send memos and progress reports to other departments, but sometimes they get so overwhelmed with their own work that they forget. The third chakra on the back is like a public relations person who runs from one department to the other and with a smile organizes meetings, makes sure that the needs of one department are heard by others, and so on, making the company run smoothly. It takes an active will to set up communication. Without this chakra working, the energy levels (departments) just get too much into their own business and forget to pay attention to the needs of other levels. If your third chakra on the back is closed, you will feel fragmented and unsure of your identity. You might also be stubborn and very determined to stay fragmented, defending fragmentation as the Self. If the back aspect of the third chakra spins counterclockwise, you might feel like you are not ok unless everyone is ok, a peacemaker, but not a true peacemaker for the sake of peace, a peacemaker for the sake of personal ok-ness. The will to communicate and unify will be directed outward into the external world, making you dependent on it.

If the front aspect of the third chakra is open but the back is closed, a person will have a strong split in their identity, and will attempt to amplify the traits she considers good and minimize or hide 'bad' ones. She will usually ignore her feelings and go only with thoughts, suppressing unwanted parts of herself. If the back is open, but the front is closed, a person will feel like they have no idea who they are, feel unsafe unless everyone is the same, will have difficulty tolerating differences, will see opinions and uniqueness as confrontation and threats to the Self.

The sense connected to the third chakra is the intuition. It is the 'feeling brain' of our energy system. You are driving and the turn comes but just before you actually turn, you have a vague sense that the road is closed. And it is, as you soon find out. Or you are looking for your lost keys and have a vague sense that they are on the drier in the laundry room... and they are. Notice that in both situations you did not know for sure, but had a vague sense. That is basic intuition. A higher frequency intuition comes when the energy moves through the fifth, sixth and seventh levels of the third chakra. Higher intuition is about directions in your life, intuiting what you are learning in the present lesson or what lesson is next. If the energy flows freely though all the levels of the third chakra, you might feel guided by your own intuition, as if you 'caught a scent' and now are following it along.

How do we clear the third chakra? If we do not live by our own rules, the third chakra holds the energy of other authority figures. We will talk more in the next chapters about rules and authority. But from a more basic standpoint, if you feel lost, as if you forgot who you are and are confused, it is because the third chakra is lacking yellow clarity energy on the mental level. How do you amplify clarity? Focus on something mental, a very simple linear thought, like 'I think of yellow' and the yellow color frequency will begin to show up in your third chakra. If you get nauseated often, it could be because the third chakra on the front is reconfiguring the identity codes, or because you have two patterns fighting in there (like your pattern and a parental one, for example). If you are talking to someone and feel pulled in the area of the third chakra on the front, you probably are being pulled, so turn sideways and the pull will go away. This type of pulling is often a controlling mechanism, someone is trying to gain control over your identity. If you have back problems, chances are your third chakra on the back is blocked and you are suppressing some parts of yourself while amplifying others. If you ask yourself 'What am I hiding from myself? What am I afraid 'they' will discover about me?' you might uncover the suppressed energy and your back will feel better.

If you want to increase your higher intuition, focus on the faster levels of your third chakra on the front and back. Sit comfortably and relax, but keep your body vertical. Bring your awareness to the solar plexus area and the opposite area at the middle of your back. Tune into the third chakra by envisioning or sensing it, like a funnel at the front of your body and a funnel at the back, connecting/touching on the inside of your body. First keep your awareness very close to the body, about an inch from the skin. You will be on the etheric level of the field. But then keep enlarging the vortex, eventually making it stand out about six or seven feet. You are now on the higher faster levels of your third chakra. Feel/sense/see if the flow of energy is unrestricted or blocked. It might be a simple feeling of pressure, as if the energy doesn't want to go there, or a feeling of heat and movement when the energy flows. Just sense it, don't try to make it into anything, allow yourself to witness it. By *keeping your awareness there* you are clearing the chakra, helping it to direct flow into the higher levels, thereby increasing your capacity for higher intuition.

The **fourth chakra,** the heart, is one of the main human chakras. It is a very important energy center because the human species learns through the heart. Not a mental sort of learning, but an experiential type; this is how we become wise. The heart is a gateway into the higher levels of the Self, a pathway between the personality we live with every day and the higher, wiser part of us that only sometimes comes out. When the heart center is functioning well, we have continuous access to that wise part of ourselves.

The heart chakra has two aspects: the front, located in the middle of the chest close to the physical heart, and the back, between the shoulder blades. The front of the heart processes the consciousness of compassion, kindness, love and connectedness with all life. If this chakra is balanced and open, we feel connected to the whole world, we are able to love not just people close to us, but all humans, all animals, the planet, et cetera. An open heart allows us to feel the whole person, not just what is presented to us. Kind of like 'seeing the good in people', the heart shows us that there is a capacity for loving and kindness even in the most closed off, scared and acting mean/angry/rude person. The open heart also can tell you if something is not true, if someone is lying about their feelings. With an open heart we are able to love without the expectation of being loved back. We do not necessarily give love to others; we allow it to flow between us and them. The energy that this Universe is made of is unconditional; it is this pure unconditionality we humans call love. Universal energy equals Universal love, it is one and the same. Universal love energy can be twisted, diffused, pressured, or turned inside out, and we experience all these variations in different ways (as anger, hate, pleasure, joy, terror, cruelty, curiosity etc.), but before they were modified to make the diversity of expressions, they all were originally love. Since everything in this Universe is made of love, the heart chakra directs only this love energy towards someone; love cannot be separated into love and non-love, everything is love. The front of the heart chakra also transmutes the lower chakra's frequencies into higher ones. It does so on every level, serving as a true gateway from the lower personality to the higher. This connects to the action of the physical heart, which we will go into later. But the energy of compassion is the main one running through the heart.

You are talking on the phone with your husband about your daughter's summer camp, he barely listens for a few minutes and then says sharply 'get to the point already', you call him 'insensitive bastard' and slam down the phone ... yet you know of the difficulties at his job lately and also your tendency to ramble. Feeling remorseful with a clogged heart chakra you call him back and, igniting compassion, tell him that you know what stress he is under and will discuss this issue later. Compassion is the energy of recognition of the Self and the other, and they coexist in love.

If the front of your heart is closed, you will have difficulty loving unconditionally, instead expecting something in return for the show of love. If someone experiences a lot of pain and the heart closes, it might make the person cruel and cold. This is only a defense from pain. If she faces what is in her heart, the chakra will open again, changing cruelty into kindness. A closed heart also makes it very hard to trust heart feelings, so one tends to expect the worst in people, relationships and situations. A person with a closed heart deals with life more by their chosen rules than by moment-to-moment experience. Since life is ever-changing, choosing rules once and then following them for one's whole life is not going to work, and a person who does that will have to find other ways of experiencing love (it might be through accomplishment, or ego power, or even cruelty and control). This is one of the major causes of heart attack in the physical body—the heart chakra is saying 'enough, we have to open up and run energy here' and the physical heart has to compensate. If the change is too abrupt and the old patterns have to be broken, the physical heart may have a problem, hence the attack.

If the heart chakra is strong, but spins counterclockwise, a person will try to get the feeling of love from others by constantly giving love out. You finally got a short vacation for yourself and flew away into tropical paradise. You do not know anyone there, but it is good, because you wanted to 'get away from it all'. Yet soon you find yourself agreeing to go to dinner with your hotel neighbors, people that you do not even really like. They invited you and you did not want to disappoint them by saying you would rather sit alone. You arrive at the dinner where you do not want to be and carry on a conversation, trying to be nice to everyone. You did not know that other people were invited, and everyone eventually gets into a heated discussion on a topic you do not really care about, but yet you find yourself calming and cheering everyone and even promising them that you will go somewhere tomorrow with each couple at the table. Before long your entire vacation week is filled with activities that are meaningless to you to please people you do not really care to know well. Your heart chakra is spinning backwards, pushing you into pleasing everyone around.

You are at a business meeting with two other companies, attempting a joint venture. Everyone sits at a large table in the plain-looking conference room. You are part of a team of four people representing your company. In a short while conversation heats up, everyone is trying to show why their proposal is better, and they are interrupting each other and pushing their point. You emotionally withdraw from the room and wonder: 'Why can't we just all get along, be friends and love each other? Why do they have to be so mean?' Your heart chakra is huge and spinning backwards, pulling you away from reality.

Pay attention, this is important, for all of you I-want-to-fix-the-world-through-loving-everyone and Why-can't-we-all-just-love-each-other types. Listen up! 'Everything will be ok if I only love enough' is not going to work. If you have this belief system, it means your heart is spinning backwards, the chakra is too big and instead of 'feeding' you it tries to 'feed' the whole world! It is an enormous energy drain on your system, and it requires the use of other chakra's energy or even their reserves, if nothing else is available. This overuse of the heart depletes you, creating emotional and physical imbalances. We will talk in the later chapters about why this belief system is not appropriate for this planet, but for now just remember that it makes the front of the heart too big and spins it backwards.

The back aspect of the heart chakra is positive will, or the will to act. It is like a large propeller behind our back that moves you forward in life. Free will is the ability to choose action. We really only have two choices: to act or not to act. How we act is secondary to having the freedom of choice. The will center of the heart allows us to feel the power of that freedom. Any accomplishment requires the use of will, otherwise we do not have enough discipline to follow through. If the will center is closed, you feel like you have no choice, you are at the mercy of circumstances, other people, God. Usually this happens when the front of the heart is overactive and draws all the energy into itself. We feel like we have no choice but to try to please and love the whole world with *our* energy.

When we face a decision and have to act, especially in circumstances requiring bravery (from entering a burning building to finally telling your mother you do not want her to call ten times per day), the back aspect of the heart can get very large. This is a normal occurrence. This is why when a person finally decides to act, s/he tends to straighten the spine and pull the shoulders back—we are creating space for the will center to open. But once the action is on the way, it usually does not require such a massive amount of energy and the will chakra shrinks back to its normal size. Problems arise when the will chakra stays too large all the time—it overrides the heart. A person with a chakra like that will be afraid of his feelings and want strength through the mental and conceptual levels, dishonoring his emotional/feeling side. He will perceive feelings as a weakness and attempt to override them with intellect.

Ideally, divine will (Soul's will) and our personal will are the same. This happens when the will center is active and balanced with the front of the heart. Then life (divine will) seems to align with what we want, what we choose is accomplished with ease, help is available and so on. If the back of the heart is too large and also spins counterclockwise, an overactive will is projected out. That chakra takes energy away from the front of the heart first, making the heart center small and the will center large. This depletes the rest of the energy system. A person with this configuration sees divine will in opposition to personal will, and life seems to be against her. In this situation accomplishment is only possible through overriding others, that is, through control. She wants to own life, control others and even her own feelings.

Hank arrives at his son's football game. In the parking lot he has a problem with the way others are parking, thinking they are 'idiots' and 'need to take parking lessons'. The game begins and in the first quarter Hank disagrees with the coach, who pulls a particular boy off the field. Hank believes the coach is an 'idiot, who has no idea what he is doing' and that 'the coach is trying to sabotage the team', when he, on the other hand, is the team's only hope and he knows that that boy had to stay in play for the team to win the game. The coach has to calm Hank down and ask him to sit back on the benches. But just a little into the second quarter Hank disagrees with the referee and almost runs onto the field yelling at him. The referee is, of course, also an 'idiot and knows nothing about the game'; instead he is there 'to get Hank and their team'. The game is interrupted again, Hank's son is embarrassed about his father's behavior and hides behind the benches. Hank continues loudly insulting the coach and the referee, eventually yelling that 'his son is better than this game' and that 'he will find a better coach for his son'. He grabs his scared and embarrassed son and proudly walks back to the car, the whole drive back yelling out loud about the unfairness of the situation and the stupidity of the coaches. Hank's will chakra is spinning backwards, huge, taking energy from every other place it can. Because of it other chakras do not have enough charge and Hank does not have enough consciousness there to help him see what is happening. How can he fix this? Hank can take a deep breath and focus on the needs of his son, this will bring more energy into the front of his heart and begin to correct the imbalance.

How can you open your heart? For the front of the chakra you can tune into someone or something that brings feelings of love to you—your pet, your garden, your child, the beautiful sky. If you find it hard to see the good in a difficult situation, allow your heart to open more by lying on a yoga ball or anything that helps you to bend backwards. To help your will open up, lift your arms to your shoulder level and move them towards your heart, then with a force back, pushing your shoulder blades together. Repeat this a few times, this brings more charge to your will. You can also balance the heart aspects by moving energy from the larger one to the smaller one. If you feel you are too controlling in a situation, your will is too big. Focus on the back of your heart, then imagine the energy moving through your body into the front of your heart, you can place your hand there. Allow some time for the flow to occur, and you will begin to feel more trusting of the situation. Or if you are trying to help everyone and missing yourself in the process, the front of your heart is too big. Tune into it, then imagine energy moving through your body to the other side, also move your arm as in the previous exercise to open the will. Energy will flow to the will center and the heart will get smaller as a result. If you want to use color, there are a few appropriate ones. If you are too far in your will and need to open the heart, use rosy pinkish energy. If you have difficulty loving the Self, bring kindness to yourself by using pine tree green.

The **fifth chakra** is located at the throat and at the back of the neck. The throat aspect represents self expression and taking in life 'as is'. This means that if the throat is functioning well, we can receive life's circumstances as they come, no matter what they are, with trust and the assurance that we are going to learn through them. The truth of our being is the consciousness in the throat. This does not mean some high-and-always-positive truth. It means the truth of the moment. It can be 'right now I am angry', or 'I am terrified', or 'I hate my child right now'. Most of the time these are fleeting emotions and chances are you are not angry or terrified all the time, and the hatred for your kid was probably brought on by his overly loud computer game, re-peating itself over and over in the living room. But nevertheless these are real feelings; they are true at that moment. If we allow ourselves to know this truth, we have a healthy throat chakra. If we filter our feel-ings, only allowing ourselves to know about the 'good feelings' while feeling guilty for the 'bad' ones, the throat chakra gets clogged and weak. Notice that I am not saying you have to speak this truth out loud. Sometimes it might be appropriate, but not always. We get so used to filtering what we are saying that we begin to filter the knowl-edge of what is happening internally. Before long we are not aware anymore about particular types of feelings we tend to judge, trying to trick ourselves into believing we do not feel them anymore at all. The throat chakra is similar to the third in that it runs the consciousness of our unique Self. Just as the third chakra's identity is unique, the truth of each one of us is also unique. And so the main reason we clog up and shut off our throat chakra is the fear of our uniqueness, which also translates into the fear of being different. We tend to subscribe to soci-etal belief systems, feeling bad that our personal truth does not always match societal requirements, and we shut ourselves off.

You are twenty-five years old and live with your mother. She tells you that your haircut is just awful and you should try another one instead. She goes with you to the hair salon where you get the new cut. Your smile is shining as you tell your mother how grateful you are that she noticed the horrible mistake you made choosing the previous haircut and for her help in correcting it. Your throat chakra is stuffed up and looks like it caught a cold. If you allow yourself to let go of the fear that clogs it, you will notice that you really liked your previous haircut and hate this new one, and the only reason you went for it was the fear of being a bad daughter if you didn't listen to your mom.

Sometimes speaking your truth is the most important thing. It allows you to anchor your Self in the situation, make your uniqueness known. This is especially necessary in relationships. In any situation we feel something on the lower levels first, then the higher ones. It is great to know the higher truth, but if we ignore the lower one, we miss out on the humanity of our Self.

You are wearing a sensual new dress, preparing to go out with your husband. He does not comment on the dress. You arrive at the restaurant and you are turning sideways, slowly taking off your coat, making sure he sees the dress. He still does not comment on it. The entire dinner you are upset and snap at him about his choice of restaurant. He still doesn't see the blasted dress! You arrive home and you are definitely not in the mood for romance, you feel ignored and unloved. You go up into your bathroom and, breathing deeply, tell yourself that you are more evolved then this, that the dress does not matter, that you wanted love and affection and he did give you that. You tell yourself that you love yourself and with a smile step out into the living room. Your husband is completely confused, unsure of your shape-shifting from a frustrated bitch to a loving wife. He thinks you are nuts, but you feel evolved and breathe deeply. You went from the lower truth to the higher truth too quickly, and because the lower truth was not expressed in your throat chakra you both missed out on the humanness of your relationship. What could have happened is that after breathing deeply you walked into the living room spinning your throat chakra and told your husband that you were really frustrated about him not noticing your dress and that you really wanted him to comment on how great you looked in it, but that you also completely know that he loves you and that the dress is not that important. You name both truths, higher and lower. This is done without blame, more as a report on your truth. Your husband then can tell you that he thought he did comment on the dress, because the whole evening he thought how gorgeous you looked, but could not understand why you were becoming more and more frustrated and mad at him by the minute. The exchange of lower and higher truths together (even if they are opposite) brings more depth into relationship.

If the front of the throat chakra spins backwards, we project what we believe is coming to us. Instead of taking life as it comes, we look for the fulfillment of our expectations. In other words, if you expect the world to punish you, you will attract circumstances that will feel like punishment. If in your eyes the world is dangerous, you will receive situations that will feel dangerous. This happens because inside of us we already have these unresolved energies: we resolve that we need to be punished, have judgments, safety issues and so on and when the throat chakra pushes this internal truth out, we perceive it as external reality. To correct this we need to find the causes for these imbalances (what makes us judge or feel unsafe)—the truth about what we are really feeling inside, not the external projection. This opens up the throat chakra and slowly changes its rotation.

The back aspect of the fifth chakra is self responsibility. If it is open and healthy, we have a clear understanding of how to respect and honor the Self, how to take care of ourselves. We know when to say 'no' to something and are comfortable with our uniqueness. A clear neck chakra brings the experience of success into our lives and a healthy pride in our accomplishments.

If the back of the fifth chakra is closed, you are in terror of failure. Self honoring does not work, and you end up working too hard yet never succeeding. Working your butt off, you feel a victim of bad luck and become resentful to life for not providing you with better opportunities. You are not being self responsible, not taking charge of your life.

But our favorite configuration of the fifth chakra on the back is, of course, the counterclockwise spin. We poof up the neck chakra, make it very large and spin it backwards, attempting to be responsible for everyone around us but ourselves! You can never be responsible for another being, it is impossible. You can keel over trying, but it will still not happen. We attempt this impossible task, feeling horribly ashamed when we do not succeed. Every person is a unique being with his/her own path. If we spin the back of the neck chakra backwards, we cannot be responsible for our Self because it projects the energy out instead of taking it in. One action cancels the other. Self responsibility is extremely important, because it allows us to change things. If you do not like how life is, change your Self to align with it differently, you cannot change life. Self responsibility gives us the power to create balance in our aura, relationships and life.

Your best friend is an alcoholic and you drink socially with her to keep her company. This bugs you emotionally, besides giving you a bad headache, but you are reluctant to tell her how you feel... your throat chakra is not running enough energy to tell the truth because it is twisted with over-responsibility towards the friend. Telling the truth keeps the relationships around us honest and authentic, while helping us to find out more about ourselves.

Both aspects of the fifth chakra function similarly to the heart in that they have to be balanced; if not, then the larger one takes the energy from its smaller twin. If you are over-responsible and attempt to take care of everything and everyone, you will not be aware of your truth (i.e., the back of the neck chakra is too large and the front too small, and probably both spin counterclockwise). If you put too much energy into the front of your throat, you will end up projecting your internal truth, pushing it onto others and life, and then getting disappointed that there is no success.

The fifth chakra's sense is, of course, sound. Not just audible sound, but any sound, including internal sound. Since it is the gateway into the fifth level of truth, it is capable of perceiving any energy through sound. Each cell has a sound, each frequency has one. But in a broader sense the fifth chakra is about our ability to listen to ourselves and to others. If this chakra is clogged we listen, but we do not hear the truth. One of the ways to open up your throat is to make a sound. Not a word, but a tone, then another one and another one, continuous smooth tones. It can also be a sound authentic to the truth within: if you are angry, then roar (of course do not forget self responsibility and do it in your car or a closed room); if you feel pity, make an annoying whiny sound; if you are happy, do not stifle the laughter. I think you get the idea. For the back of the neck chakra you can try slowly rotating your head from side to side and from front to back. And don't forget to go into self responsibility (you can make a statement out loud like 'I choose to take care of myself').

The **sixth chakra** is well known and often called 'the third eye' because of its location at the forehead. It actually acts as an eye into a less dense world of mystery. The third eye has two aspects, the front and the back (on the back of the head). The front of the third eye chakra is responsible for envisioning. Anytime we want to envision something, to come up with an idea for something we do not yet know or to see ourselves or others differently, we use the third eye. When it is balanced, it represents the ability to envision the Self in wholeness, we see ourselves as a precious/powerful/satisfied being, connected to the Universe. The third eye also helps to translate higher energies into something our personality can comprehend. It allows us to use visual images as a tool to explain something linearly that would otherwise be unexplainable due to its simultaneous nature. When we are looking for a particular block, trying to figure something out about ourselves, the third eye will often provide a picture of some event that can help us connect to the energy trapped in that block. It could be metaphorical, mystical, an actual energy configuration, in the present or in another lifetime scenario, an insert from a movie you saw that explains what you are feeling, et cetera. The third eye does not look at matter as our physical eyes do—it looks at the rest of the Universe in its totality. Most humans, because of many fears of their uniqueness, are afraid to open the third eye, and after birth instead of growing this chakra tends to diminish. But we can open it back up. This does not mean that we all will suddenly start seeing energy and angels all the time, but you will regain the capacity to perceive more of reality beyond the physical world.

People often say that they would do anything just to 'have their third eye open', assuming it means they will see energy beings around them and theirs and others' auras. It is way more complex than that. Third eye vision comes with a price: your identity can no longer be associated with the normality of the status quo.

You are sitting in a chair and across from you on the other side of the table is another person. With your physical eyes you see yourself, the other, a table, chairs and the walls of the room somewhere farther away. All these things are perceived as separate objects (hence our attempts to treat the physical body and the entire world as if it is a machine made of separate parts). Now imagine the room is filled with multicolored smoke (some transparent, some very dense and opaque) and that you and the other person sit in an even denser oval-shaped cloud of smoke with structures of different colors, like scaffolding inside the cloud. And of course don't forget your skeleton, it is sitting right in there across from the other person's inside that complex cloud, a skeleton with organs hanging around it. The table, chairs and the walls are almost invisible, they are transparent, you are in an endless space that is filled with blobs of color slowly floating or moving very fast (inside your personal bubbles and also in the whole room), everything looks like a mixture of floating ribbons, tails, vortexes, clouds, spirals, blobs, et cetera. Also, between you and the other person are long cords with tiny bubbles and other colored things flowing inside. Would you have a clear idea of who you are if the whole world around you looked like this all the time? Could you drive? Could you simply walk on the street or talk to another person? I am clairvoyant; this is part of my journey on Earth this time. By the age of two I figured out that people around me do not see what I saw and that to them the 'real things' are only the things I can 'bump into', namely, solid matter. It took me a while to learn to drive, because I focused not on the shape of the car, but on the energy field of the trees and drivers, which are much bigger than the car's shape. Having this ability from birth, I had to find a way to live with it, and I have adapted. It is very different when someone opens their third eye this much suddenly, after having spent years building their identity on the solidity of things. Could you feel sane if suddenly you did not know what was around you? The answer is no. Even the energy beings that everyone so much wants to see do not look anything like what we *think* they do. We think in terms of separation, so we assume that a non-physical being will be just sitting in the room with all of us physical ones. Separate from us!? This is not true, there is nothing separate from us, to some extent everything is always connected, so that in a room of multicolored smoke you might focus on a bright cloud or other shape until you realize that you are not looking at a thought-form or an emotion, but another consciousness, a being. It can then open up into its original form or project a picture into your third eye. Eventually all humans will be able to use their third eye in this 'full open' way, but today we build a lot of our identity on matter and still see ourselves separate from other people, trees, animals, tables and walls. Everything has to be balanced. When we live in balance with the planet and do not need to drive to the store for food, instead manifesting that food in front of us, our identity will be able to handle full third-eye vision without any issues. But we can learn to use our third eye for everyday things first, then it will begin to tune into energy. How does that work? If I asked you right now to describe to me what your living room looks like, even if you are not in the living room, you will see a mental image in your head, right? It's a picture of your living room in your mind's eye. You are *seeing* your living room, yet you are not present there, the picture is reviewed through your third eye. In the same way, with more clearing and processing you can *look* into yourself, some other life of yours or into the future through the third eye. In your regular life the third eye can become a very useful tool in translating (remember, that is one of its main functions) reality to us.

It is rare that the third eye is 'too big', but sometimes we end up making it too long. Like a telescope it stretches in front of us, protruding forward in the auric field. This happens when we are trying too hard to see something, like 'what job should I get next?', 'where should I move?' or 'is this guy the right one?', et cetera. This overly stretched forward configuration might feel very uncomfortable, you might have a headache from it or feel pressure and stuffiness as if you got a cold. If you are in this state for a while you might not be able to concentrate and it will start working against you—you are trying to get more ideas and answers, but instead are able to focus less and less, after a while you feel like you are 'losing it' and are ready to chop your aching head off. It is all because the stretching of the third eye takes energy from other chakras, especially the solar plexus one (third chakra on the front). The energy of clarity cannot exist in the solar plexus chakra after a while of this over-activity in the third eye, and we get tired and confused. This is why it is always a good idea to ask something once, when you are really ready to get the answer (like during journaling or meditation), but stop yourself from asking the same question over and over. If we do not get an answer, there are usually only two reasons: we are either afraid to see it, or it is not the correct time for us to know it. If you are afraid, you need to get more energy into the front of the fifth chakra to unblock the personal truth of that fear, and then the third eye can provide you with the answer (this is when any focusing technique is helpful). If it is not the time to know the answer, you will feel that you do not have a strong logical solution (there is none or there are too many) and you do not feel an intuitive pull towards anything. In both situations there is no reason to put all this extra energy in the third eye, it will only make it harder on you.

The sixth chakra on the front can also help us create the life we want. If you can envision something, you are capable of doing it and having it. Usually we cannot really envision ourselves as sultans or presidents, we can have mental images about these positions in life, but cannot actually completely submerge ourselves in them. But things like seeing yourself healthy, or in a different job, with a particular mate, in a new car or a place, these we can truly envision and hence bring into existence. The third eye allows you to experience the vision as if you walked right into it, like trying on the clothes from that picture for a while. When we can completely submerge ourselves into the *experience* of the vision, we begin to unravel fears and blocks in the way of it and to attract supportive circumstances.

As a child your grandpa tells you about the vineyards in France and you dream yourself there, in the magic of it all. Fast forward to now: your job as a computer specialist requires more than seventy hours per week, and France is a long way away. In your busy life you do not have any space to even think of a trip, the childhood dream is long forgotten, rationalized as 'immature'. One day in a newly built grocery store you pass by the French wines and remember...the child in you wakes up and defends the validity of the dream, it becomes real again as the visual images begin to speed through your mind's eye. By the time you exit the store, you decide to go for it. In your sixth chakra the vision of you actually *in* France is amplified. You visit the local travel store and start looking at the books and pictures of the vineyards, you cannot resist searching the web for more information, you begin to have dreams of France. Next week you master enough courage to ask your boss for a vacation so you can schedule your trip. All of this aligns the intention in your aura. You will be walking through the vineyards in France, tasting wine, in just three weeks. This is how the sixth chakra works.

If the third eye is clogged, it becomes the source of limited self vision, and a person will have difficulty coming up with new ideas. S/he will have limited ability to change, because we have to envision what we are changing into first (not the same as 'know mentally'), before the intention for 'going for it' can happen. If the sixth chakra on the front is spinning counterclockwise, we project our ideas about life onto life, and the images of how we *think* life is (due to our fears, blocks and past traumas) become our reality. We then see ourselves in accordance with these projected images, justifying our behavior. If you are afraid to be used, you will push the image of being used through the third eye onto reality (seeing yourself as already being used), which then will attract the circumstance of someone using you—then you feel justified in seeing this world as a user. Or you think you are fat or ugly. You might have been taught that by your parent or a sibling, but either way, this image of you as fat/ugly gets projected through the third eye and before long other people begin to notice your weight or features you are not comfortable with. People might comment on them positively or negatively, but for you the result is the same: your self image as fat/ugly just got its external 'proof'. To correct this you need to envision yourself as balanced, happy and beautiful (not necessarily thin, because that will be not your truth, but a reaction to your fear of being too fat), then sit with this new vision of Self. You can meditate on it, journal about it, you can encode it into your psyche every morning and night when you brush your teeth, it does not matter how you do it, as long as you keep reminding yourself of it. Eventually your external world will begin to reflect the new vision, giving you support for internal transformation (courage to challenge the blocks associated with the negative belief).

Noticing the self judgments that external reality reflects to you and correcting them with a more balanced, unconditional vision of Self changes the counterclockwise spin of the sixth chakra into a correct clockwise one. Since no chakra is separate from your psyche, the chakra is not some 'thing' you can manually manipulate to change its spin from incorrect to correct. To make this, and any other, chakra spin properly clockwise and stay clean, you have to work with an issue connected to it (in this case a negative Self vision), and the consciousness of processing the issue will adjust the chakra, reflecting your progress.

The back aspect of the third eye is about how to make ideas a reality. As you can imagine, this is a very import chakra! Have you noticed how some people seem to be able to get a lot done, have great ideas and accomplish a lot, while others tend to dream a lot, but nothing ever happens? The front of the third eye provides us with ideas, while the back helps us to see the ways these ideas can be manifested. You want a new kitchen in your house. Your third eye is working overtime as you envision the most beautiful cabinets made of cherry wood, beautiful hardware, lovely marble countertop, new large cooktop, you see yourself having breakfast with your honey at the tall island, sitting on the barstools, chatting about life while you are having a glass of hot chocolate… then you walk into your existing kitchen. You are scared, overwhelmed and discouraged. You have no idea how this magnificent idea can come into being, it seems impossibly large. Your sixth chakra on the back is blocked. If you open it up, you can envision the steps to your goal, like writing up the kitchen ideas, looking around for a designer, getting rough price estimates and even budgeting your project, creating a savings fund and a time estimate for your new kitchen. All these steps dream the new kitchen into being, moving it from the higher vibrations of an idea to the lower vibrations of matter.

There is always some reason for why a certain chakra is closed. If the front of the third eye is open, but the back is closed, a person will have a hard time making things happen, while having lots of ideas. This usually means on some deeper level he does not want to make decisions associated with the goal, does not want the responsibility of it. There must be an unconscious judgment of material reality as too slow and insufficient. He does not want to be here, in physicality, but since he is here, physicality is blamed for its speed of manifestation—it takes steps, sometimes many steps, to make something happen here, but a person like that will want the creation to be instantaneous. He is arrogant in his belief that he is above physicality, desiring to be an ideas-man while someone else takes care of him (and his ideas). If you have difficulty making ideas come to life, look for these symptoms so you can begin to clear the unconscious blocks to manifestation.

If the situation is reversed and the back of the third eye is functioning perfectly, while the front is clogged or spins counterclockwise, a person will also be in trouble. If your third eye on the front is closed, but the back is open, you will not have many ideas, but be a great 'working bee' to help other people's ideas come to life. But if the front spins backwards while the back is open, you will have some twisted ideas about life and be able to manifest them successfully. Imagine a woman who gets hurt too many times by lovers breaking her heart. She develops a belief that 'men are there to be used for money, nothing else' and this image of herself using men for their money is in her third eye. The back aspect also spins, enabling her to actually use men successfully. She is creating a reality where she is limited in her love expression, but perhaps gets a well-off lifestyle. Or imagine a man who believes that 'everyone is out for themselves'. With this image in his third eye he projects that he can do whatever he wants and can take anything from anyone, because they will do the same to him. If the back of his third eye is working, he might become a successful criminal.

One of the ways to open the front aspect is to give yourself permission to freely use your imagination. We often judge ourselves without even knowing it, not allowing the freedom of our imagination to unfold. You might start to envision yourself in a more expensive house, or with a partner of your dreams, but then shut yourself off with 'don't waste your time, this will never happen'. The purpose of imagination is not to come up with affordable and doable scenarios, but to open up the limitations of our linearly oriented mentality. Feel free to imagine anything, no matter how improbable it is (but it has to be about you, not about how you want your kid to succeed or your mean neighbor to be a nice person). As you are imagining something, if you are afraid to be disappointed you might have a very hard time envisioning anything outside of linear limitations. So I suggest you look at your imagining not as a roadmap to what and how things will happen but as an exercise, as if you are coming up with probable endings to a movie or something like that. This trains your third eye to be free of the limitations imposed on it by blocks in the aura. To open the back aspect, you just need to work with the resistance to manifestation and have discipline (the will chakra) help you in creating structures for manifestation. Before long energy will begin to flow in that chakra and you will see the results.

The last of the seven chakras is the **crown chakra,** which is at the top of the central vertical tube in your aura. It acts as the bridge between the human energy system, including the physical body, and the Soul. When the crown chakra is open and healthy, we feel connectedness with the Universe, being a part of All That Is. Spirituality becomes an experience, not a dogmatic idea or a mental concept. This experience is unique to each person, it cannot be easily explained in linear words. It is a transcendental state of being. Through the crown chakra we can comprehend infinity, whereas to our personality infinity is an abstract concept, not an experience, because we live in a finite linear reality. The crown chakra is also responsible for a sense of purpose in our life. Faith (not to be confused with religion) is the gateway to purpose, which rewards us with feelings of peace, belonging and wholeness. This purpose in life is not a direct linear plan. Humans often make the mistake of thinking that their purpose in life has be a particular career, or marrying a certain person, or writing a book/making a movie, or starting some campaign, et cetera. It is never this linear; it cannot be. The crown chakra receives guidance from the Soul about a particular type of learning we are here to do. The Mission Alpha of each human is still to get their Soul connected into their body, which eventually turns the physical body into Light/consciousness. Built into this main 'mission' are smaller ones about particular types of learning. Someone might choose to learn courage, and he can do it by becoming a firefighter or a single dad. Or speaking up for yourself can be learned by getting a job as a public speaker or by telling the truth at a family dinner. The energy of the crown chakra is what guides us into these situations, magnifying the intuitive feeling that 'this is *it*, this is my moment to do/say something'. This is the purpose we are talking about, the access to the synchronicity of the Universe. The crown chakra is not only accessed when we are in meditation, its power exists as spirituality 24/7.

If the crown chakra is open but spins counterclockwise, a person will have a desire to override the spirituality of others. He will want to see his spiritual experience as the 'right one' and other types of spiritual expression as the 'wrong ones'. A person like that is a fanatic, his faith is blind—he has a 'blind' crown chakra. He will either look for someone with a spiritual expression similar to his and follow them blindly, or he will make his own religion or cult. He will appear powerful because the energy flow in his crown chakra amplifies his higher frequencies, and people tend to follow leaders like that. But it is a dead end, because instead of supporting others in their spiritual self discovery he will attempt to dominate them with his beliefs. The backwards crown spin is usually based on fears of 'disappointing God'. This condition projects energy out of the crown, pushing the actual Soul consciousness away, hence the person feels disconnected from God. He then bases his relationship with God not on actual transcending experiences, but on dogma, mental understanding and fears, all of which are limiting. But now, in order to stay connected to his idea of God he has to 'do everything right' by his beliefs. Out of this comes a desire to dominate others, because their submission becomes proof of his 'rightness'.

When the crown chakra is closed or isn't working correctly, we lose the meaning of everything and life becomes black and white, boring and stagnant. Usually in this configuration the structural levels and the will chakra will be strong, so that the configuring of this person is not dissimilar to a computer. His personality will be based in physicality or on linear reasoning and he will have no idea what others are talking about when describing some spiritual ecstasy. He will see life as mechanical. He might find meaning for himself in his career's advancement or family, but will not have a sense of a larger purpose.

The sense connected to the crown chakra is inner knowing. It differs from the intuition in that it is certain. Remember we talked about lower intuition being a vague sense about something and higher intuition being a sense of being guided. Well, in the crown, consciousness is much more focused. Ever felt like something just 'dropped in' your mind? One moment you had no idea about it, the next you knew for sure? Like knowing that you must go for that job, or you just have to turn right as you're driving, or that you will come to know this girl/ guy way more intimately. All these are common experiences from the crown. The more complex ones include being energetically download- ed with a new language and, when confronted, suddenly being able to speak it, or instantaneously remembering in detail another life you had with a person you are meeting for the first time as you are shaking their hand, or witnessing a car accident and without medical training knowing exactly what and where the driver is injured and what to do to help her. The crown chakra is a gateway into the seventh level, and it is capable of understanding whole concepts at once. A concept on the seventh level is like a complex program that can be downloaded into the crown and integrated immediately (like with the language example: not learning it, but just knowing it).

How do you open the crown chakra? By experiencing stillness and connectedness. If we meditate or otherwise focus on 'I am God', we raise our consciousness to match the Universal range. Do not repeat a million times 'I am God'; this is not about chanting it. Say it slowly (it doesn't have to be out loud) and breathe deeply, holding the mean- ing of the statement, perhaps repeat it again when the meaning begins to dissipate. Another exercise you can do involves your body. Sit with your back straight (you can be cross-legged or on a chair with legs apart), relax, and interlock your fingers. Do not tighten, let the energy guide you. Place your interlocked hands in front of your third chakra about four to five inches from your body, take a slow, deep breath in, then slowly exhale. As you breathe, feel the energy between your third chakra and your hands. Raise your hands above your head, fingers in- terlocked, but extend both index fingers when your hands reach the crown chakra position. Again inhale and exhale slowly, as you envi- sion energy moving into (inhale) and out of (exhale) your crown. Then breathe in, envisioning energy moving into your crown, and move your hands to point down (in front of your body at the lower belly) and exhale, envisioning energy moving out of your root chakra into the Earth. You can repeat each step more than once, just keep them equal (e.g., four times at the third chakra, four times at the crown, four times from crown to root).

Structural/Electro-Fluid/Magnetic Balance

The human energy field consists of two complementary forces (pure intense energy charges): structural/electric and fluid/magnetic. These forces are also yang and yin, light and dark, male and female, active and receptive, doing and being, logical and intuitive, right and left, up and down and more. Notice that the first force in each pair is the synonym to the structural and the second force, the synonym to the fluid. These two forces are opposites, even though they are part of the whole. The structural force represents straight line movement, active force, the known/the light, male polarity and is electric. The fluid one represents wavy movement, receptive/passive and the unknown/dark, female polarity and is magnetic.

Why is it important to get this? Because all of us naturally have more of one polarity than the other. This makes us all unique, no one is exactly 50/50. When we know which polarity is predominant and which is harder for us to deal with, we stop blaming ourselves, get a grip and resolve our action/inaction issues more efficiently. (You will have a better idea of which polarity you have more of from Chapter 3). Becoming 50/50 is not a goal; it is not a format for a human. We tend to see this 50/50 as perfection and then blame ourselves for not being able to embody it. But actually humanity's uniqueness is based on not being 50/50. Each individual has his/her own ratio of these two forces, creating many more exciting alignments with other humans, like trillions of pieces of a puzzle, all different, able to fit together in complex and beautiful ways. The simplistic beauty of this resonance is Love and Grace.

Structural and fluid energies are supported throughout all the energy levels, they do not just exist in one spot somewhere in our aura. We have a predisposition for a particular polarity that is set up by the Soul in accordance with karmic patterns and the lessons of each lifetime. It is a very complex process. The genetic line into which a Soul is going to incarnate is chosen, and it has a particular atomic structure that will enable it to easily anchor the chosen polarity.

How does atomic structure anchor electric or magnetic energy? It does so by means of tiny, subatomic particles called fermions and bosons. Fermions are tight forms. They choose identity and determine to stay in form; they are electric sub-particles. Bosons are energy clouds; they are charged fields and are magnetic. Each person is born naturally with more fermions or bosons, determining their dominant polarity. But we do not always follow this sub-atomic blueprint. If you are naturally more magnetic, but get scared of being so open and also get trained that electric is more safe/responsible, you might end up trying to act more electric. This tends to bring a lot of pain from not being able to relax into the Self. You will still feel like you can 'never do it right' or match up to other 'electric types'. Or you are naturally more electric, but forced by societal standards to play a more magnetic role. You will feel unrealized, unable to express your potential.

Does that mean we can only be whatever combination of sub-atomic particles that we originally have? That would be true if we didn't have one more type of these particles—a neutral one. This particular sub-particle is capable of becoming a fermion or a boson. What determines it? Well, our science has only now just become aware of the existence of these particles and, of course, says that 'it is random'. Actually it is our consciousness that determines what that neutral sub-particle will become.

If we are in fear/judgment/guilt/shame, we defend against our Soul's plan and tend to activate not the balancing particles to our nature, but the opposite. You might be just learning to be more magnetic and come into a body with a little bit more magnetic then electric energy. Your Soul's plan was to activate even more magnetic energy for deeper experiences. If you got scared, your neutral sub-particles would freak out into fermions and you would become more electric, which wouldn't serve your evolution. If you come in to learn the electric side, but because of karmic patterns incarnate into a slightly more magnetic body, you can activate more electric energy over time and balance them. But if you are afraid of the electric and choose not to look at that fear, the neutral sub-particles will become magnetic, tuning you into a magnetic mess instead of a balanced, powerful identity. These forces are very powerful in the energy field and even more in the body (because it is denser). When we recognize what polarity is dominant in us and the direction of our journey in life, we feel guided to a correct polarity.

There is no 'ultimate correct polarity'; it depends on the life's plan. Unfortunately we get taught that one polarity is more powerful/important than the other. This is not true; they are equal powers of this Universe. If you recognize an internal bias toward a particular polarity, work with it, make it more conscious, so that you help your system to let it go. This will support your neutral sub-particles to change their polarity into the *correct one for you* for that time. The correct polarity balance leads to the amplification of life force.

There are two main ways to access life force. One is through the external environment by osmosis, like in the high mountains or the woods. The other is by internal creation, the sparking of the two polarities. Without this spark we cannot access our Soul consciousness and bring it down to the cellular level, and invite it into our lives.

Since we cannot always just get up and go to the woods, we are better off learning how to do this internally. Then even if you are in the dead energy of an office with fluorescent lights, you still can generate your own life force. Another useful piece of information is that when we generate life force ourselves, we add to the environment; that is, we support Life. It seems only fair to 'repay' the Universe for its support of us by at least occasionally supporting it, don't you think?

When there is enough ability to use both the electric and magnetic, more life force is built. Life force is generated through the bouncing between the polarities. If we are always using only one side, we significantly limit our production of life force. This makes life feel hard, as if we have to do everything by ourselves without any help. If the production of life force is constant, life becomes more effortless and we have the support of Universal energies. Not only that, we feel genuinely alive because we *are* in a very personal relationship with the Universe.

Boundaries

There are two types of boundaries, natural and artificial. We are all familiar with the artificial boundary. It is a fortress-like rigid defense system, the maintenance of which requires us to use lots of our own energy. It walls us off from a direct experience of life and deadens our sensitivity in a weak attempt to make life less scary. We get little result in comparison with the energy output. Yet we still wall ourselves off, afraid of the unpredictability of Life and our place in it.

A natural boundary is generated by the up and down pumping of energy in the vertical tube; this creates the centrifugal force that becomes the natural boundary. This boundary is supported completely by the Universal energy flowing through the vertical tube from all over the Universe and Earth, we do not have to use any of our own energy for it (our energy is the neutral Universal energy encoded with our field signature, and it is much better to have a constant inflow of Universal energy into your system than to recycle your own charge time after time). The natural boundary encourages our exploration of life, while defining our personal space. It acts as a container for individuality at the same time as it allows life to be shared.

Why is this boundary necessary? Why don't we just live without it? Without healthy and clear boundaries (and without the artificial ones) it feels like everything happens at once, and we feel overwhelmed and insane. We experience everyone else's emotions as our own. It becomes very difficult to have an identity, our individual thoughts over-merge with the social consciousness of family, friends, political and religious organizations, country, and then we cannot think/feel for ourselves. A person like that is left with being told what to do and how to be.

Most of us humans did not read the part of the 'manual' that says we have the innate right to exist, which would have allowed a healthy, natural boundary. Instead we learned to create an artificial one as a defense against the perceived danger of the external world. Inside this artificial fortress is a *false* sense of safety, false because this safety is dependent on keeping others out. The more energy a person puts into maintaining the fortress walls, the less energy there is to create within his/her life and for vitality and happiness. In other words, we take energy away from the vertical pump of our energy system. The boundary is a container, not a screen. We get so scared of 'not being right', or being something terrible that we believe we are not supposed to be, that we try to use the artificial boundary as a sifting screen to hide from us what we are afraid to know about ourselves. Instead of resolving issues, learning more and creating, we are hiding behind our self-draining artificial boundary.

To correct this one needs to bring awareness to the vertical flow of energy within the vertical tube, claiming the identity's right to exist no matter what, without restrictions, judgments or limitations. Focusing on the up and down movement of energy supports the flow. Make sure you have a full range of energy movement inside the tube from the very top of your head through the area of the pelvis and into the legs with no restrictions, then back up, again and again.

Color and Sound

Everything in the Universe is made of energy, of differently vibrating matrices. Color is a form of perception, and so is sound. Depending on who is experiencing the vibrations of energy, the *range* of her/his perception will define how much s/he sees or hears. What we humans see with our physical eyes is a tiny percentage of the totality of the frequency range of the electromagnetic spectrum. Our physical vision sees less than one percent of it! Just think about that, you see only less than one percent of life! As one of my non-physical friends used to say: 'All these perceptional limitations and humans still have the audacity to claim that they know what life really is!' Although humans can perceive some colors and sounds through the physical body, almost ninety-nine percent can only be perceived through the energy field. Color, if not seen through the physical eyes, is perceived through the sixth chakra, the third eye. So much has been written about the third eye, yet there is still a lot of confusion and preconceived ideas about how seeing energy through it is supposed to look. Most of the confusion is based on our placement in the consciousness spiral. Humans were 'asleep' for a very long time and have just lately began to dream themselves awake. So erroneous ideas about sixth chakra vision are also the result of where we are coming from—a very long sleep. In the spiritual traditions of many cultures the ones who 'remembered' and 'knew' something from ancient, more conscious information attempted to explain the unexplainable to the ones who did not remember and did not know. The attempt was flawed from the beginning, because this information could not be explained, only personally experienced. But because of collective sleep this experience was almost impossible. Until now, of course...

Sound, if not heard through the ears, is perceived through the fifth chakra on the back of the neck. We humans had this experience of non-physical sound in the sleep state. It originated from two very different sources, though: one was from our guides and enlightened masters of previous ascensions, and the other was from beings interested in the control of the planet's sleeping population. This is why we have so many warnings, fears and horror stories about 'hearing voices'. In modern culture it marks a person as insane, schizophrenic, paranoid, et cetera, because during the low-consciousness phase humans were not able to discern from whom the sound was coming, and we have forgotten that we are the creators. We believed all the sounds were coming from someone 'bigger than us', and hence we worshipped it and became victims of it. Energy sound does not only mean a 'voice'. Non-physical guides often sang to us while we were asleep. Hearing words, a voice, is the rarest and the most unusual form of perceiving energy from the fifth chakra on the back.

But back to color for a moment. White light divides into many color rays. Each planet can anchor specific color rays; some are predominant and others are secondary. Our Earth has seven main color rays. These vibratory frequencies feed all life on the planet, including us. These are the main seven rays of Earth: red, orange, yellow, green, blue, indigo and purple. This is why our chakras tend to process these color frequencies as the main fuel for maintaining us. The red ray relates to strength and vitality, orange to creativity and sexuality, yellow to mental clarity, green to feelings of love and kindness, blue to truth, indigo to insight and purple to wisdom.

Color can be used as a tool to move energy, to clear blocks, to enhance boundaries, let go of fear and old trauma, amplify experience and more. When someone feels depressed, s/he has too much gray, but very little orange, the color we need for vibrancy. So if s/he wears orange clothes or looks at the orange color, the energy field will start to resonate with that frequency, amplifying it and feeding her/him. If a person feels angry, s/he has too much red color and not enough yellow and green. An overly mental person uses too much yellow, while an overly emotional person doesn't have enough of it. Physical fatigue occurs with too little red color, as does nervousness and the inability to remember. When someone is withdrawn and cold, they have too much blue color in the field. Just like the planet, we do not have to have all the colors in the same amount, so contrary to popular belief we do not have to look like a rainbow!

Sound is a type of perception based on pressure and motion. What does that mean? It means that a sound is what happens from the friction of directed energy moving through undirected energy. When an arrow penetrates the air, its movement makes a sound. This sound is the friction of the directed arrow against the undirected air. Since everything is somehow directed and undirected at the same time, depending on one's viewpoint, everything has sound. This friction is also a thickening of space, hence the pressure. The consequences of that pressure are the colors we see (physically or energetically). Imagine a bullet shot through the water. The bullet itself would be the directed pure energy, the 'cutting' of water as it moves through; the pressure/motion, would be the sound; and the waves and ripples of this movement would be the color.

Sound is best used to move emotional and feeling energy. Sound as energy exists in our aura and in the physical body. When we are balanced and healthy, we sound like an orchestra playing beautiful music. When something is out of alignment either in the energy system or the physical body, we sound like an orchestra when they are tuning up before the concert: everyone is trying to play their part, but not together.

Sound is fluid but it can be structured into very complex formations. When we make a sound, we shift energy by giving it thickness, a heavier presence. This is why if we proclaim our intentions verbally, we make a stronger energy statement than if we only think them on the inside. When people chant, they fill the space so much with sound that it weaves a complex energy fabric. This energy structure can support a particular flow of feeling and emotions. This is why we can feel very different, even euphoric, entering a space where people were chanting for a while. If someone sings (using words or only sounds) what they are feeling—pain or joy, loss or remembrance, we feel what they are presenting to us. This is because the friction of the sound created by them shapes our own fluid energy levels into similar patterns. We do not just think 'oh, this sounds sad', we feel that sadness in the song. The same could be done, and was in the past, for healings. A scared child could be calmed down by a mother's song, because it represented safety. Traumatized animals relax with calm, peaceful sounds. We sleep better with the sound of a waterfall, waves or distant birds. If something particular hurts, whether physical or emotional, we can start by giving that pain a sound; be prepared that it will probably not be a pretty and harmonious one. That sound in itself can elevate the pain. How? Remember that sound is a 'thicker' energy then regular energy? So if we have difficulty releasing pain, because it feels too elusive, the sound gives it extra 'weight'. If your intent is to move this pain, to release it, the 'weighted' pain is easier to direct with intent, and so it clears faster and with more grace.

CHAPTER 2
The Body

CHAPTER 2

The Body Systems

Material 'stuff' is the same as energy 'stuff', but is significantly slower. Matter is energy, even though it looks and feels solid. Matter has a very slow vibration, so slow we do not perceive it as a vibration at all, but think it is solid. The slowest frequency in the energy field is the physical body. The body structure acts as an anchor point for the entire energy field. A system is an organizational arrangement of energy. Systems exist on every energy level and can overlap and interact with each other. They are relational and always involve some sort of internal movement or circulation of energy.

The body systems mirror many energy patterns on different levels of the energy field. Just as the emotional, astral and unconditional levels of the field are fluid, so are the digestive, circulatory, and lymph systems in the body. Structural levels such as the etheric, mental, truth and conceptual relate to the structural systems of the body, like the skeletal, nervous, respiratory and the skin (integumentary). The other body systems also relate to different levels and patterns of the field.

The purpose of this entire sub-chapter is to help you see that everything in the body relates to consciousness or the blockages in it. There is no such thing as a physical disease, really, only consciousness imbalances that affect physical wellbeing. We are conditioned to give over our authority to doctors who are supposed to know what is wrong with our physical body. No one can know better what is going on inside of our consciousness than us, and so we are the top authority on all the physical conditions we have. Doctors can give us more information and offer ways of helping the body's healing, but in the end we are the healers, not the doctors. When something is wrong in the physical body, people tend to automatically run to the doctor or emergency room out of fear—fear that our body is betraying us, as if it has turned on us and now is working against us, making us feel sick. This only creates a larger rift between what we see as 'us' and the physical matter we are in. In reality it is all one being, we are energy and matter. Actually, if we only remember that, we can see any physical difficulty as a message from the body, not a punishment or betrayal.

Let's begin with the **digestive system.** The digestive system represents the ability to take life apart, to assimilate its components. The energy boundary is important to the health of the digestive system, since it helps the production of stomach acid, facilitating digestion. The digestive system takes food in, then apart; assimilates it, then discards the unnecessary components.

When someone has difficulty digesting, they do not have enough discernment in their energy system, which relates to the amount of acid they produce. Then the stomach sees all different kinds of food as one and gets overwhelmed, and cannot take it apart. Sometimes we under-assimilate the nutrients or take in more than we need. When we do not take enough, this connects to the non-deserving issue in the second chakra, or scarcity on the emotional level. When we take too much in, we also have scarcity on the emotional level, but deal differently with the issue and take in more 'just in case'. This especially relates to carbohydrate (for comfort) and fat (for support of a weak boundary) assimilation.

If a person has problems with constipation/elimination, it represents the resistance to let go, an issue that connects to the emotional level of the energy field. The energy patterns will look tight and overly rigid. To work with that issue a person will have to look at their relationship to abundance/scarcity, and allow in the little things of life, have what they need when they need it, rather than stockpiling (not only in food intake, but in *all* activities of his/her life). Also if there is an emotion or a feeling that a person does not want to let go of, but should, the physical digestive system will match the emotional over-digestion by creating constipation. Hence the physical condition can be easily resolved by letting go of the over-digested emotion/feeling (like holding a grudge, or refusing to stop worrying, or beating yourself up with a particular judgment, etc.)

In the case of food allergies a person's energy field allows in only a very narrow range of vibration. The restriction is due to beliefs, many karmic patterns, and of course genetics. Each food has a particular vibration. If this vibration is incompatible with the energy field because of the restriction, we have an allergic reaction to that food. The allergy also always relates to issues of weakness in the root chakra and the boundary. Why? Because when we have a particular restriction pattern in the energy field, but the root chakra is strong, generating a healthy boundary, then this restriction pattern will affect the body only occasionally, reminding us of its existence so we can work on it. But it will not override the body's natural defenses and processes, and a person won't have an allergic reaction. It does not mean that there is no issue at all; if the restriction is there, so is the issue and it needs to be addressed. But the physical symptoms might be milder, maybe diarrhea or constipation, or indirect digestive symptoms like toxicity, headaches, etcetera. Any time there is a food allergy, we should look at what we are resisting in the consciousness of that food. Milk product's consciousness is nurturance and comfort, strawberries are sexual self love and exposure of intimate self, peanuts represent internal relationship between three things: our stability, how much energy we allow ourselves and the shared energy of the heart (If we give too much with the heart, we might not have enough energy and not feel stable in life, or if we hate our life and do not feel stable in it, we won't have enough energy to love ourselves). Some people have an allergy to soy products. Soy is a feminine consciousness, a very smooth female charge. If someone is either afraid of the feminine (but needs it) or has too much of it (and needs to develop more masculine components instead), their system will develop an allergy. When a person has a belief that animals should not be eaten, s/he might develop an allergy to meat (reversible by changes in that belief). Or, if you died in another life from eating a fish dish that was poisoned by your jealous sister, you might have an allergy to any healthy fish in this life.

As you know, many of our medical chemical drugs precipitate allergic reactions due to their toxicity. This is an example of when a body's natural defense says 'I do not have this poison in my vibrational range, so I will throw it out' and we end up with diarrhea or vomiting. If a person is afraid to get sick again with whatever he needed the drugs for in the first place, his body will still have an allergic reaction, but probably create constipation instead of diarrhea.

Ulcers occur when acidity touches what it shouldn't touch, a stomach or intestinal wall, for example. When the boundary is not strong, a person sees certain life conditions as his/her fault. Actually, everything that happens in our life is directly related to our internal energy-consciousness state and perception; external conditions are consequences of internal ones, but they are not 'our fault'. Fault implies guilt, shame, something we've done wrong to arrive at the undesirable result. If we see life that way, feelings and emotions of guilt create overly acidic conditions in the physical body, leading to high toxicity, acid reflux and ulcers. How many people do you now with acid reflux? How many people do you know who feel guilty? Many years ago my nonphysical guides told me that guilt is a waste of time, energy and space. It is a human illusion, created to avoid self responsibility.

High toxicity is a direct result of stress. The energy boundary is weak and a person takes into her field everything, unable to discern what is hers to 'digest' and what is not. Overwhelm is a natural consequence, followed by fear that life is somehow unsafe. Defensive mechanisms are activated in the aura and in the physical body, leading to higher acid levels, and toxicity rises. But because of the original lack of discernment, the body cannot figure out what to do with the extra 'stuff', so toxicity stays and continuously pollutes the system. This is why if we want to detoxify ourselves we always first have to clear overacidity. Alkalizing is required for toxicity to be able to move out of the body. On the emotional level the counterpart of this is processing guilt, clearing it out, changing one's perspective on life.

The liver is a major component of the digestive system. It discerns what is dangerous and what is safe, breaking down harmful substances and excreting them as harmless. Without a healthy, balanced liver we cannot 'digest life' properly. The liver manufactures cholesterol which is necessary for every cellular membrane (which reflects the strength of our energetic boundary) and for the production of hormones (adrenaline, estrogen and testosterone—the amount of life force we allow ourselves); stores sugar (responsible for helping our life to flow effortlessly); converts food into proteins, carbohydrates and fats (supporting the interface with external reality) and creates proteins needed for blood clotting (self containment). Energetically, besides discernment, the liver deals with the fire element: anger/hatred and passion/compassion. The three main malfunctions of the physical liver are 'fatty liver', cirrhosis and hepatitis. Fatty liver means that the liver accumulates too much fat, which happens because it is unable to discern properly. On the emotional level this connects to the perception of life as overly fast and overwhelming; the fire element is suppressed by the water element and goopy fear. The condition of cirrhosis means that some liver cells self destruct and become nonfunctioning scar tissue. The fire element has turned on itself and burned out. Emotionally, cirrhosis looks like self hatred and irresponsibility. A person stuffs his hatred, because his beliefs do not allow him to have it, but stuffing the hatred is in turn not a self-responsible behavior. Every human being has the right to feel anything, including hatred, and it is your responsibility to allow yourself to experience your emotions. What we do and how we act from our emotions—that is where responsibility comes in and you do not want to act on hatred, for example, even though it is ok to feel it. Hepatitis is inflammation of the liver; in other words, too much active fire element is stuck in the liver and we do not allow it to come out. Medically it is said to originate from a virus that got into the liver. Actually all these viruses are programs for the use of fire element in the body and we always have a multitude of them, but most are dormant. Sometimes when we are processing a particular issue it activates one of these programs, creating a weakening, and we will then experience the virus either by activating it internally or by attracting contact with it. Hepatitis A is related to not enough discernment of Self versus the other, leading to the confusion of fire in the liver, hence the virus usually is water- or food-borne. Hepatitis B is based on a person's desire to have life reflect only the positive fire element (i.e., only compassion and passion). The negative side (hatred, anger, jealousy) is alive in that person, that is, she feels these emotions too, but her beliefs do not allow these feelings space. This very charged fire element gets trapped in the liver and overcharges the blood, hence this virus is usually transmitted by blood. Hepatitis C is similar to B, only it has a component of self blame to it. A person stifles her alive, 'negative' fire in the liver, desiring the world to be 'only good', but blames herself for it not being so. Any hepatitis can be very active and sudden (acute), constant (chronic) or dormant (the person is a carrier but has no symptoms). An acute situation develops when there is a particular issue with the fire element this person was dealing with and it is active on the emotional level, where it is being processed or actively fought. A chronic condition means an ignored issue and dormancy often reflects a karmic weakness pattern, which if worked with consciously, will never activate.

The **circulatory system** relates to sharing, fullness and grounding. All the issues of the heart, blood vessels, bone marrow and the blood itself, spleen and the thymus are part of this system. The blood carries the red color ray and, like a flashlight in the dark, the red light in our blood guides our body home—to the planet. Without this frequency in the blood we could not live. The hemoglobin in the blood needs to be synchronized with the frequency of iron in the planetary core in order for us to feel stable and anchored on the planet. When someone is sick or undergoes some highly toxic drug treatment, their blood loses red energy and becomes a washed out reddish-gray; a person might die from this (which is why it is good to keep red colored things/clothes around people going through serious physical difficulties).

The most common circulatory imbalance is cold hands and feet. The vertical energy tube becomes narrower at the bottom due to resistance to being here on Earth, and this makes the lower two chakras tight and small. The root chakra is the main supplier of red color frequencies and in this situation it is the smallest. The blood then is depleted of the red ray and the physical body limits the red energy that it still has to the torso, for the survival and functioning of the vital organs. And so hands and feet do not get proper circulation.

High cholesterol is an inflammatory response to seeing the world as an enemy and having to protect the Self. This depletes the red ray in the blood because it is supporting the inflammation, not the health of the blood. Then the body is forced to produce more cholesterol to put out the fire of the inflammation. When we try to reduce the cholesterol, we are not looking at the root of the problem. The root of this problem would be lack of safety due to the perception of life as an enemy. Remember that the root chakra represents safety, right? If it is not functioning well it is because a person doesn't want to put energy there because of a belief in danger, but by not putting energy there s/he in turn creates exactly that—the perception of danger. Danger creates inflammation and the red ray in the blood is drained by it. When the red ray is fully functioning in the blood we are so filled with vitality and true strength that there is enough room for all points of view. Danger can coexist with safety and we become balanced.

Heart attacks begin in the fluid levels of the energy field. Continually ignored emotions cause congestion and pressure in the field. For example, a person feels anger or jealousy, emotions he does not feel good about, and instead of processing them, feeling them through and balancing them, he ignores them as if they did not exist. If any of the difficulties we feel were processed as we go along through life instead of stuffed for later, there would be no backlog and hence no heart attacks. If we look for the cause of heart conditions in genetics, we only prolong the issue, making it karmic. To correct the situation we need to look at the unresolved emotional issues and simultaneously give ourselves kindness. The energy of self kindness is essential for heart health and maintenance. *It is self kindness to move emotional energy, instead of trying to pretend to be 'strong' and not feel the emotions.* Don't you wish you were taught that as a kid? It would save humans a lot of trouble, pain and hospital bills to remember that, eh?

When you begin clearing up the backlog of issues, begin processing and readjusting, restructuring your life to match your Soul design, you might have heart arrhythmia. This does not mean there is something physically wrong with your heart. The electric current that runs through the heart and makes it beat in the correct rhythm is based on energy field dynamics. Our heart beats to whatever pattern we have on the structural levels of the energy field and the rhythm matches the electric programming of the etheric level. When a block is being processed and cleared, it affects the structural levels down to the etheric one, which frees up the electric current and adjusts it. Then our physical heart adjusts. If the processing is gradual, in other words if we live life consciously and clear blocks at a steady pace, this electric adjustment is small and constant, and the physical heart hardly notices. But if we go through big changes, emotional trauma or process something large and integral to the whole identity of our being, the etheric level cannot adjust right away. And so it keeps the old electric pattern and the new one at the same time. What is your physical heart to do? It tries to match the pattern, but there are two of them, so it jumps from one to the other, back and forth, creating an arrhythmia. It might actually physically hurt or feel like there is a bird in your chest ready to fly out. This will happen, it cannot be prevented. But it is not harmful. How does one deal with it? When your heart starts jumping, first go through the usual questions in your mind (Is it a physical symptom of over-exercising? Was there some potent stress just now? Did you drink too much alcohol? Are you actively afraid of something right now? How is your left arm feeling? etc.) You might find your answer that way (chances are it is not a heart attack at all). But if there is no answer, then it is an electric current change. Know that it will pass once the etheric level switches from the old pattern to the new, take breaths as deep as you can and relax as much as possible (imagine yourself being a rag doll with no tension at all anywhere), you will be just fine. Once the heart adjusts, the arrhythmia is gone.

Blood pressure issues occur because of emotional fluctuations. If someone has high blood pressure, they are pressing, pushing, forcing something emotionally, which creates high pressure in their emotional level and the sharing/circulation of energy cannot happen correctly. For example, if a woman tries very hard to give her full attention to her child, her job, her spouse, her parents and her friends (I am sure you know one of these women, right?), she is forcing energy interaction. It does not happen naturally this way, and so if she does not address the issue it will develop into high blood pressure. Low blood pressure limits the supply of oxygen and nutrients to the cells and the removal of wastes from them. If someone has low blood pressure, they are giving up emotionally on something, refusing to incorporate some naturally occurring energy, or feel that changes come too quickly and they try to slow them down artificially. For example, if a woman does not like her life situation (relationships, career, or simply the amount of pain in the world) she will reduce her emotional level circulation, either giving up on 'trying to change things' or slowing down the uncomfortable feelings, which after a while will affect the circulatory system by creating low blood pressure. Sometimes blood pressure jumps up and down, and a person can have very high blood pressure one moment and very low the next. This happens when we emotionally fluctuate between forcing ourselves and giving up on it, then forcing again, then giving up. Energy circumstances always precede the physical reaction, sometimes by a few minutes, at other times by hours or even days. With chronic physical conditions an energy imbalance exists most of the time. A few people have low blood pressure in their normal relaxed state. It does not create the usual symptoms of dizziness, lightheadedness or fainting; they are balanced and relaxed, and they usually live longer too.

The spleen produces and destroys blood cells. There are two energy programs for the spleen, which is why it has two functions as if it were two separate organs. One part, the white pulp, produces antibodies for the immune system and the other part, the red pulp, takes out of circulation and destroys defective/old red blood cells. The red pulp part also stores platelets needed for blood clotting, which we used to be able to dump back into the blood stream when needed (if injury occurs); even though humans have lost this ability, many animals still use it. The most common imbalance of the spleen is its enlargement. When a person has some other physical difficulty and tries to escape it by floating out of the body, s/he becomes ungrounded and the spleen tries to compensate by getting larger. Why? Because the larger its size, the more blood cells it can trap and destroy. It tries to help us eliminate the cause of our fear (of another physical condition) by taking damaged cells out of circulation. If we stop running away from the fear of physical difficulty, the spleen will get better. Another common reason for an enlarged spleen is self hatred. When a person does not feel full on their emotional and astral levels, the sharing of energy cannot happen and self hatred triumphs, taking over. The spleen then acts on its orders (to reduce fear), taking in and destroying more blood cells, getting larger and then taking even more. In the physical body this can lead to anemia due to too few red blood cells (diminished amount of red ray in the blood and ungroundedness), bleeding problems due to too few platelets (unclear boundary and weak root chakra) or frequent infections due to too few white blood cells (emotional level self-hatred and self-punishment energy). If self hatred is unprocessed, the spleen continues to enlarge, trapping healthy blood cells; that is, we 'eat ourselves'.

Anemia is another somewhat common imbalance of the blood. Anemia means that either there are not enough red blood cells or that hemoglobin in them is reduced, both minimizing the amount of oxygen carried by the blood. Oxygen is like prana or pure life force, it is necessary for life. When we have emotional challenges related to fullness (feelings of not-enoughness, self hatred etc.) and/or etheric level challenges leading to ungroundedness (not wanting to be here on earth, mistrust of the physical body, judgment of the reality we live in etc.) we disrupt the proper consumption/metabolism of oxygen. If the root chakra is too weak, it cannot supply the red ray to the blood, and so iron in the body is not synchronized with iron in the planet. Difficulties on the emotional level lead to the diminishment of vitamin B12, C and folic acid. Iron, vitamins B and C, and folic acid are essential for red blood cell production, and without them a person becomes anemic.

The lymphatic system relates mainly to the unconditional fluid level of the energy field. The lymph has no propulsion, it moves only when the muscles move it, just like the energy of unconditional love, which only flows when we use it/intend it. Lymph acts like a sponge, absorbing everything we do not need and taking it all out of systems it no longer belongs in. Lymph can go everywhere and absorb anything, just like unconditional love energy.

A lymph node can become clogged if we either avoid living through something or if we absorb something we are not supposed to. Let's say there is a certain difficulty in your life, perhaps you came to a point when the relationship you're in isn't working anymore and you have to make a decision about it, but you do not want to face that. You avoid it. The difficulty is absorbed into the lymph and the unconditional level is blocked. Because you avoid it, the lymph node directly involved in this issue will become clogged (swollen or even inflamed). It takes extra physical effort to move the lymph again, and that effort can unclog the node, but if the issue is not addressed, the node will become clogged again.

The second reason for clogged lymph nodes (and sometimes the whole lymphatic system can stop functioning) is over-absorption. When our unconditional level has a weak boundary, we absorb everything. Yes, everything: the stress of our boss at work, the worries of our spouse and the difficulties of our children at home, the pain of our parents, the suffering of animals on this planet, sometimes the pain of the whole world (from watching the news, reading the shock-value information in the papers etc.). It overloads the unconditional level and so the physical lymphatic system stops functioning properly. People with serious physical imbalances in the lymph system always have this energy configuration—a weak boundary on the unconditional level, because they are processing something through their system that is not theirs to process (from the whole world or from one particular person). This does not mean that one should not live with an open heart. But there is a big difference between taking on the pain and trying to process it internally versus resonating with the pain and feeling compassionate. *Compassion means witnessing and honoring the painful process with an open heart and no judgment, not 'taking on' someone's pain* (which is impossible anyway, because we live in our own perception of reality).

The **urinary system** deals with the balancing of fire and water elements, and it relates to the processing of internal fear and the feeling of belonging. When the kidneys and bladder are healthy, we have a balanced amount of fire and water elements and they do not fight for domination with each other inside of us. Since the planet has balanced fire and water, if these elements are in peace within us, it results in the feeling of belonging here on Earth. We always have fear, it is one of our natural feelings, but it is supposed to flow through and be processed quickly, which is exactly what happens when fire and water in the aura are in synch. If fire and water do fight, it generates large amounts of fear, which we end up storing in the kidneys. This leads to the perception of life as dangerous and we do not feel that we belong in it anymore. If physically the fire and water elements are off, it results in psychological 'off-ness' (the stifling of fear and the pain of not belonging). To balance internal fire and water one needs to let fear exist, without using it as a 'stop sign' (as an excuse not to act). This allows life force in, hence fulfilling belonging.

The kidneys act as filters, taking excess sodium and water and toxic waste products out of the blood. Inside each kidney are millions of little nephrons (tiny filters). Energetically they are fire-water balancers. On the etheric level there are three structures for filtering, which the physical body mimics. If a person has kidney stones, the stones are usually a product of the rejection of the water element. Calcium carries the love vibration and connects it to the water element; if a person is not metabolizing love/water properly too much calcium is released into the blood, which then accumulates in the kidney, forming stones. To dissolve these stones, sound waves can be very helpful (literally having a drum, a voice or a speaker a few inches from the body and vibrating), lots of water and, obviously, a shift in consciousness. Uric acid stones are products of too much fire in the kidney, too much acidity. They can be cleared by making urine more alkaline; that is, by balancing fire and water.

Everything that the kidney decided is not needed in the blood, extra water and toxic waste, is pushed into the bladder through tubes called ureters. When a person has a bladder infection, it is because there is too much fire element in the bladder and that overabundance attracted an overgrowth of bacteria. The imbalanced fire in the bladder indicates that that person is 'pissed' at life. Changes in the potency of emotion can range from mild frustration to full blown, angry dissatisfaction/tantrums about life not fulfilling expectations. The potency of the emotional charge matches the severity of the bladder infection, of course. Sometimes when we are processing an issue of dissatisfaction we get a bladder infection. Even if it is severe, it will not stay long. But if there are chronic bladder infections, a person is lacking the water element (love and connectedness) and instead of the feeling of similarity and an openness to other points of view, places demands on life to match his/her expectations. These expectations do not have to be positive. For example, 'I am unlovable' matched by people trying to help might make this person very frustrated; or, 'I need drama to feel alive' while there is a calm period might make that person mad, resulting in a weakening of the bladder. You might want to take cranberry powder or juice, use orange and silver frequency for your bladder, and take a natural antibiotic like Golden Seal Root (which will pretty much artificially add the orange-silver and help the immune system). Only if all of this does not help take an artificial 'medical' antibiotic, since your brave suffering will not benefit you either, just make sure you have applied all of the other methods first. But the main point here is that you need to really look at the issue itself in order to clear the condition and prevent its recurrence.

The **skeletal system** relates mostly to the etheric level. The etheric level acts as a template for physical bones. The bone structure learns to assimilate nutrients, to stay resilient and alive, as it was programmed by the etheric level. This programming is constantly adjusted according to our needs and our state of being. If the programming is off, though, bone structure follows an irregular shape instead. This can result in a crooked bone, an overly tight tendon or a deadening of the bones. Planetary energy is supposed to run through the bones, acting as a stabilizer. If the etheric energy level does not have a sufficient amount of planetary energy, it cannot support the skeletal system properly. Also, the skeletal system is like an armature for the rest of our body systems, a structure that holds everything in place. When we are unsure of our main structure, that is, lose our internal balance ('I do not know what to do!?' or 'How do I feel stable in the midst of this difficulty?' etc.), our etheric level weakens, leaving the bones more vulnerable.

When one experiences a broken bone, the bone breaks precisely in the area where the etheric level has already become weak. This means that the etheric level needed attention, and it got attention by affecting the physical level. Now, as one pours awareness into the poor broken bone the etheric level gets the love it needed and allows the bone to heal. The physical circumstances leading to the breaking of the bone are irrelevant to the etheric level. But if we stay angry at ourselves ('how could I be so stupid?!' or 'I deserve this, I should have been more careful and watched where I was going' etc.), and pay more attention to the circumstances than to self love, we limit the flow of healing energy love into the etheric level and so the bone heals much slower and with complications.

Problems with ligaments and tendons being stretched or torn relate to overriding the physical body's needs with the will. In the energy field the heart chakra on the back, responsible for the will to act, gets huge, taking the extra charge from the root chakra, which in turn becomes very small. The root chakra feeds the etheric level, so when the root is small the etheric level suffers, limiting the support for the skeletal structure. Because of the overly potent will center the under-supported skeletal system tightens, hence the torn/stretched/injured tendons and ligaments. But there is one more consequence of this situation besides the physical condition. When the overall state of the ligament/tendon is too tight and rigid the emotional and astral levels of the energy field cannot deal with the circulation of emotions. We either feel too overwhelmed by feelings or afraid to feel them. The first step in addressing this situation is always the opening of the root chakra.

Osteoporosis is unfortunately a common physical imbalance, especially among women. Human bones need calcium, phosphorus, vitamin D and other vitamins and minerals in order to keep them at a healthy density level. Calcium is the most important component that is missing during osteoporosis. Energetically, the calcium ion carries the frequency of love, the self-oriented type. The energy of love is allowed in according to the main structural understanding of the life we have. If a person sees loving the Self as a positive and necessary component, the structural levels will support that frequency. But if we judge self love as 'bad behavior', our structural levels do not include it. As you probably have noticed, many women tend to love everyone around them, but not themselves, and if they do, a lot of times it is not true self love but either conditional praising or rebellious pushing. We are not taught how to self love, considering it selfish, especially for women. But without true self love we cannot metabolize calcium properly, and together with hormonal changes, not enough movement and an unhealthy diet, this can lead to osteoporosis. If we train ourselves to self honor and self love, we can rebalance our absorption and distribution of calcium, allowing the body to recover and rebuild health in the bones.

Another dysfunction of the skeletal system is arthritis. In osteoarthritis cartilage-synthesizing cells produce too much collagen and other components, making the smooth surface of the cartilage rough and unable to move properly. The energy of the protein collagen is related to the structural support of fullness and satisfaction. If on the emotional and astral levels we are never satisfied and full, we encode that into our structural levels, which affect the etheric charge of collagen. This sends a message to the etheric level to produce more collagen energy, so we can experience fullness and satisfaction. Collagen builds cartilage. If its charge on the etheric level is increased, so is its physical production, which eventually disables the joints. In rheumatoid arthritis the immune system attacks the tissue that lines the joints, scarring them and eroding bone, cartilage and ligaments. This physical imbalance is similar to osteoarthritis because it also relates to satisfaction and fullness, but different because it is based on anger. Rheumatoid arthritis usually involves imbalances in the liver. Energetically, the liver processes anger. When a person is really dissatisfied with the reality they are in and angry about it, the energy of this dissatisfaction swells up in the liver, sending a message to the immune system that life is dangerous and we better defend ourselves. This energy configuration puts a person at odds with the world, creating a physical response to attack by the autoimmune system. Since there is nothing outside of the Self to attack, it attacks the Self. Such a person would usually also have a belief system that everything is black and white, in absolutes, allowing for nothing in between, no cushioning, hence the deterioration of the lining in the joints. Arthritis is best rebalanced by finding ways of internal satisfaction, instead of looking for it in outside reality, and by processing anger.

Fibromyalgia is one of those medical mysteries, no one really knows how and why it happens, except that it is painful, occurs more often in women and is usually connected to stress. Well, energetically all people with this physical condition look the same: their aura is frozen in fear. The fluid emotional levels barely function, filled with fatigue, depression and/or anxiety, and unable to regenerate, while the structural levels are overly tight and rigidly frozen, as most of the energy is used for the cryogenic support of the fear. This fear is always connected to the root and the crown chakras on the etheric level, although it penetrates all levels, and usually comes as karmic inheritance from other lifetimes. A person like that fears life, feels endangered in it and wants to escape it by going into the faster frequencies. The higher vibrations are perceived as safe and the lower vibrations closer to the physical level as dangerous. Fibromyalgia is pain and stiffness in tendons, ligaments and muscles. Energetically it translates into the perception of the lower frequencies as painful and a stiffening of the structural levels in the hope of escaping that pain. The origin of this frozen fear is often very far back many lifetimes ago, amplified every time it got carried into a new incarnation. The way to work with this imbalance is to find/acknowledge the fear, face it, allow small doses of it to flow through the emotional levels and feel it; its defrosting alleviates the physical symptoms.

The **nervous system** is an electrochemical communication network. It relates mostly to the structural levels of the energy field, especially the etheric and mental. The nervous system acts as a bridge between the etheric and the physical. A little bit here on physical anatomy: there are billions of nerve cells in the body, the neurons. The main part of each neuron is the cell body, which has many branches, the dendrites, for receiving messages, and one long arm called an axon. Information from the energy field gets transferred from the etheric level to the nerve cell body, then the electric message moves through the axon, becoming chemical and physical. The next nerve cell picks up the message, translating it again into electrical impulses. This is how we get messages transferred throughout our body. The informational flow usually happens in one direction, from the etheric level into the cell body, then through the axon to the dendrite of another neuron. The synapse is a gap, or a contact place between the neurons. This is where neurotransmitters are secreted by the axon for informational transfer. Each axon is wrapped in a myelin sheath, which functions like insulation around an electrical wire. The myelin sheath corresponds to the less dense space in the etheric level structures. The etheric lines are connected to the structural parts of the cells; the 'empty spaces' relate to the fluids and the internal space of the cell, plus to the myelin sheath. It acts like cushioning for the informational flow, and when disrupted, it fragments the information. In multiple sclerosis this is exactly what happens: the myelin sheath degenerates, attacked by the person's own antibodies, and the nerve deteriorates, unable to function without the insulation. If the magnetic component of the etheric level (the 'space' between the lines) can recharge properly, its physical counterpart, the myelin sheath, can regenerate and repair itself, saving the nerve.

The physical brain (which is not the same as the Mind) is designed for maintenance of the body, not the functions of the mind. We overwhelm our brains with extra stimuli only because our other 'brains' are not functioning properly. What 'other brains' am I talking about?! There are two more 'brains', one is located in the physical body in the solar plexus area and is designed for processing emotions, and the other is located outside of the physical body on top of the head and is designed as the 'main brain' for thinking, reasoning, processing, informational access and so on. (This 'brain' looks like a horizontally positioned egg; if actively used it is orange in color, it is the 'Soul brain'.) But here we will mostly talk about the brain located in the head. This brain is a coordinator. It reviews all the available information and makes decisions accordingly. Its decision are based on precedents, it builds knowledge on what it already knows. Some information we are aware of and it seems logical to us, but we are not aware of other information that the brain has and when it bases a reaction on that unknown information, it looks like a creative approach to us. When we remember something that occurred in our life, we access this store of information in the physical brain. But when we remember some ability or knowledge from another lifetime, something that did not happen to us in this incarnation, we are only using the physical brain as a translator, the information comes into the higher nonphysical brain above the head and then gets translated through the physical brain to our comprehension. The brain needs lots of oxygen and so it requires about twenty percent of the blood flow from the heart, and lots of sugar.

One of the most common nervous system problems is headache. If it is not a symptom of another physical imbalance (like high blood pressure, tumor, infections) there are two main reasons for headaches. One is the overly large amount of electric charge around the head. This occurs when a person either literally thinks too much (i.e., is over-analytical/mental for a prolonged period of time), or when the root chakra is weak and most of the energy floats to the crown chakra. Both conditions create an overly potent electric charge in the top part of the field. When the mental level is very busy, a person thinks a lot, trying to figure something out, and they generate extra electric charge that has no place to go. All electric energy has to be evenly anchored with the magnetic. If there is not enough magnetic in the aura and/or the root chakra is too weak, it ungrounds the electric charge. Extra electric energy can be tolerated only by two chakras, the third on the front and the crown. Once the third chakra is filled up, the crown takes over, creating pressure in the physical head. That pressure is what one experiences as a headache.

The second main reason for a headache is over-responsibility and anxiety about measuring up to the expectations (of others or of the Self). The back of the neck chakra gets either too big or spins backwards, pulling on the nervous system structures on the etheric level, creating tension. That etheric tension translates into a physical tightening of the neck muscles, which limit the flow of blood to the brain, hence the headache.

Migraine is an electrical storm in the head on the physical and etheric levels. During a regular headache there is only a build up of the electric charge, but no movement in it. In migraine a pressurized electric charge on the etheric level begins to move, triggering a storm in the physical brain. Energetically, migraine looks like a real storm, with lightening, bright flashes, circling energy resembling little tornados and so forth. Physically, the arteries to the brain begin to rapidly shrink, then release, and this narrowing/widening triggers all the surrounding pain receptors. What starts up the storm? It has to do with the balance of electric and magnetic charge. We cannot exist with too much electric charge; at some point when the amount of electric energy gets overwhelming, the aura naturally tries to rebalance the electric by shifting into more of the magnetic. The third chakra on the front is minimized so it cannot generate more electric energy, hence one of the common migraine symptoms—nausea. The sixth chakra on the front, which connects to the pineal gland in the head, expands to a large size, trying to reactivate the magnetic in the head, hence the other common symptom—sensitivity to light. Because magnetic energy is a receptive energy, one of the best ways of dealing with migraine is to go into seclusion, into a quiet dark place, and allow the magnetic charge to rebuild. Once it can match the electric charge, the pain subsides.

Vertigo, or extreme dizziness, is medically explained by abnormalities in the ear (infections, pressure etc.) or in the nerves connecting the ear to the brain or in the brain itself, but energetically it is caused by ungroundedness. When a person does not have enough energy in the root chakra and 'floats out of the body', their energy field moves upwards significantly, creating a less-than-normal pressure in the lower part of the field and overly high pressure on top. This high energy pressure is the most extreme in the etheric level, the closest in frequency to the physical. That is what the sensitive ear structure often picks up, and further pressure is registered in the nerves and the brain. Vertigo is rebalanced by moving energy down significantly, in the shape of a physical body, and by activating the root chakra again. The oval shape of the aura is misplaced upwards during vertigo. To correct the situation, envision the oval moving slowly down until your body is in the center, then even a little farther down (so you are closer to the top of the oval than the bottom; it is an over-shoot, but it will correct the vertigo).

Anxiety and panic attacks are responses to energy moving too quickly through the energy field structure and hence through the neural network. When we compare ourselves now with how we want to be and notice a big difference, we run the energy through the nerve cells too quickly, and freak out. In the fluid levels of the field there is an expectation that we have to match what we imagine we have to be/achieve in order to feel safe/receive love. The structured levels run this energy towards the goal. If something has to be done so we can receive love, that love is no longer unconditional, and we become dependent on the action or particular state we believe we have to be in to enter safety. For example, a person believes he has to have a certain amount of money in his bank account, but finds there to be less than expected. He might have an anxiety attack because his ability to feel safe is dependent on the amount of money in the bank and the energy just went too fast through his structured levels, amplifying the discrepancy. Or a woman might worry a lot about everything, the wellbeing of her kids, the diet of her husband, the walking of the dog on time, her job situation, the repair of her daughter's car, and so on. She keeps tuning into how it all 'should be' and runs energy too quickly through her structural levels, only to find that it is not at all how it 'should be', so her emotional level freaks out and the etheric level speediness is matched by physical anxiety or even panic. The energy experience of the anxiety attack is like lightening traveling in and bouncing off the inside of the energy field without being able to ground itself. The root chakra is not able to pull this lightening storm into the planet and therefore disperses it. If we can have enough awareness during the attack, we can focus on the root chakra and self ground by using intention. The other way to correct these imbalances is to slow down the energy flow through the etheric level by anchoring safety and love in the present ('I am ok *right now*', 'I am safe', 'The world will not end if this doesn't get done today', etc.)

Bipolar and manic-depressive conditions have similar symptoms, and so they are considered to be the same thing from the medical viewpoint. But if we look deeper at the causes of these two nervous system imbalances, we'll see that they are quite different. Bipolar imbalance is based on the inability to choose which, fluid or structural, pattern a person wants to use at any particular moment. This back and forth motion in the nervous system creates instability and culminates in erratic behavior. In the energy field the consciousness of this person keeps jumping from the fluid/feeling levels to the structural/reasonable levels, creating a confusion of identity. Usually the third chakra on the front, responsible for self understanding, has a hard time dealing with this kind of jumping of consciousness. The nervous system is given conflicting signals as the third chakra twists, trying to accommodate the flipping. To correct this behavior a person needs to develop an inner witness for the 'flipping', so that there is always a part of the personality on the 'outside'; this stabilizes the third chakra and the nervous system receives more coherent messages. It is only possible, though, with emotional level flexibility and a feeling of fullness ('Everything is ok', 'I am centered', etc.)

In manic-depressive imbalance a person has a particular emotional pain that they are trying to avoid feeling at all costs, while their Soul wants them to resolve the situation by finally facing the pain. They feel an echo of the suppressed pain and fear the full extent of it, clogging their emotional level with fear. In this overstuffed state the emotional level cannot circulate energy almost at all and a person becomes chronically depressed. That pain is usually karmic; it was brought from another lifetime into the present one, so it might not seem very logical to the current personality. But the Soul keeps triggering that pain so that it can come up to the surface, be felt and processed and finally cleared. When a person feels the pain coming up, they flip to the artificial wellness of the manic state. That wellness is run on the structural levels; it is not an emotional type of actually feeling great/happy/satisfied/powerful/joyful, but a simulation, a concept of wellness from the mental and other structural levels. It is a defense against feeling the pain, and a person will do anything, including becoming hostile, to prove to others and himself that he is 'doing just great'. If the karmic pain is an old pattern the Soul will be determined to clear it and hence trigger it more often; if resisted, a person will have more manic episodes. If the pain is somewhat new, there might be fewer manic states. Manic behavior is an avoidance of feeling emotional pain, hidden by fear. To resolve this imbalance a person must face the pain instead of running away from it. Feeling the pain will diminish the fear, clear up the emotional level and alleviate depression, at the same time erasing the need for manic avoidance of the experience.

Chronic fatigue is also a nervous system imbalance. Remember, for the nerve cell to have electric charge to give to another nerve cell, the information from the etheric level first has to be delivered to the nerve cell body. If the informational impulses flow too slowly through the energy field, they are unable to spark the nerve cells. The red color energy is missing from the root chakra and the etheric level is too silvery and washed out (instead of being blue and charged). This usually occurs when a person is more concerned with using their energy for others instead of themselves. A person's higher consciousness then creates a 'stopper' for this behavior. S/he has to address it and cannot over-give further. The etheric level's low amount of energy is not enough to stimulate the nerve cells and they do not get their electric charge, diminishing their ability to function normally and to focus well. Sometimes a person with chronic fatigue imbalance might have swollen lymph nodes because the nodes are overwhelmed with unprocessed emotions. When we give out too much energy and all our awareness is focused on others, we cannot adequately process our own emotions, fluid levels get clogged and lymph nodes swell. This also leads to difficulty feeling the Self as a separate person. The way to correct chronic fatigue imbalance is to pay attention to personal emotions, letting go of over-concern for others, disengaging from them and recharging the Self. Once the Soul sees that the personality is serious about the change, the 'stopper' is released and the nerve cells receive a normal electric flow of information.

ADD, attention deficit disorder, became much more common on our planet since consciousness began to evolve faster. A person with ADD has too much active electric energy flowing through their nervous system and they have difficulty focusing their attention on any one thing. The amount of information available in the external world increased a lot lately, and we are bombarded with it. Also, conscious awareness grew, especially in children, allowing them to receive many more informational impulses from other energy levels simultaneously. But the nervous system is not used to this amount of information/electric charge, and freaks out. The freak-out resembles a live wire, jumping and moving unpredictably. What the Soul is trying to teach the person is to calm down, to receive the flow of information more as rain instead of focusing on every drop; to be present in the moment. We are learning how to be present/still instead of having to always do/act, following Soul's desire to become more flowing and magnetic, in synchronicity with life. Adding strength to the energetic boundaries will allow a person with this condition to stabilize and contain their random dispersal pattern of electrical energy. Also, training in expansion/contraction of their awareness is supportive, building familiarity with the extended field of awareness.

The **respiratory system** of the body connects to the capacity to experience perceptual freedom. Perceptual freedom is a balanced state of the energy field, it exists on all the levels and in all chakras; it is the openness and internal knowing of free choice. When one breathes deeply air enters the little sacks in the lungs called alveoli and then gets delivered to the blood through the capillary walls. Carbon dioxide from the blood is deposited in the lungs to be exhaled out. If there is not enough oxygen, the brain sends a signal to the lungs to breathe faster and deeper. But when we squeeze the air out of our lungs by following an emotional reaction (fear, the perception of danger, shock, etc.) instead of accessing the body's balanced programming, we minimize our capacity for freedom. The amount of freedom we can have is in direct relationship to the amount of air we can take in. If we are breathing shallowly, we do not allow our lungs enough space to exist. That space is an essential component of feeling free, because our energy system reads the physical lung function/rhythm/space as its capacity for freedom. Taking deep breaths is important for practicing an increase in the perception of personal freedom.

Asthma is one of the most common imbalances of the respiratory system. During an asthma attack mast cells located throughout the tree-looking pipes called bronchi, release histamine and leukotrienes, causing the muscle of the bronchi to contract and mucus secretion to increase. This narrowing of the bronchi makes breathing harder and spasm-like. Not only does it become laborious to let the air through the bronchi into the lungs, the membranes around the alveoli cells get thick and it takes too much effort for the oxygen to cross that thickness. What triggers this physical reaction of the mast cells? It is the perception of the danger from pollen, pet dander, dust, smoke, cold air, etcetera. It does not mean that there is actual danger—it is a real perception in the person's body—but the danger is not real. In small amounts cold air or pollen will not damage the body, but nevertheless the body perceives them as deadly. Certain chemicals can bring on asthma attacks (from heavy industrial stuff to food preservatives), and these are dangerous to the body because they act like a poison. In that case a defensive reaction to send white blood cells to the site, and produce mucus and spasms is warranted. So why does the body react to the other not-really-deadly substances (even in small amounts) as if they can kill? It is an emotional perception, not physical. Just as with other allergies, there is a rejection of the frequency of a particular allergen because it is not included in a person's frequency range. Only in asthma, this is not just any range, but the frequency range of freedom. If dust/cockroaches/dander triggers the attack, chances are that the person feels this world is imperfect and limits her/his freedom in it to 'only the good stuff'. This extends to the asthma jumpstarted from animal dander: one might actually love animals and yet be unable to be around them because of the personal freedom limitation that 'animals have to be nice' instead of seeing them as 'wild creatures'. Or if the attack is triggered by pollen, a person is feeling the pollution and reacting to it (it can be a judgment of the planetary pollution or fear of personal pollution). When an attack is started by inhaling cold air, a person feels danger from external reality but is unable to build a bridge and find safety, which limits his freedom and jumpstarts the attack. The emotional and astral levels during the asthma condition get too stuffy, while the etheric level becomes too weak. Normally the etheric level acts like a lining between the emotional and physical, filtering messages from the emotional level and telling the body which messages need a physical response and which ones do not. But the undercharged etheric level cannot correctly filter the messages and the body reacts to the emotional experience. Asthma is always based on the fear of life which limits the freedom a person can have in that life. Asthma begins at the point of shock experienced in the energy field. An experience of shock sends a message of danger to the energy field, putting it on high alert. This tends to trigger other lifetime's traumas and fears. If a person has a lot of unresolved patterns in the emotional and astral levels, they are more likely to develop asthma. In the physical body the origin point of shock usually happens at the fetal or newborn stage, but asthma itself can develop from that shock later in life. In order to work with an asthmatic condition, first a person needs to look at the limitations created in his/her conceptual understanding of freedom, rather than at emotional components. Questions like 'what limits me?' and 'what do I feel I need so I can be free?' can be helpful. Since there are no real limitations to the Self and one does not need anything in order to be free (we are always free) the answers to these questions can guide a person to the origins of his asthma. Then every time the attack begins, a person has to remind himself that he *is* safe, that there is no actual danger, and intend to be open to all life.

Pneumonia is a manifestation of the fear frequency in the lungs. Physically it is an infection in the alveoli usually caused by bacteria, but sometimes by a virus or fungi. Bacteria invade the lungs, making breathing shallow. Fear is the reason that invasion occurred, because the presence of fear energy changed the etheric blueprint of the lungs and weakened the boundary, allowing the infection in. Pneumonia appears after a cold or flu or often when a person is in the hospital, or after surgery that weakened the physical body. It also often occurs in infants and the elderly. Why? Different fears (of the same category) cause it, and they determine which bacteria (or virus, or fungi) are going to enter the lungs. The category is always the fear of freedom, but it is experienced differently. A person experiencing a cold or flu might be afraid to be limited and to have to miss work or other necessary activities, someone after an operation might be afraid of the limitations of a painful recovery, an infant might have a fear of physicality altogether seeing it as a major limitation to the Soul, an elderly person might fear loss of independence, etcetera. Working with these fears consciously will process and release the energy of fear from the lungs and significantly speed up the recovery.

Smoking is a very common way to create artificial fullness and artificial freedom in the lungs. When one does not allow consciousness to fully enter the lungs, it creates an energetic vacuum that calls to be filled. The smoke acts as that filler. Smoking tends to jumpstart one's system artificially when one does not have enough natural freedom and fullness. A person usually has a fear of being trapped by life (relationships, beliefs, fears, circumstances, deep feelings, etc.) and rebels against that fear either by destructively defying life, or by pretending s/he is above life. Refusing to face the fear of entrapment, defiant behavior and arrogant irresponsibility only mask the absence of true freedom, and it is freedom that this individual longs for. The fire element in smoking substitutes for grounding and the energy of passion. Without being grounded we cannot absorb oxygen correctly (hence the feeling of entrapment) and passion for life is a necessary component of wellbeing. Without passion we become limp, tired, bored and unfulfilled. Smoking is psychologically and physically addictive because we get hooked on artificial fullness—the type of fullness that we do need to be present for. Natural fullness means a person is present in their life with curiosity and passion, grounded in the body and allowing it to be a component of themselves (not just 'some thing dangling down there somewhere').

The skin is the most easily recognizable boundary for physical identity. If you don't know the difference between your body and another's, you are in big trouble! The integumentary system of the body acts as a natural boundary for the physical level, and is a component of the force-field-like boundary of the energy field. When one's energy boundary is not very strong, the skin tends to have issues.

Redness and inflammation of the skin are related to the issues of self hatred in the second chakra on the emotional level. Often as the chakra processes this energy, even if positively releasing it, the skin will break out in a rash or eruption. This is part of the Self-healing process. If we get mad at the body for making our skin look ugly, disgusting or not the way we want it, we take away the energy from the healing process of release of hatred. The body is trying to correct the emotional imbalance by releasing the 'energy of ugliness' through the skin and requires our cooperation. Sometimes when a person is not taking good care of themselves emotionally and/or physically, the body will create a patch of scaly or itchy skin to get our attention. That patch will be present as this person processes the issue, which might be couple of days or many years (and usually will not respond to any physical/medical treatments). Once the issue is no longer there the skin disturbance disappears.

Dry skin is a result of an overly electric boundary. Ever notice that people with thick, healthy moist skin are magnetic and earthy? Our boundary is a definition of ourselves. If you feel tense and nervous in connection with the world, ungrounded or forceful to prove your individuality, and push against the world, your boundary will be overly electric and skin dryness will reflect that. A sluggish attitude towards the world, the 'low floating' of the root chakra instead of a healthy grounding and over-association of the Self with the rest of the world will make your boundary overly magnetic, resulting in too oily and unhealthy skin. But an electromagnetically balanced boundary paired with a charged root chakra gives the skin moisture and a glow with health you can't get with any make-up.

Is it healthy to tan? No. You do not want to roast your boundary! What's healthy is to receive energy encodements from the sun's rays, but not to tan the skin. It is very confusing how tanned skin is considered to be a sign of a healthy person, yet it is actually very unhealthy to tan. We tend to think that someone who is tanned spent lots of time outdoors, played sports under the sun, perhaps lay on the beach during vacation, while we slaved in a boring fluorescent-lit office. Maybe she is rich, so she does not have to go to work, or perhaps she is adventurous, daring and a sex goddess to boot, so let's all get very tanned and then we also can feel rich, sexy and free! The problem here is partially commercial propaganda, partially our Soul memory. We remember cultures that were free and curious and connected to Soul reality much more than we are now, as being dark skinned. Some were genetically darker, while others had white skin, but spent such a long time outdoors that their skin got tanned. These were more conscious cultures and they did receive informational energy from solar light, while being able to either neutralize or block radiation. The reasons they could do this before were that they were more connected to their physical bodies and, of course, the rays of our Sun were not so deadly. The planetary magnetic field was stronger and the ozone layer was much thicker, and the skin could deal with the sun's radiation better. Conscious advancement has nothing to do with a tan! It is true that 'outdoorsy and sporty' is healthier than a 'couch potato', but the tan should not be used as a marker. Today's couch potatoes tan on the beach, often resembling beached whales, while 'sporty sexy and fit' are riding their bikes or running with a thick layer of sunscreen on. If you still like the idea of a tan, there are two things you can do. One is to use a sunscreen and if you truly spend lots of time outside, you will get an even glow anyway; two, use a sunless self-tanning lotion or a spray-on 'fake' tan. The Goddess/God is within, and if we remember that, our skin reflects it!

Hair is a component of the skin. Often when a person begins to progress spiritually, their hair might start to fall out. Not completely, of course, but there is a noticeable thinning. If you panic because you think that there is something wrong and that is the reason for your hair loss, then you are actually adding to the stress that the nervous system is already experiencing from the evolutionary changes of the energy field. What does that mean? When we learn to expand our consciousness more, the energy field becomes more sensitive, making the physical body also much more sensitive than we are used to. We end up sending significantly more energy in and out of the crown chakra on the top of the head. This shocks the nerve endings throughout the body. Eventually the shock clears out as the physical body gets used to the change, but while it is happening, we might lose hair. One of the ways to compensate for the nervous system overload is to make sure that the root chakra has a lot of charge all the time, to balance the crown. This pulls some energy away from the head and gives hair a chance to stay attached to our heads. Yes, if you are permanently ungrounded, prepare for baldness. It is true that for most men baldness is a genetic pattern but, first of all, we do not have to follow genetics, it is an unconscious choice; and second, if a man is very grounded and is working on enhancing his Soul identity versus his genetic one, he can slow down and even stop the balding process. Most other species of this Universe, much more advanced than us humans, do not have hair at all. Humans went for an extravagant attempt at evolution while keeping a full head of hair. It has never worked before, or only with very few exceptions, but there is a first time for everything...

But the most common reason for hair thinning is stress. The main reason anyone has stress is because they are trying to move through life faster than their root chakra can keep up. A person becomes ungrounded and the nervous system freaks out, sending massive amounts of energy to the head in attempts to compensate. This delivers a potent electric charge into the hair follicle, shocking it. The hair then cannot stay rooted in the follicle because its etheric level connections were severed by the electric shock, so it falls out. This hair loss is fixed by grounding and slowing down the pace a bit, so that the root chakra can maintain a balance with the crown and the hair follicles can receive the etheric nourishment they require.

The **endocrine system** is a master operating system for the whole body. The endocrine glands relate directly to the chakras, being fed by their particular energy. Each endocrine gland is a mechanism for the reception, transmutation and delivery of etheric energy into physical form. Endocrine glands produce and secrete hormones into our bloodstream. Hormones are messengers and coordinators of the body's internal processes. They are made from proteins or derivatives of fat. Hormones attach to cells using specific receptor proteins and that either changes the permeability of cellular membranes (then specific substances can enter that particular cell) or alters the codes of the cell's receptors (so they produce new substances, acting as a second messenger). Isn't it amazing how these simple actions of the endocrine system maintain balance in our bodies?

Far back on the spiral of consciousness, before human physical form became what we know it to be today, we were different, more conscious, responding to the flow of life force directly. The full potency of the light/dark matter dynamic of aliveness was available to the physical form, and each cell receptor was capable of receiving information from it. Then, as consciousness diminished and the gap between the energy dimensions became larger, the physical vehicle had to adjust to the changes in order to still be able to receive Soul light. The etheric DNA (an etheric level component of our physical genes) was de-stranded, ending in only two etheric strands, a match for the two physical ones. This made the physical form capable of many adjustments, including growing the many different glands that we now call our endocrine system. Before there was only one gland with a direct energy pathway to the crown chakra, the present time pituitary gland, and that produced only one hormone. We do not have this hormone in the body anymore, instead it was broken down into many smaller and less complex formulas; these are our hormones today. The pituitary is still the master gland, maintaining all of the others, but the energy pathway is rewired now and the hypothalamus part of the brain serves as the monitor of the flow. Instead of receiving the life force through the cell receptors we now do it through the glands. First the energy field of a person relays the message to the endocrine system, then the glands translate it into hormonal messages and create a different pattern on the etheric level of the energy field. The etheric level then sends electric impulses into the nervous system, completing the loop.

The <u>adrenal glands</u> are connected energetically to the root chakra. Their function is to control the fluid and mineral balances (affecting heart rate, blood pressure, sweating, levels of potassium/salt, etc.) of the physical body. They are involved in the production of the fight/flight hormone epinephrine (adrenaline). This hormone is designed to put the whole body on alert: breathing quickens and the heart beats faster, pumping more blood to the muscles and away from the digestive system, and the pupils in the eyes dilate to take in more light—now the physical body is ready to either fight the attacker or to run from him. The problem is that this mysterious attacker is not usually physical. The emotional component of the adrenals is safety. In the imbalanced state the emotional component becomes 'body terror'. What does that mean? Well, when we feel safe energetically, our adrenals receive the message about body maintenance and vigor. But when the feeling of danger shows up in our system (emotional fear, mental stress, situations when we feel inadequate, or our beliefs are challenged, etc.) we transmit this message of danger into the adrenals, which in turn respond as if there is a physical danger by releasing their hormones accordingly. This affects the etheric level, which sends a sharp, fast and very uncomfortable electric charge into our nervous system that we experience as 'body terror'.

Resistance to being in the body and using the root chakra improperly makes adrenals underactive. The symptoms of this physical imbalance are the same as the severe symptoms of a person whose root chakra is blocked. Because of the absence of the flow through the root there is no clear boundary within which that identity can exist, so that the person does not want to stay in the body and floats out a lot in an attempt to disconnect from the body. It is important to recognize how our physical body and all the energy levels are connected, and how we create our own issues, including the physical ones. Underactive adrenals make a person feel weak and tired all the time, dizzy and nauseated, lose weight and dehydrate, lose her appetite and develop aches in the muscles (due to a blocked root); also, the skin becomes darker as if tanned (due to the Soul's attempt to keep life going by artificially strengthening the boundary, which in the physical plane is the skin). Obviously this is a severe case, but when someone is depressed on the emotional level, s/he to some extent transmits the same message to the adrenals, trying to close the root chakra when s/he does not want to be in this world. If you notice these physical symptoms, look at your relationship to life, are you trying to escape it into some imaginary world? Have you become mechanical in your life, instead of alive? Do some exercises to open and charge the root chakra and process the emotional stuff that goes with it. And watch your body respond.

Overactive adrenals have the opposite cause—the desire to overpower life, instead of to escape it. It is still based on the fear of life itself, hence it is not a true power position. A person attempts to fight life, generating more hormonal release from the adrenals. If there is too much testosterone and the like, a person becomes 'more male', that is, an overly electric, imbalanced aggressor on the energy levels and physically more short tempered, with a lower voice, more hair on the face and body etcetera, and increased sex drive—the distorted desire for life. If too much corticosteroid is produced by the adrenals, then a person's boundary suffers the most, leaving him exposed to a life that s/he fears. This leads to a thin boundary and stuffed emotional and astral levels in attempts to self protect. Physically this is mirrored by the improper distribution of body fat. Yes, stress can make you fat! In a person with overactive adrenals that generate large releases of corticosteroids body fat accumulates first at the belly (the second chakra trying to protect itself), then on the rest of the torso, leading to weakened bones and muscles, while the skin becomes thin, bluish and bruises easily (weakened boundary). The overproduction of the other adrenal hormone, aldosterone, is a response to an indecisive root chakra and aggressive and frightened emotional level. When we want to fight and run at the same time, we split the charge in the root, making our adrenal glands respond in this way. Physically, levels of potassium in the blood drop, making a person feel weak, tingly and sometimes even paralyzed. All these scenarios are extreme cases, but when you notice your emotional level response to life is off, be kind to your adrenals! Or the other way around, if your physical body is showing you through mild symptoms that there is an emotional issue affecting your root chakra, do not ignore it, process it and help your body.

The ovaries and testes are connected energetically to the second chakra. These glands, as you well know, are responsible for the sexual development of the female and male physical bodies. The emotional component of these glands is joy or, in the imbalanced state, resistance to it. Infertility is one of the common imbalances, and the reason for it in the energy field is that a person is afraid to use her/his second chakra either at all, or during intercourse. Most Souls desire to enter this world through parents that have healthy energy bridges during intercourse, that is, their second chakras are working well. If a couple has an orgasm, all the better, but even if not, if there is pleasure, it makes it much easier for a Soul to enter in conception. When a couple is attempting to 'accomplish a child', or to resolve their personal or relational issues by bringing a baby into that relationship, the conception usually will not happen. When partners are not sure if they want to be together (and stay a couple out of guilt or responsibility, but not love), their second chakras are not in synch, creating discord during intercourse. Since eggs and sperm carry the second chakra charge of their owner, if that charge is off, they cannot relate to each other and 'miss'. If there is a problem with the sperm itself or its delivery, a man might have fear of responsibility, fear of physicality in general or overly electric, forced goals in life that do not allow him to have self love and pleasure energy in his second chakra. He needs to look at these issues. If there are not enough healthy eggs or the uterine lining does not support pregnancy, a woman might be carrying too much guilt in her second chakra instead of pleasure, or perhaps she is unable to give loving pleasure energy to herself, instead giving it to other people (then her own Soul will not allow pregnancy to occur, since she will give all her love from the heart and the second chakra to the baby instead of herself). In this situation a woman needs to clear up the guilt or shame she might have, and definitely practice self loving and giving pleasure to herself (not 'rewards' but actual pleasure).

The <u>pancreas</u> is connected to the third chakra and it is instrumental in the regulation of blood sugar levels. Besides secreting digestive enzymes, the pancreas secretes insulin and glucagon, hormones necessary for the metabolism of sugar. The emotional component of the pancreas is the sweetness of life, or its harshness when imbalanced. If the pancreas is in a balanced state, life feels effortless. If it is out of balance life is perceived as hard. Diabetes is a malfunction of the pancreas/third chakra. The sugar molecule stays in the blood too long because of the lack of insulin. The job of insulin is to regulate the balance of sugar in the blood. Insulin helps to transport glucose into cells so that it can either be used as energy fuel or stored for later when needed. In type 1 diabetes the pancreas does not produce enough insulin, making the blood too 'sugar-full'. Energetically, this means that a person has himself convinced that life is too hard and that there is not enough sweetness for him, and the third chakra holds this pattern, blocking the energy of effortlessness and sweetness in his pancreas. Since he cannot live without the sweetness of life, yet his third chakra energy configuration does not allow it, he artificially creates sweetness by holding sugar in the blood too long. This pattern actually makes his life overly hard and everything takes extra effort, because natural 'sweetness' is missing. In type 2 diabetes the pancreas produces enough insulin, but cells do not respond well to it, developing insulin resistance. This means that that person is convinced she does not deserve an effortless flow of life, and she either has a belief that she has to suffer or that she has to work hard for it to have value. She does not know how to hold on to the sweetness of life, so she artificially creates this 'fullness' by holding on to the physical sugar in the blood. Either way, although this third chakra pattern allows the life flow to come through the pancreas (it produces insulin), it fights that life force inside the body (insulin resistance in the cells). An energy component of bringing these situations into balance is to rebalance the third chakra first by remembering that you are a part of the Universe filled with sweetness and effortlessness. If instead we see our world in a limited way, see only pain and suffering in it, forgetting the wonder, the pancreas becomes limited in its capacity to receive life force, creating a physical imbalance.

The thymus gland is connected to the heart chakra. Its function is to produce hormones that stimulate white blood cell development and differentiation. T-lymphocytes are a type of white blood cell that is very important for our immune system. They migrate from the bone marrow into the thymus for 'school' where they learn how to differentiate the Self from non-Self, divide and mature. When they 'graduate', the thymus releases them into the lymphatic system, where they serve as 'immune surveillance'. The emotional component of the thymus is compassion, unconditional love and nonjudgment. Only with these energies can our internal immune surveillance function correctly, when white blood cells do not destroy life, but rebalance it, do not judge, but differentiate. When the thymus is not balanced, we hate and judge, and our white blood cells seek enemies. There is no compassion and understanding of connectedness, but instead a desire to separate and kill. The autoimmune disease arthritis is also closely related to the imbalance of the thymus gland. Antibodies are sent against the body's own cells instead of against invaders. Antibodies are the proteins produced by the immune cells that aid in the destruction of 'non-Self' tissues or organisms. This energetically relates to the feeling that life is a struggle and that we have to 'work hard' in order to engage and overcome this struggle.

The thyroid gland is connected to the fifth chakra. Its function is to control cellular metabolism and the rate of oxygen consumption. The energy component is freedom of self-expression/lack of it and self-responsibility issues. When we have a healthy understanding of the Self as a part of the Universe and are able to be responsible for our role in it, the front and back aspects of the fifth chakra are healthy, and so is the thyroid gland. The two most common thyroid conditions are hyperthyroidism and hypothyroidism.

In an overactive thyroid condition a person has the feeling that there is no space for self expression, and that she had better 'hurry up' while she has her very small window of opportunity. She has learned to express herself overly fast. This makes the throat chakra flip outwards, unable to hold its shape due to the absence of the flow in the middle and the too-quick movement on the outside of the chakra. It looks as though the fast energy flow is blasting the throat chakra open, while the middle is empty. Meanwhile the back aspect of the fifth chakra becomes very narrow, compressing energy and restricting the flow, contributing to the emptiness in the middle of the front aspect. The innate energy speed of frequencies like love and self kindness is slow. An overly active thyroid deprives itself of the slow energies, it becomes devoid of love and kindness.

The underactive condition relates to fear of self expression and an 'allergic' resentment to self responsibility. If we are afraid of self expression, we end up minimizing the Self's presence by lowering the charge on the etheric level and almost erasing the boundary. That way we are 'not here' and hence feel less in danger. This person weakens the clarity and strength of his boundary by moving the energy power away from the throat and into higher energy levels away from the etheric one. Because the etheric level is not strong, power doesn't get up to the throat and instead sinks, dispersing into the hips and creating a false default boundary. There is no freedom, since this person is in reaction to a perceived danger in life and feels that he has to minimize the Self to survive. His thyroid gland does not get energy from the etheric level or from the fifth chakra, and so the internal processes in the physical thyroid cells slow down, making the thyroid underactive. If this is your situation, I would suggest that you look at the fear of self expression and your perceived danger that if your opinion/creation is different than someone else's, you will be 'in big trouble'. Working with this issue alone will begin to bring energy into the fifth chakra and rebalance the thyroid.

Radiation also affects the thyroid. The energy consciousness of radiation is the igniting of deep feelings, but by splitting apart the atomic structure, radiation amplifies the deep magnetic power of feeling. If a person gets a high dose of radiation, it can break apart his internal structures and bring up to the surface a deep magnetic component that this person might not have been consciously connected to before. Because radiation collects in iodine isotopes and the thyroid absorbs iodine, the radioactive iodine can break apart thyroid structures on the etheric level, resulting in a damaged thyroid or thyroid cancer. If a person received an overdose of radiation, the etheric level of the thyroid and the fifth chakra will be affected for sure, but the physical damage will depend on how that person processes the radiation. If she allows deep feelings to come up and does not succumb to fear, she will be self responsible, the back and the front of the fifth chakra will support the thyroid and the physical damage will clear. If, on the other hand, she freaks out, goes into fear and then tries to 'normalize' the situation by being logical, she will have to deal with the physical component of the etheric damage. Either way, especially in a child, if there is damage to the thyroid, there is radiation involved. But it could be the type of radiation we are aware of (like an accident with radioactive material resulting in a worker getting a high dose of radiation) or that we are not aware of (like the cosmic type of radiation that, because of particular karmic patterns, can focus on one person more dramatically). A person with such a condition should be encouraged to look at his/her deep feelings, witness the breaking of some mental/conceptual structures without fear of that process, allowing the fifth chakra to recuperate and rebuild.

The pineal gland is connected to the sixth chakra. Its main function is the production of melatonin and serotonin hormones, which regulate the sleep cycles of the physical body and the consciousness cycles of the etheric bodies. When there is enough melatonin, we can rest well and sleep deeply. Enough serotonin keeps us alert and positively motivated. The emotional component of the pineal gland is clarity of insight into the overall design of the Universal matrix. When the sixth chakra on the front and the back is open and clear, we have healthy pineal function. If you have symptoms of unrest, insomnia and often have a slight depression, the level of hormonal production is low. This means that in the energy field your sixth chakra on the front is clogged, which is perceived as a loss of direction and confusion. If in this situation the back of the sixth chakra is closed/clogged, you will feel like you do not belong, do not know how to live, how to 'function properly' in life. If, when the front is clogged, the back of the sixth is overly charged, you will feel mechanical, confused and lost, looking for someone to give you directions. Either situation messes up the hormonal balance of the pineal. To correct this situation you need to do some energy exercises for the sixth chakra, clearing it. Also, try to see the 'bigger picture' of your life, look at the larger patterns, instead of focusing on the 'to do list'. These intentions will allow the flow through the clogged sixth chakra, clearing it and rebalancing the back aspect, in turn helping the pineal glad to regulate hormonal production.

As we mentioned in the beginning, the <u>pituitary gland</u> is the master gland. Its main function is to control the endocrine system. It produces the hormones that stimulate all other endocrine glands in the body. Energetically, it is connected to the seventh (crown) chakra. Its emotional component is the experience of unity/oneness. The amount of life force we allow ourselves (adrenals), the strength of our boundary (skin), our mood, alertness, perception of physical and emotional pain, self love (ovaries/ testes), the amount of freedom we feel (thyroid), the sweetness of being alive (pancreas), the metabolic rates of our interface with life and physical processes, our presence in the physicality of our body and the feeling of belonging to the Universe/Earth/our body (having balanced amounts of water in the kidneys)—all these depend on the health of the pituitary gland. When the pituitary is not working properly it indicates imbalances in the crown chakra, leading to the perception of life as meaningless. A person either cannot experience/comprehend Universal unity, or sees her/himself as isolated from it. All other functions of the endocrine system are thrown out of balance. Life force and the boundary diminishes, freedom is trapped in the perception of pain and harshness, a person feels like s/he does not belong here (in the body/on the planet/in the Universe). This situation can be remedied by building a bridge of consciousness between the Self and the Universe. A person might tune into her/himself for about ten minutes, then to the larger picture, the world or the cosmos. If s/he is overly mental, s/he can start by writing a small paragraph about the Self, then about the world (any larger view would do—the country, the planet, the cosmos, the Universe, etc.), then write one more paragraph on the Self, and one more of the world, and so on. For a feeling type of person, tuning into the Self and then into something 'bigger than the Self' (like a tree, the sky, the Earth, etc.), moving consciousness back and forth between them, will build the bridge. Practice that every day and eventually there will be a connection, you will begin to see yourself as part of the Universe. Do not try to make the 'bigger picture' pretty. If you perceive the world as painful or cruel, but try to pretend it is 'sweet and nice and pretty', it will not do anything. Instead, let yourself feel/write about the true perception you have, then see if you can find something, anything, no matter how small, that is more positive (like 'the world is cruel, but it has beautiful beaches with sand and turquoise water' or 'there is pain and suffering on the planet, but there is also ice cream and sexual pleasure', etc.). This is more honest and will begin to clear up the crown chakra, positively stimulating the pituitary gland.

We have already talked about the **immune system** in connection with many physical issues, but let's look at it separately. The immune system is responsible for knowing the difference between the Self and the other, and it relates to the conceptual level of the aura and the root chakra. It acts as a military system, collecting intelligence, and is alert to defend its territory when needed. Problems begin when it confuses friend for foe, or vice versa. This confusion happens because of the perception of certain energies as enemies based on a belief of what is beneficial and what isn't. Often we confuse a challenge for an enemy, instead of a teacher. This triggers the root chakra. We begin to look for safety by moving into the higher chakras, further up in the vertical tube, abandoning our root chakra connection to the earth. The root chakra shrinks. At this point our white blood cells become hypervigilant and overactive and move into attack position. The energy of the immune cells becomes erratic; they 'lose perspective'. Sometimes this means that the 'propaganda' of the belief is so strong that the white cells blindly 'shoot' what they are told instead of using their inherent intelligence, or they begin acting as scared soldiers, shooting everything in sight. The solution is to bring awareness back to the root chakra, returning 'sanity' to the immune cells. The strength of the root then circulates the energy up and down the vertical tube, bringing the conceptual level into relationship with the physical body. All the beliefs we hold on the conceptual level have to be anchored in the physical, or they become self destructive. When the root chakra loses stability and shrinks, the conceptual level disconnects its communication with the body. It is like a general who watches a war on a computer screen and has no idea of how his or the enemy troops are actually doing. Root chakra charge is essential for a healthy immune system. The second chakra also plays a very important role, supplying the physical immune system with life force and potent orange energy—it is fuel for the immune strength. If the root is strong and the conceptual level is communicating with the body, but the second chakra is weak, a person will not have autoimmune issues, but will probably have colds or mild infections often, because the strength of the immune system is low. To amplify your immune system, use cobalt blue and bright orange-red together; to combat an existing autoimmune issue, first amplify blue and gold/silver frequencies, then add blue-orange. Use these frequencies in meditations or intend for them to be present when you are sleeping every night, and you will recharge your immune strength.

Physical organs from many systems are part of our immune defense mechanism: lymph vessels and nodes, thymus, liver, spleen, tonsils and bone marrow, even lungs and intestines. The ingenious design of the immune system is in its readiness, just as in a country where there are always the military and the reserve, stationary hospitals and make-shift facilities, etcetera. Similarly, our immune system is a net of many organs. For some, their main job is as part of the immune mechanism, while others participate only when needed. Just like if there is an accident, an ambulance will carry an injured person to the nearest hospital, the lymph nodes swell because the lymphatic vessels drain the infection by carrying it to the nearest area where an immune response can be organized. The human immune system also has access to the memory files of any antigen it has ever encountered, so that if it meets it again, the response can be swift. The reason the body can do this is because the etheric level stores these memory files for the immune response. If the etheric level is healthy, charged and balanced, the files available are not just on the antigens already encountered, but also on the ones yet unknown to the physical body. Every human has a wealth of information inside their energy field. The etheric level holds the balanced template for the body with every file we will ever need. But things go wrong when we either block/clog/tear/undercharge/uninhabit our etheric level, or when the other energy levels override the wisdom of the etheric. In the first scenario, a person is not willing to be in the body or in their life, so the etheric level is weak, injured and/or undercharged. A person in the second scenario has beliefs or emotions that override the natural systems of the etheric level, disrupting the immune system. The human body can heal itself of ANY disease, because the files for any possible scenario are there, on the etheric level, explaining to the immune system what to do. If we are unable to heal something, from a simple cold to AIDS, it is because the information from the etheric level has difficulty being applied. If someone truly believes he will not 'catch a cold' while everyone around him is sick, he actually will not get the cold, because the etheric level will work with the body in such a way that the frequency of the cold will not resonate with the body. There are kids in Africa being born to mothers with AIDS but who do not have that virus active in them, because it is not part of their Soul Contract for that lifetime, hence there is no resonance of the mother's virus with the fetus' body.

We never 'catch' a virus; viruses are internal programs from the etheric level. We have every possible viral program inside of us, and every possible solution too. When we need to process something, our etheric level can activate a particular virus. By experiencing that virus we can clear the energy we have already processed/released on other energy levels. For example, the influenza virus represents many different types of our fear and victimhood. A person is working with being conscious about her fears and tries hard to not be a victim in her life. She processes this energy on the conceptual and emotional levels. She feels good about herself and that she is finally succeeding in being the creator of her life. Then she creates a flu, she is sick as a dog, has high fever, sore throat, is achy and exhausted, congested, can't hear herself over her own coughing and sneezing. Did she fail? Was all the conscious clearing in vain? Any issue can be completely cleared only if it is 'unhooked' from the physical body. What is happening is that she has cleared the higher levels of the issue and now the lower ones get their chance. Her etheric level activated a flu virus program to help her discharge the fear and victimhood from her physical self. If she is able to maintain a creator attitude and not become a terrified 'victim' of the flu (the Soul's test), she will use the flu symptoms to complete the clearing of her issue. Her immune system then will be able to access the programming for clearing the flu from the etheric level and she will get well sooner.

Cancer

The word cancer brings immediate fear into most people's consciousness. It is because over the years we projected an incredible amount of our own power into the consciousness of cancer, hence not only maintaining the terror, but amplifying it. The cancer archetypal energy sits on the astral level of the planet; it is our creation, not a planetary one. For any astral charge to exist on the planetary energy grid, it has to be supported, otherwise the energy dissipates. The planet Earth does not support the cancer charge, we human beings do instead. Every time one does not own his fear of cancer, it gets placed into the archetypal cancerous charge on the astral planetary level. When you feel the fear of cancer, this charge is the same as the cancer energy on the planetary astral level. They get synchronized and end up amplifying each other. You might then feel overpowered by the fear of cancer, but it is not cancer that is overpowering you, it is the cumulative human fear of it. Owning the fear of cancer and not projecting it out anymore means a person understands that s/he created cancer and because it is his/her creation (obviously an imbalanced one), s/he can heal it, s/he is in a creator mode, not in a victim mode anymore. It is very important to take the power back from cancer.

Myth #1 is that 'it can happen to anyone', 'no one is safe'. That is not true. Cancer is an energy issue of lack of internal space. When we try to follow what is expected of us instead of what we are curious about (which comes from the Soul), or when we fear some part of our internal world so much that we suppress it, we create an internal lack of space. A good example is that of a man who was taught to not express feelings and emotions, because they make him look weak. He grows up unaware of his feelings, convincing himself that he is strong. He creates prostate cancer... Or a woman who was taught to always be nice and love, love, love everyone. She grows up 'breast feeding the world', nurturing everyone but herself, always being nice. She creates breast cancer. The issue of space is different in each one of us and the type of cancer depends on the specifics of how we do not give ourselves space.

Myth #2 is that if you have cancer in the family, you have a high risk of getting it yourself. Again not true. The only reason it looks this way is because instead of being self-sufficient human beings, we run life from genetic patterns—the stuff we incarnate into and then inertly follow. If a family has an issue with anger, for example, incarnating into that family will amplify your issues with anger. But that does not mean that you, like the other family members, will get liver cancer! If you follow the genetic path in not only amplifying the issue with anger, but not dealing with it (or doing it whichever way the rest of the family members with liver cancer did), you might also create the same cancer. But if you give space to this amplified issue of anger in your life and process it, then you will be dealing with an energy process, not a physical one—that is, no cancer.

Myth #3 is that cancer is a death sentence. That is definitely not true. When a person hears that they have cancer, the first feeling is usually just that—I will die. Then comes the question of its curability. Medical professionals talk about 'cutting cancer out', survival rates, and how many years after surgery or chemo people in a similar condition are alive and cancer-free. There are two very important things to remember here. One is that everything is curable because everything in the physical body is controlled by consciousness. Two is that statistics are for computers, not living beings, because each of us is a unique creation. Even in the grimmest of situations that, statistically, is a sure death sentence, a person can prolong physical life and even reverse the condition. It is done not by overriding the body, but by processing the blocked energy and helping the body heal itself. No one can stay alive for the sake of loved ones, it happens only because of a person's own choice, from a passion for life.

Myth #4 is that cancer is an 'evil attacker', an enemy we have to fight with everything we've got. This is also not true. Cancer is a response to a problem and the body's way of attempting correction. Cancer is not a random occurrence but a consequence of a severe energy imbalance. When we see it as an 'evil attacker', we give it power over the Self. We become the victim and Cancer stands the victor! Cancer is not separate from us. Understanding that is the first major step in healing it. Because of the fear that cancer brings up, a person with this physical condition energetically tries to separate from the cancerous cells in their body. This is a very human (based on an animal) response to a dangerous substance, the same as if you were in proximity to an open petri dish that you know contains a lethal virus, you would try not to touch it or maybe even hold your breath so that none of it can interact with your system, and then try to make the distance between you and it as large as you can. But this is not a correct response to something that is created from within one's own system. The dish with a virus is outside, it was not created by one's energy field or body, but cancer is. To some extent we all have this cancer energy program in our auric files, because we all have some issue with personal space. But if we are working with it, the cancerous pattern stays as just that—an energy pattern we are processing. As we talked about before, any physical condition is an indication that an energy block has been in the field for a very long time and on many, if not all, energy levels. Any block, including cancer, starts with an erroneous belief/concept. Like 'Anger is harmful so I should not get angry'(instead of allowing anger to exist, but controlling its expression) or 'Everyone should do good all the time'(instead of seeing how negative 'bad' is a part of a human lesson), or 'I can never fall apart, I have to be strong, so others do not worry about me, they have enough to worry about already' (instead of allowing space for personal pain and processing, letting go of over-responsibility for other's happiness), etcetera. Beliefs like these then penetrate the field, blocking unconditional love for the Self, misaligning us with our own higher truth, creating drama, scarcity, suffering, isolation, confusion and so on, until the block eventually makes its way into the physical body. Since we did not pay attention to the issue, it was allowed to arrive into the physical plane, and left to the resources of the body. The body is not equipped for reprogramming beliefs, so it responds it the only way it can—by creating extra cells in alternate patterns (not based on a balanced, healthy blueprint). Some of these new codes are random, some are from existing genetic files of previous cancers. These cellular mutations are the body's desperate attempts to clear the energy block. The reason they end up as harmful instead of healing is because the energy block that the body attempts to clear originated on the conceptual level, the furthest level from the physical body and inaccessible by it. If you had a precious child in your arms who was suffocating and you already tried the basic techniques of help, what would you do if there was no support coming? You would try everything you could come up with, right? Even if you had no idea if it would work, you would try anything you could think of in your desperate attempt to save that child. Relating this metaphor to cancer, the physical body is the adult, while the child is a balanced, healthy Self. When we are not in balance (an erroneous unprocessed belief about space exists on the conceptual level and penetrates further and further towards the body), we hand our physical body a 'suffocating child' (the unprocessed block) and the body, left to itself and unable to get any help from the rest of the energy system (since that is where the block comes from in the first place) is desperately trying to help. In this desperation, it tries different cellular configurations, anything that *might trigger the energy block to be processed.* And so our physical body gets our attention by creating cancer, and we start to process our issues of lack of space and recreate balance. If a person sees herself as a victim of cancer, she has already done two things to sabotage her healing: one is that she pulled her energy away from the cancerous cells (abandoning the body even further), two is that in seeing cancer as some evil creature attacking her she gave her power away to it (actually fueling cancerous cells instead of healing them). Healing cancer means first of all not abandoning the physical body, and second, creating space for the rest of the Self. Remember your Mission Alpha? The primary agenda of the Soul is always to get into the physical body, not to escape it. If a person with cancer works on the issues of lack of space and is present in their physical Self, they can heal the cancerous program and get back to health.

How does cancer happen? When a lack of space issue is not processed for a long time, the genetic makeup of the cells associated with the energy block gets altered. This does not always result in cancerous growth. If the internal understanding of the Self is strong, the third and root chakras are clear, and the immune system is functioning properly, the physical body is able to destroy the cancerous altered cells before they replicate the wrong code and become established as cancer. But if one is not in the root chakra and the identity of the Self is not clear, one ends up disassembling a healthy boundary and living off genetic/karmic patterns instead. This confuses one's immune system and the cells growing with abnormal codes multiply and invade surrounding tissues. Pretty much any time there is cancer, the physical state is no longer based on a healthy etheric blueprint but is instead overridden by the unhealthy pattern of the energy block.

If a baby has cancer, it is because the very prominent karmic issue of lack of space is also mirrored in the genetics this Soul incarnated into. If genetics were not supporting the issue, the karmic pattern alone would not have manifested cancer at this early age (only later if this person further ignored the karmic issue). This does not mean that if genetic factors show chromosomal abnormalities that a newborn will have cancer. The genetic factor alone is not responsible for cancer; we as the Self are responsible. You can be born into a family with a particular genetic mutation resulting in cancer, but if you do not have a karmic issue similar to theirs, or have it, but work on it, your energy field will not allow cancer to materialize and your immune system will destroy any cell that uses that family genetic makeup.

Environmental factors do not cause cancer, but can make a precancerous condition activate further. For example, ionizing radiation from space (also in atomic bomb explosions and in x-ray machines) is related to the way we humans process passion for life. If one is overly exposed to that radiation, the body might experience burns and other injuries but it will not result in leukemia (the typical cancer associated with ionizing radiation) unless one has issues with passion. Asbestos carries the energy of entrapment, while uranium relates to free expansion—both are said to activate lung cancer. They do not cause cancer, but if a person had the issue of lack of space for internal freedom, which is associated with the lungs, and then was overly exposed to asbestos or uranium, the physical body might end up activating cancerous cells. Viruses do not cause cancers either. But it is probable that if an issue has already created an activation of a particular virus and that issue is continuously ignored, it might develop into a cancer.

Cancer is always paralleled by high toxicity in the body. That is one of the first things to correct physically. Why is toxicity there? Because when one does not process something for a long time, it stays in one's energy field, affecting the body by slowing down the natural cleaning process. Energetic toxicity created by stagnant, unbeneficial patterns and blocks brings on a similar condition in the physical body. This amplifies acidity, making it even harder for the body to detoxify.

123

Here is a simple plan to detoxify the physical body, which is necessary if there is any imbalance, especially with one like cancer: take colloidal minerals, coral calcium, alkalizing solutions (baking soda in water, teas etc.); drink green mixes (with barley grass, chlorella, spirulina, etc.) at least two times per day; take very good probiotics; eat organic fish and beans three times per week and do not eat beef, pork, pies, cakes, any dead food (over-processed and with preservatives) or candy. In other words, maximize nutritious intake in the most available form, alkalize and do not eat chemicalized food and too much wheat or sugar. And do not forget physical exercise—moving the body helps to absorb and distribute all these nutrients properly, helping the body.

If a cancer program is in the energy field and it arrives into the physical body, why does one particular organ or system become cancerous first and not the others? That is because the consciousness of the energy block focuses on a particular physical place. So, depending on the type of cancer a person has, s/he can figure out what was the original issue that created that cancer and work on processing and clearing it. Here are just a few examples of different physical anchors of the cancers. Reading about why it happens might help you to take your power back from the fear.

Ovarian cancer is the issue of space for female creative power. When a woman suppresses her internal life-giving power, she might create ovarian cancer. Giving birth to a child is just one of the expressions of this power, but not the only one. The feminine creative power is a connection with the creator's mystery.

Prostate cancer has to do with not giving space to emotional support. In world culture today, in general, men are taught to be overly structural and stoic, and hence they are unsure of how to incorporate their feminine nature into their personality. Even if a man is very emotional, his emotional nature might be at odds with his conceptual understanding of what it means to be a man. If a man is overly dependent on his mother for emotional support, his body also might create cancer in the prostate. This type of cancer travels very slowly though the energy field into the etheric level and the physical body. Because of that slow speed this type of cancer tends to show up much later in life, even though the issue that created it the originated much earlier.

Skin cancer is a sign of not enough space in the personal boundary. The energy boundary can be overly rigid, like a thick wall of glass, which takes an enormous amount of energy to maintain. This represents fear of life and the desire to over-control the external environment. Or the energy boundary might be almost nonexistent if a person does not want to self differentiate, choosing instead to stay merged with the world. This puts extra pressure on the only existing boundary—the physical skin, and so the skin cells mutate, trying to support the boundary.

Colon cancer has to do with not giving space to life as it comes, and instead trying to control it. Usually this means that a person is not willing to see the reasons for the existence of dark, destructive energies (like cruelty or hatred), wanting the world to match their idea of balance based on the 'good only' diet.

Bone cancer represents the scarcity of internal flexibility. Not the elasticity of the physical body, but of the personality. In other words, if a person has very strong idealistic, fanatical, religious or just plain rigid beliefs, they will put extra charge into their bones, erasing any space for the fluid, flexible type of energies. Bones then try to compensate by creating cancerous tumors. The type of bone cancer (origins in the cartilage, bone itself, the bone marrow, etc.) is determined by the type of rigid beliefs.

Leukemia is cancer of the blood, and it is related to the lack of space for passion. When a person does not have passion for life, the desire to live fully, to engage in life, she can create this type of cancer. Also, all sorts of issues with sexual passion relate to this condition. That's one of the reasons that leukemia often develops in kids just before full puberty—the karmic pattern of fear in connection with sexual passion gets activated just when the hormonal levels begin to change.

Cervical cancer is not caused by the HPVirus, as is often said. It is true that the virus and the cancer tend to go hand in hand, because if a person's issue weakened the etheric level of the cervix's blueprint and activated the virus but she still refused to work with that issue, it might materialize as cancer. But if one is told she has this virus it does not mean she will have cervical cancer, instead she needs to look at it as an alarm, a message to pay attention to the issue that activated the virus in the first place. The cervix represents a direct connection between the physical and divine; the original fetal cells from conception are in the cervix. Physically it might not seem logical that the cervix connects to the brain or to something divine, but it does energetically. There is a direct link between the physical cervix and the brain. The original cells in the cervix are the first matter 'spot' that the Soul touched when it incarnated; it is the anchor point. When energy runs smoothly through the cervix, it activates a direct pathway to the brain and the crown chakra, hence connecting the Self to the divine Soul Self. A woman can block the charge in the cervix (which also destroys its connection to the brain) if she is afraid of her feminine divine power, or afraid of orgasmic energy. Aggressive energy also shuts off the flow to the cervix, especially that of being abused sexually. If a woman was raped, she might have the abusive charge from that event stuck in her cervix's memory, blocking the circulation of life force there. Either way, if the cervix gets a limited amount of energy its cells will be challenged, and that might activate a virus there. Not dealt with, these cells can become cancerous. If the situation is more severe and the flow of energy to the cervix is blocked completely, there is no space for sexual divinity, which results in cancer. Resolving cervical cancer is not accomplished by the 'everything has to be cut out' attitude (especially when it is used simply as a fear-based precaution); instead, this woman needs to really seriously look at her issues with sexuality and divinity. The problem might be in her not seeing the connection between being a sexual female and her Soul's creative playful powers, or she might have a fear of letting go into her sexual ecstasy, perhaps she has an overly rigid protective layer of energy around her cervix (because of sexual abuse or issues with control), etcetera. Working with these issues of lack of space helps to clear cancer from the energy field. This might stop a precancerous condition from becoming cancerous, or if an operation was necessary and cancerous cells were manually cut out, from any recurrence.

Concluding this very charged, scary topic, I want to mention again that it is essential to take the power back from cancer. If you know that cancer represents a very particular energy program in your energy field, you can work with the issues of personal space that you know you have (we all have some of these) and prevent an occurrence of cancer in your physical body.

Fluid and Structural Dysfunctions

One of the other ways to categorize physical body problems is by the energy type most involved. Dysfunctions of the fluid energy levels, like emotional, astral and unconditional, create a very particular set of physical issues. If the energy on these levels is stagnant, polluted, compressed or overly stretched, we tax the physical systems and organs related to these energy levels. This produces physical dysfunctions; some are small and temporary while others are lifelong, difficult-to-break patterns. If you are processing stagnant energy, it also might activate cold-like symptoms, because your physical body will match the energy charge that you are clearing. When the structural (etheric, mental, truth, conceptual) energy levels are off, they affect the physical body in their own unique way. Overly rigid, tight, brittle, idealistic, fanatical, overcharged and other patterns like that make the physical body respond by tightening in places where it is not supposed to. Personal processing of these patterns can create physical symptoms also, but they last only as long as the energy processing continues. Why is this important to know? Because if you notice that you have one particular physical symptom showing up again and again, you can help clear it by balancing and clearing the issue on the fluid or structural energy levels. Let's say you get infections often. It might be hard to figure out exactly what particular issue is creating them, but you know that they are a sign of dysfunction on the fluid energy levels. You can then look at the previous chapter about energy anatomy, and use one of the exercises to clear and charge your fluid levels. As you do that, you might actually find out what was the particular issue that was calling for your attention by creating the physical infections. But even if you do not find it consciously, your efforts will help to balance the fluid levels, hence alleviating the physical symptoms.

Here are some examples of fluid and structural dysfunctions.

FLUID DYSFUNCTION	STRUCTURAL DYSFUNCTION
Depression	Bone/joint pain (no lubrication)
Colds (stagnation)	Flu/fever
Overweight	Anorexia
Chronic fatigue syndrome	High blood pressure
Alcoholism	Cancer/tumors
Bronchitis (mucus)	Clogged arteries
Infection (invasion)	Arthritis
Diabetes	Broken bones/torn ligaments

Cellular Joy

There are two basic factors that limit our capacity for joy. One is our attitude toward life and the other is the number of joy receptor sites on the membranes of our cells. These two factors are interconnected. Every person has a genetic predisposition for the number of joy receptor sites, but we can teach our cells to grow more of them by changing our attitude and redefining what gives us joy and pleasure.

What is joy? Joy is a slowed down, densified light (of a very high frequency), which as it enters a physical cell, creates a chemical reaction inside that cell. Joy is a different energy than happiness, which is an attitude. Joy is also different from pleasure, which is a melting relaxation into second level emotional energies. Joy is not an attitude in itself; it is a frequency, and each of us can tune into it, allowing our physical body to receive it. The Universe is filled with the frequency of joy—a yellow-orange ocean of joy permeates everything. The movement of atoms is charged with the excitement of joy. It exists without our permission, it does not need to be generated or created, it is infinitely there already. We human beings can choose to tune into it or not. Joy is independent, our interface with it does not change anything for joy, but the conscious anchoring of joy can surely change us.

In the physical body, cellular receptors are molecular configurations made of amino acids or proteins. Each receptor is attuned to a particular frequency, like a radio station receiving its home signal. When we have these particular receptors coded for 'joy radio station' we are capable of receiving joy into our cells. The frequency of joy, after it enters the receptor site, passes through a cellular membrane. This feeds joy energy to the internal workings of each cell, giving us the physical sensation of joy in the physical body—that is cellular joy!

Cellular joy occurs in the body for no particular reason known or given by the mind. It is a state of alive excitement, the cells are just 'turned on'. When we think we need a reason to have joy, our physical and emotional levels actually block the joy from entering us. This is because the imposition of reason makes the joy conditional. *Conditionality kills joy.*

When the joy frequency has reached the inside of a cell, the DNA material is activated and produces chemicals that reinforce the physical state of joy and amplify the energy state of joy. There are genes for the chemicals that support joy in the body. Specially encoded 'joy' peptides are the chemicals that come out of the DNA code; they circulate through the blood stream, feeding all of the body cells with the frequency of joy. This is the way joy energy is translated into joy biology.

Our genetics preprogram us for high joy capacity or lack of joy. Based on how our ancestors related to joy, we build a certain number of coded messengers in our DNA material following the ancestral pattern, and usually this just sucks. Parental problems with joy become our own, limiting our ability to make joy cellular. We can deal with this issue by changing our attitude towards joy, reinforcing our own pattern, hence overriding the genetic inheritance. Genetics are only the basic matrix, preinstalled when we incarnated into this body, and it is up to us to add our own programs, personalizing the 'device'. As we examine our thinking/feeling in relationship to joy and use this curiosity to enhance the number of receptor sites, we expand the range of possibilities of joy perception. Tuning into Universal vitality on the atomic level increases joy perception. Curious thoughts do the same. Feeling the magic of life and yourself as a piece of a very large, awesome puzzle of the Universe (God) amplifies joy in the body. When we understand how thought changes biology, we reinvent ourselves, increasing the capacity for joy in our lives.

Physical Pain

Physical pain is not a punishment, neither is it an attack on our wellbeing. When a person projects her internal authority of physical body-self onto something external, it separates her from her body, making pain seem as a punishment or as an attack, that is, an enemy. What does this mean? Ok, here is the basic rule: the Self and the physical body are one. When we do not see the body as a part of ourselves, we go against that rule, making it harder to clear physical pain. Now, why would someone not see their body as part of themselves?, you ask. Isn't it kind of normal to assume that we are the body? Well, not really, considering all the painful experiences we have had in it, time after time. When the body's reactions to life's circumstances seem to us as foreign, mean or even cruel, it is an indication that we do not see the body as part of the Self. We then end up blaming the body for betraying us, for giving us pain. When we have a cold, we do not normally go 'why did I create this cold today?', right? We think how inconvenient it is, or maybe that 'we are bad' and 'why is it happening to me' sort of thing, and we ultimately end up blaming the body for doing it to us, for interrupting our life. But in truth we did create the cold, the body did not do it to us, but did it as a part of us. The same cold without being physical might look like self pity on the emotional level, confusion on the mental, whining on the astral, and so on. We usually do not go 'you, bad emotional level, you gave me self pity!', or 'I would have been just fine if not for you, pesky mental level, making me all confused!'. We see these internal reactions as part of our creation, yet the same reaction on the physical level gets a bad rap. Why? Because of our illusory perception of the physical body as solid, we tend to separate our ideas of the mind or feelings, from the body. This leads to the perception that we do not have authority over that part of the Self. We are the only authority, the creator of everything, for our physical body. But when we relinquish our rights to it, we project the healing power outward, and become victims of the body. It feels like being at the mercy of chance, waiting for the body to throw us into another painful experience.

If a person carries a lot of fear and guilt, and has a predisposition for water and/or the air element, she will perceive physical pain as a punishment. She will think that she did something wrong (or be afraid that she might have), and then, because of not seeing the body as part of herself, the pain will look like punishment for her wrongdoing. A person with an abundance of the fire and/or earth element, and with tendencies towards anger, stoicism or control, will see pain as an attack. His gut reaction will be either to fight back by all means available (including medical), or to resist 'giving into the pain'; in fact, ignoring it.

But what is physical pain? *Pain is a message.* Yes, please re-read the last sentence. We give a lot of power to pain because of the separation from the body (victimhood); this only makes the pain scarier. But physical pain is the body's way of telling us that we are ignoring something inside. When one is in physical pain, it is a sign that the body is forced to reject the life force due to some configuration in the rest of one's energy field. If the aura is balanced, the body is designed to receive pure life force in a constant abundant flow from the etheric blueprint of health. When we block that transmission by our beliefs, fears etcetera, the body is left on its own, giving us pain as a sign of its struggle. This pain is a message to our conscious awareness to pay attention to the imbalances in the energy field and to listen to the wisdom of the body. By attuning to the message, decoding it and, hence, releasing the rejection of life force, the body can heal itself.

As we know, pain is a brain function. If we burn a finger, the message travels through the nervous system to the brain, which in turn registers this message and decides how to react. This is based on the perception in the brain. The brain receives the message and references back to past experience in order to know what just happened. The brain would not know the pain of the burned finger unless it had experienced it before. This past referencing is one of the biggest issues we face when dealing with physical pain. The brain connects circumstances to perceptions, creating pathways of anticipation of the event because of the similarity of circumstances. But every moment is unique, right? If the pain is received as a new message and decoded, the energy configuration creating the pain can be cleared up, resolving the pain. You might get a cold a couple of times per year, but the reason for it every time might

131

be different. If the pain is chronic, it usually represents a habitually ignored message. A chronically sore and tight neck might be a sign of over-responsibility and trying to control/do too much, chronic constipation might represent the inability to let go and the desire to not miss anything, while chronic allergic reaction tells us of defensiveness towards life, and so on.

Once the pain has shown up we need to make sure we do not ignore the message or try to cover up its significance. Often, pain's message is not what we want to hear, especially with chronic pain. Knowledge of the energy system can help you to decode the body's messages. Depending on the origin of the pain you can connect it to the correlating component of the aura. Even the vaguest message will make itself known if you stay focused on decoding it. The problem is that we often give up too easily. We try to figure out why the pain is happening, but we either block the answer by fear, or we get the answer but do not like it so much, that we refuse to see it. When attempting to decode your pain, first release the fear. Remember, fear of pain only makes the pain scarier, so make a pact with yourself that for the time of searching for an answer you will set the fear aside, you will be brave to receive whatever the answer might be. If the fear of the answer is overwhelming, see it as a gray smoke around you, then breathe it out of your space until it is reasonably clear. Then attempt again to decode the message. This is not so much for finding the physical cause of pain, which is actually secondary, but for the energy reason. Why is the physical cause secondary? Because the body never causes the pain, our misguided beliefs and energy imbalances cause physical pain. The faulty energy configuration creates faulty physical functioning and rewiring of the body's processes, which we feel as pain. The physical reason might be important for dealing with the physical situation, but it serves only as a temporary solution unless one clears up the energy situation. It does not do much good to find out that chiropractic adjustments help your neck's pain, if you then have to visit the chiropractor every couple of days for pain relief. But if the actual energy issue causing the neck pain is resolved, then the physical support of a chiropractor is needed only as maintenance. A kind self investigation for the origin of your pain will lead to a more powerful relationship with your physical body, releasing old patterns of victimhood. Pain is not an enemy, but an internal alarm, reminding us to pay attention to the issue at hand.

Cellular Regeneration and Conscious Sleep

Nobody likes to get old, but it seems an inevitable result of living, right? Well, not exactly. Aging is a programmed result, not an original design. In the original design an individual receives life force without filtering or blocking it, and s/he does not get old or die. A clear, permeable boundary allows the life force to enter, and the Self then experiences this life force freely, completely, unconditionally. This unrestricted experience allows the energy field to stay clear of karma, since everything gets processed as it enters, nothing is stored for later. In this format the physical body, being a lower vibrational component of the Self, is constantly replenished by the etheric level perfect blueprint of health. There are no imbalances, hence no physical issues. Each cell receives an abundant amount of the Soul's light and retains its perfection after each cellular division. There is no aging and no death. This being/creature will live forever, unless s/he decides to terminate her/his existence, or transfer it into some other frequency reality. Sounds great, eh?

But we are somewhat far from this balanced creaturehood. We have lots of karmic experiences to deal with, lots of stress in life and lots of societal patterns to clear, all of which have changed our original blueprint into what it is now. However, this does not mean that we cannot change our speed and severity of aging. Probably we won't be able to live forever, but we can live much longer and much healthier. Youth is not as elusive as we have come to think. Most of it has to do with attitude. If we decide that it is normal to get slower, fatter and diseased as the time goes by, it will happen. On the other hand if we decide that aging can be very slow and graceful, kind, that we can feel and look fantastic at any age, it will become our reality. The absence of sexual energy plays a very large role in getting old. Sexual energy is the life force itself, it is a dynamic aliveness without which the physical body has no reason to exist. If a person keeps their sexuality alive (which does not necessarily mean 'has sex a lot'), s/he will be able to stay youthful for a very long time. When we shut down our sexuality because there is no partner or we feel unhappy/unattractive/scared, we actually speed

133

up the aging process. Why? Because our physical cells need the juice, the passion for life, to stay charged. Without sexual energy the karmic, societal and genetic patterns take over cellular function.

What does aging really look like? Cells always multiply, this is what keeps us alive. You do not have the same cells in your body today that you had a year ago or even yesterday. They replace each other to maintain the organism. But unfortunately each new cell is not an exact copy of the mother cell; it loses some of its vigor with replication, following a self-diminishing pattern that causes aging. When DNA divides many times, the ribosomal (protein encoding) part of the DNA is prone to instability. Repetitive instability sequences lead to recombining of the same ribosomal DNA fragments to each other, resulting in numerous illnesses and but mainly, aging. Sometimes there is a small ribosomal DNA backup created as if the mother cell was afraid to forget something. This copy is useless. The actual genetic material is divided, half goes into a new cell, but that redundant small genetic copy stays behind. The more of these copies there are in a cell, the junkier it gets, and eventually it is unable to divide and dies. Why would we create these unnecessary copies? Because we are afraid of life. The fear of being in the physical body forces our cells to multiply their 'protein factory manuals' to ensure survival. Then due to different beliefs and feeling patterns, these copies mingle together and generate physical problems and aging. When we live with passion and excitement, our DNA is packaged tightly inside the cell, which means less of these redundant ribosomal copies. But when we fear life, we try to slow it down so we can better control it, which leads to loosely packaged genetic coils that are prone to fear-based dividing decisions. The cellular component called mitochondrion is fueled energetically by self love, kindness, nurturing and being in excited presence with each moment. When we have these energies flowing freely, our mitochondria have a great time! They fuel the production of special enzymes, which make our DNA coil tighter, hence minimizing genetic junk and reducing cellular diminishment. These supercharged mitochondria also amplify the body's ability to heal and to clear toxins automatically.

Certain genes and proteins encoded by them are fear based, and so they amplify cell diminishment. In other words, the more fear we feel, the more we are in resistance to life, the faster we will age. But if we face life with excitement and wonder, with curiosity, then we charge the genes and their proteins responsible for destroying cellular mutations. This means we can de-age! Not just halt the aging process, but reverse it. Inside each cell, in the nucleus, mitochondria, cytoplasm, there are particular enzymes, which are part of an automatic regulatory program for anti-aging. Our cruelty and judgments kick this program off-line, instead allowing our imbalances to dictate cellular processes.

The belief in aging is a psychological 'clock' that translates into biology for a subscriber to that belief. The average human body clock programs cells to divide, diminish and die, therefore creating a limited lifespan. The human clock is based in chronology, in linear time. Lately, due to dimensional energies being more coherent and to increased awareness, time feels faster to us. From the Soul level, this brings greater emotional experience in every moment, but from an imbalanced human perspective it tends to speed up the clock. In other words, lately it might feel like we are running out of time. This is one of the reasons for such an expansion of the cosmetic surgery industry and all sorts of ways of making the body look younger. On the social scale, there is urgency (and even a low-level panic) about getting old, and a resolve to do whatever is possible to stop it. But since the idea of the clock is based in victim consciousness, the clock cannot be stopped. It can only be discarded. The biology of aging is created by a belief, which is a conceptual level program. A perfect blueprint of health contains another program, the one for cellular regeneration. But it is only accessible when social, genetic and karmic patterns are not overriding our curiosity for life. *Curiosity fuels cellular regeneration.* The more curious we are, the more passion we have, the more desire to live, the more vitality and health, which in turn makes us younger.

The abundance of time plays a key role in the body's ability to regenerate. Luxury of time is spaciousness on the fluid energy levels. If that space is too compressed, we have stress (feel overly mental, mechanical etc.). If that space is overly open, we also have stress (feel too emotional, overwhelmed etc.). And stress is a killer of regeneration. It takes time to bring fluid levels into balance, because fluid energy is slower than structural. You give yourself that time when you take a deep breath in the middle of some task you're involved in, or by stopping everything you are doing and walking outside into something more spacious (a larger room or the outdoors), or by imagining yourself in the peaceful 'perfect place' (a meadow, a beach etc.). This is the true balance of time and space.

One of the most efficient ways of cellular regeneration is sleep. Not any kind of sleep, but a deep, consciously regenerative one. The brain opens to receiving the 'magnetic ocean' of the Universe/Source without any distractions from everyday life, the energy flows through aligned levels into the physical body, maximizing access to the blueprint of perfect health. This promotes the clean-up of negative patterns, affecting general health and especially aging. By aligning with the Universal energies of balance, we become out of synch with negative vibrations, and this releases/dissolves them. During this type of sleep you gain access to your Soul's remembrance, which often allows a different perspective on current events and a view of the bigger picture. This sleep also builds familiarity with other-dimensional energies, eventually expanding your conscious comprehension of the Universe. It allows us to gain access to other timelines, leading to growing abilities and knowledge of the expanded realities of the Self. Often during our awake state we download lots of energy information, but cannot integrate it right away and put it on hold. Then when we sleep, because the cells are in the regeneration mode, this information 'hanging' in the energy field can finally integrate.

During the correct mode for cellular regeneration, cells have the capacity to multiply and get stronger with each replication, not weaker. The cells of an enlightened being not only regenerate with each division, but learn and, infused with more light, become immortal. This is what it means to 'turn body into light'. It makes an enlightened being in a sense immortal, because the cells will evolve without ever dying until that being chooses to terminate existence in matter. But this is an ideal, not a typical human pattern, obviously. We would be glad to age more slowly and live healthier, right? Using the information about cellular regeneration (including that of a consciously regenerative sleep mode) we can in general expand our healthy life span.

One of the exercises you might use for activation of the cellular regeneration processes is alignment with the Universal Pulse. This pulse is a rhythmic transmission of intelligence between our own body/energy field, our Sun, the Galactic Sun (which is the black hole region in the center of this galaxy) and the Universal Central Sun (which is the conceptual center for this Universe). To activate regeneration in your body, do this exercise before you fall asleep each night, it is very expanding and soothing. Tune into your physical body and relax, as if you are floating in the large bubble of your energy field. This stabilizes your cells. Then breathe deeply and slowly, tuning into the Sun of our solar system. Try not to just think of it, but feel its warmth, experience the golden light etcetera. This recharges your cells. As you are feeling the Sun, move your awareness to the Galactic Sun. Feel the black velvety energy of the galactic center; there are no sounds, no light, it is perfect peace. Allow yourself to experience this peace, float in its void. This helps your cells to let go of any habitual, harmful patterns. Then expand to the Universal Central Sun, just intend it and witness what happens. It usually feels as if one is coming from a dark tunnel (Galactic Sun) into a very bright light. You might hear the sound of music, or see many different colors in motion, or only a very bright white light. Whatever your perception is, let yourself stay with it for a while. This regenerates your cells. You can end here (it is ok if you fall asleep in this step), or you can then reconnect to your own body and your own internal bright light (your Core Star), to anchor the regeneration process. Enjoy!

Metals in the Body

Energy anchors differently in particular types of matter. High frequency electrical charges conducted through precious metals in the physical body create the feeling of bliss. We can feel the bliss emotionally without the use of metals, but to have a physical bliss sensation metals have to be involved. Heavy metals carry frequencies that support physical and sexual sensation. Radioactive elements activate deep feelings. Trace elements give the physical body the ability to perceive high frequencies. If we use metallic energy in the body correctly, we benefit tremendously in health and consciousness. By removing erroneous and limited beliefs about metals, you can learn to change habitual unbeneficial relationships to the metals in your body, creating emotional/mental balance and physical health.

Because of the dense nature of most metals, they tend to further activate our fear of being here, in matter. Because we are afraid of metals, we often project our power onto them, as if they are more powerful than us and can harm us. In general, human beings do not use a lot of metallic energies, they seem somewhat alien to us, cold and often reptilian. But using metallic energy correctly in small amounts is very beneficial. Each chakra responds to a particular metal frequency. In other words, if we have difficulty with a particular metal (allergic reaction, poisoning, inability to assimilate, etc.) it means we will also have difficulty in the corresponding chakra. Knowing that, when the physical condition associated with the metal is overly difficult, we can approach it from the chakra cleansing perspective. Working with the issue in the chakra will allow energy to flow through the corresponding metal, helping our efforts to clear the physical situation.

Platinum has a fast vibration and connects to the crown chakra. Platinum energy is very cold. This is the reason why when one connects to a very high frequency, one gets physically cold—the crown chakra takes in the energy and it runs through platinum in the physical body. Platinum is responsible for the connection between the physical body and the etheric blueprint for perfect health. When we send our body's functions off course, platinum corrects them.

Silver is connected to the sixth chakra (the third eye). Silver energy is very smooth, and warmer than platinum. One has to know how to use silver metallic energy if one wants to have the ability to envision possibilities or to see energy. Silver makes our energy boundary clearer. Physically, silver enhances/charges the immune system, and also clears up the skin. But silver molecules have to be broken into extremely small sizes to supercharge your immune systems. Beware of taking large supplements of silver in its regular form, because it can turn your skin blue permanently. Drinking a cup of silver water once per day is a very good way of familiarizing yourself with silver energy. You can make that water by letting it sit in direct contact with silver for twelve or more hours (either cold water in a glass jar with a silver spoon in it [not a silver-plated spoon, but real silver], or if you have a silver pitcher, fill it with cold water). Because silver is a very healing metal, drinking silver water teaches your body to heal itself more efficiently.

Mercury is an element that brings up a lot of fear in many people for its ability to activate deep feelings, very similar to radioactive elements. Mercury corresponds to the throat chakra and relates to the expression of personal truth. It wakes up deep and very powerful feelings about reality. If a person knows their truth and does not hide from it, mercury energy will flow evenly. But if she fights her truth, hides it even from herself or from others, the energy of mercury gets overly heated due to internal friction, which can result in physical issues with mercury metal, even mercury poisoning. Mercury is not bad, as many people tend to think. It is a metal necessary for evolution, but in very small amounts. We only accumulate too much of it if we refuse to use it properly in the first place.

Gold is the metal of the heart chakra. It is warm, sunny yellow and comforting. It also supports the body's healing processes, but more in the category of repair. If a bone is broken, skin is torn, there is some internal eruption, or after a surgical operation, gold is indispensable. It works well with silver: gold repairs the damage while silver fights off any infection. Gold has the energy of compassion and nonjudgment. It does not get repelled by the destruction in the body, but goes to work to correct it. Gold is extremely useful for repairing the heart muscle after heart attack or an operation, and also in preventing heart conditions. Wearing gold might work, but only if the person is conscious about the metal. Drinking gold water is also a great support, especially if there is an urgent need for repair in the body (you can make the gold water the same way as the silver one).

Zinc connects to the third chakra. Physically, zinc is required for protein synthesis and collagen formation, reproductive organ maturation, a healthy prostate, the protection of the liver from free radical damage and the prevention of infections. Zinc energy mostly runs through the nervous system, and it balances the solar plexus area. This bundle of nerves at the plexus is the 'feeling brain' for the body. You know how when you are nervous, that spot almost hurts, right? Or if you are anticipating that something will go wrong, you might get a nagging sensation in the plexus. And if you are in love, you will have 'butterflies' there. If we use zinc energy properly, then the feelings are processed easily and there are no 'fires to put out' for our immune system, that is, the body stays healthy. If we refuse to process our feelings though, it is hard for our identity to be stable and we end up fluctuating in our understanding of the Self, taxing the immune system. The body then will use all the zinc it can get, creating a zinc deficiency. The liver becomes toxic, the skin gets more oily and acne-prone, a person feels fatigued, easily susceptible to infections, colds and flu, wounds might heal very slowly and fingernails might develop white spots. If correcting the physical imbalance with supplements, make sure not to take zinc with iron (take it at different times because their activity interferes with each other) and do not take more than 100 mg of zinc per day (less than that will enhance your immune system, while more than that can suppress it!).

Copper is the corresponding component for the second chakra. Copper holds the energy of abundance and warm support. Physically, copper is responsible for the formation of bone and red blood cells; it is necessary for the healing process, energy production and health of the nerves. If one has major second chakra issues, s/he distorts the energy of copper, making the body work harder. When copper energy is off, we struggle physically. A copper deficient person might be often fatigued, have osteoporosis, anemia, muscle aches—all signs of resisting the flow of life due to fear of pain. If the second chakra issue is not corrected, but this person takes large supplements of copper, he might end up with toxicity and depression, because copper will restore the flow of life force through him, making him face the issues of the second chakra he wanted to avoid. This is not bad, one can work with an energy block starting with a physical correction (supplements) which will trigger the emotional processing, or from the conceptual/emotional/mental place first, which helps the body to correct itself. Either way, both components, energetic and physical, will have to be addressed.

Iron is connected to the root chakra, it is a stabilizer metal for the whole body. Physically, iron is necessary for the production of hemoglobin and the oxygenation of the red blood cells, it is required for strong immune function and energy production. One has to be in the body for it to function properly. The iron in the planetary core is the same iron that is in your body, allowing you to energetically be one with the planet. When we do not have enough charge in the blood, it is because we do not want to run life force through it—it is a form of rejection of matter. This rejection leads to anemia, an iron deficiency. Other symptoms are recurrent dizziness, fatigue, fragile bones, hair loss and slow, confused thinking (as if you are in a fog). But when correcting iron deficiency make sure to not overtake iron, for it leads to the production of free radicals. And never take iron supplements if you have an infection. Bacteria need iron to grow, so the body will hide this iron from the bacteria so as not to amplify the infection by storing it in your liver, toxifying it. When trying to correct mild iron deficiency always pay attention to your root chakra first, this will help to stabilize the iron.

Metals, minerals and vitamins work synergistically; they act as catalysts in cooperative action promoting the absorption, distribution and assimilation of each other. Correcting a deficiency in one mineral requires the addition of others, not simply a replacement of the one you are deficient in. For example, to correct a copper deficiency one needs folic acid, iron and zinc. While for zinc deficiency calcium, phosphorus, vitamin B6 and copper are necessary.

When a person is able to fully use the frequency of each metal, he does not accumulate any extra metal in his tissues and there is no metal poisoning. But if he is afraid of/in resistance to the energy of any metal, his body will try to compensate by amplifying the physical amount of that metal. In other words, each metallic atom anchors a specific amount of metallic energy. When we resist the energy, we anchor less of it in each atom and the body has to accumulate more metallic atoms to receive the needed amount of energy. We end up with too much physical metal in the body so we can get the vibration we need. This can lead to metal overabundance or poisoning. Metal poisoning does not happen because we ingested too much metal, but because we resisted the frequency, accumulating extra metal. If you ingest too much metal, but have no resistance to its frequency, you will not get poisoned because the body will automatically clear it out of its systems. Overabundance of metals in the body requires physical detoxifying. But detoxifying alone will not work if the original reason for the rejection of the particular metal frequency is not corrected. Always look at these reasons first, make friends with the metallic energy that you have a problem with, tune into it, synchronize with it, play with it. There is a belief that if we tune into the metal energy, we amplify the physical poisoning. That is not true; by tuning into the metallic charge you will build familiarity with it and help yourself to clear out the energy resistance and fear, which in turn will assist your physical body's detox process.

The Consciousness of Fat

When we think of fat, we generally freak out. It has the social energy charge of poison, a national enemy. But fat is not something to go to war with. If we do, we will lose. What if you want your body to 'not have fat'? The only way to adjust the fat in the body is to make friends with it. Fat is very magnetic and fluid in its energy, which is one of the reasons why fluid type people have more physical fat. Just notice your emotional reaction to fat: there is everything from hatred, disgust and fear to shame, guilt and dread. But all of these are emotional and astral societal patterns that you end up subscribing to throughout your lives, they are not real, not true and not yours!

Fat is first of all a type of energy. Physical fat cannot exist in the body if there is no corresponding energy configuration in the aura. Energetically, fat looks like a yellow-ochre spongy goo, with slightly rubbery internal compartments that give fat its squishy quality. There are many beneficial reasons for the existence of fat, and equally, many unbeneficial ones. It acts as a buffer, slowing down the inflow of life force from the outside of us. It also cushions internal energies, so we do not get shocked. The energy of fat is heavy in comparison with many others, and so it also acts as an anchor for the whole energy field into the etheric level and the physical form. Fat can be a boundary definition, creating a thick 'wall' to differentiate the Self and the other, or the Self and uncomfortable feelings, etcetera. The energy of fat is slow, so any place where fat exists will have a slower energy flow. Fat can be packed tight, and then it loses its rubbery quality and can slow down the flow to a standstill. Or it can be a more loose energy, then it takes up too much space, which also disrupts the flow of life force because energy lingers too long in the fat and gets stuck there.

If a person is trying to avoid dealing with an issue she is facing, she might gain more fat all over her body as means of slowing down the issue, a form of resistance. That fat can be used up as soon as she stops resisting and faces her problem. Sometimes if we are processing something and too many things are going on, we might end up with 'these extra ten pounds' as a form of 'making it' through the difficult time. These fat cells usually will not go away by any dieting or exercise, but if you stay kind to yourself, they will eventually disappear once the crisis is over.

If there is something wrong with a particular chakra, a person might accumulate lots of fat around that area. These are usually chronic misalignments, lifelong imbalances, not something that happened during stress in a week. For example, if there is an issue with self love, self acceptance, guilt, etcetera (all second chakra problems), the belly might get more fat cells. Or if a person does not know who he is, trying to match or fight someone else's idea of him and so on (all third chakra issues), he might have a 'fat middle'.

If someone does not want to be in matter and floats out of her body a lot, she might use fat as an anchor to keep herself present. This means that she will accumulate lots of fat around the hips. Fat will ground her. This 'floating out of the body' reaction usually goes hand in hand with overwhelm/fear of pain, which relates to the second chakra, and so she will also have fat around her belly. A pear-shaped person usually has issues with second and root chakras. But what about people who are so very thin and ungrounded? If they are 'floaters', then why are they not fat? To accumulate too much fat a person has to spend at least some time in the body and be somewhat magnetic or very magnetic. Usually a thin 'floater' spends very little time in the body and fuels his metabolism with fear, not love.

Fat can also serve as a boundary if a person feels invaded. Often people who were abused as children develop much extra fat on their body to protect themselves. Because fat is thick, it slows down external vibrations. If there is a lot of abuse—physical, emotional, sexual—the body will thicken its energy boundary, which physically produces more fat cells. In a sense, a person will hide behind their fat. Issues of low self worth and self esteem often make a person overly sensitive to life, and by accumulating more fat she can make her emotional pain less intense. Or if a person does not have a boundary or her/his boundary has holes or is too thin, s/he will feel life as overly raw. This oversensitivity is minimized by accumulating fat cells on the body, which end up serving as a substitute boundary.

Our body cannot function without fat, since fat is the 'packing material' around organs. Energetically it cushions and properly separates the structures, physically maintaining the correct space. The physiological/emotional function of fat is satisfaction. Without fat it is not possible to feel satisfied. If we do not fear or judge fat, we have only the necessary amount of it, which allows us to experience satisfaction. But what if your satisfaction is conditional? What if you are never quite satisfied? When we place restrictions on satisfaction, it becomes unattainable. And so our physical body then compensates for this by creating more fat. This type of fat is not just on the surface, but inside, and it is much more dangerous for physical health. The liver might become fatty, the blood might have too much fat and so on. All of this makes the body struggle, which leads to even less satisfaction and even more fat. This is one of the reasons for major obesity problems. People are satisfied not with evolving in life, but with entertainment. This makes satisfaction conditional, creating a need for immediate gratification, further resulting in bad habits, a sedentary lifestyle, unhealthy diet, and so on. All leading to more fat, as the body attempts to correct the conditionality of satisfaction!

So if you want to lose some of your fat cells, look first at the issues connected with them. The best way to do that is to ask the fat cells themselves. You cannot do that by despising them, so love your fat! Yes, tune into your fat cells, don't be afraid. You will not make them multiply by tuning into them. You will find the stuck emotional energy in these fat cells that is responsible for their existence in the first place. When you tune into your fat, what do you feel first? Fear, guilt, shame, disgust, dread? These first impressions are the energies stuck in the fat. Follow these feelings deeper. Fear of what? Of being invaded? Or being hurt? Guilt and shame about what? Not being responsible or being 'bad' by someone else's standard? Why disgust? Are you punishing yourself for something? Dread about what? Not being perfect? Ask these questions, dig deeper. Find out what is behind the answers. The feeling of being invaded or hurt points to a weak boundary; knowing this you can make it stronger. Guilt or irresponsibility usually connects to trying to please/rebel against someone who you made into an authority, and this knowledge will help you to take your power back from them and change the irresponsible behaviors. Self punishment shows you that your second chakra is not balanced, which you can correct by choosing to be kinder to yourself and to value yourself more. Recognizing discouragement/dread about not ever being able to match your image of perfection leads to relief if you can learn to see your imperfections as 'perfection of learning' (or 'perfection in training'). And so on, keep decoding the messages that your fat cells hold. This will start to clean up the extra energy of fat goo in the field, which in turn will burn its physical counterpart. By examining/questioning images, concepts and beliefs that support the accumulation and burning of fat, you will unplug from the societal astral mess of perfectionistic images and perpetual dissatisfaction. Learning and evolving will become more satisfying than matching a perfect image, and your fat cells will anchor joy energy instead of all the negative stuff you found in them earlier!

Chocolate

I just could not bear ending this chapter on the topic of fat. So here is a little something much more fun. Chocolate! Why is chocolate in the chapter about the body? Because it works miracles for it! Do not let other people convince you that it is 'bad for you' or that it will 'make you fat'. Chocolate has a balanced charge and will never harm you if used properly. There is a chemical in chocolate that increases the networking capacity of brain cells. Chocolate amplifies inner brain networking by growing more synapses. It can make us smarter, clearer, more focused and balanced. It is perfect for times when you feel sluggish or confused. Another chemical in chocolate creates the feeling of being in love. When you are in love, there are very particular hormones swimming actively through your system. Chocolate elicits the same response! Because chocolate is fire-element based, when it interacts with your body it amplifies the fire in you and brings the electromagnetic balance online. Due to its 'in love' and fire qualities, chocolate is an excellent natural antidepressant and emotional picker-upper. It is a master food for the entire system just like the pituitary is a master gland for the body. Chocolate is the 'food of the gods'. And guess what, WE are these gods! Our human Mission Alpha is a fusion of body and Soul, it is godhood. And chocolate is the perfect support on this mission!

Now, before you run out to the nearest store (or a kitchen drawer) for your chocolate fuel, here are some suggestions on how to use chocolate medicinally. First of all, it is a live energy, so treat it as such, do not 'use it' but 'work with it', respect it. For your chocolate to have medicinal properties the cocoa content has to be at least over seventy percent, making it dark in color. The cocoa bean has a fast electric charge, while cocoa butter has a magnetic and slow charge. Milk chocolate has little cocoa, and the cocoa is pretty much the power of chocolate. Even though the buttery components can support you, they do not have the ability to stimulate the human brain, stimulating fat cells instead. The Diva of Chocolate is a nonphysical being overseeing the substance of chocolate on the physical level. This Diva is androgynous, it is not a woman; actually, it is a being from another star system. Maya people saw It as a male being—the Cocoa Being. You can invite It to bless the chocolate you are about to eat, this will potentate it and synchronize its energy with your body. If you are not on a first name basis with the Diva, you can synchronize your body and the chocolate yourself by holding it in your hand and tuning into it, focusing your attention on it while you relax, before you eat it. Using chocolate medicinally requires only small amounts, eaten slowly. An inch by inch square is more than enough if consumed properly. We bite chocolate only out of fear of pleasure. Allow yourself to slowly dissolve a piece of chocolate in your mouth, luxury requires the spaciousness of time!

CHAPTER 3
Awareness

CHAPTER 3

Worthiness

Everything and everyone has value to the Universe; the application of this principle is worthiness. To the Source/God, the value of any Self is the same. What does that mean, how can it be the same? A particle of stellar dust, a butterfly, you, a fish, a water molecule in a thunderous cloud, all have their own unique path of exploration. When we have an experience, go through circumstances, learn lessons, we are exploring reality, exploring God. No one's path is more important than another's. It is true that someone's path might noticeably affect many other paths (like an asteroid crashing onto a planet, or a king's decision to go for a peace treaty) while another path will appear somewhat separate and invisible. But in truth nothing is separate and everything we are/do/think/feel affects everything else one way or another. Everyone's journey is unique to God. We are infinitely precious and important to the Source. Application of this value of preciousness and importance onto a matter-vehicle-based form (i.e., us) is what we call worthiness. Self-worth is an internal perception of this worthiness principle.

The essence of the Self that is transmitted from the Soul level into physicality at birth must pass through a 'shrinking' process in order to incarnate. It is this shrinking that is at the base of all feelings of unworthiness. The shrinking process is necessary. Why? When we claim the body by attaching to physical cells at conception, we minimize the Self a bit to 'fit in' to the narrow focus of physicality. Like condensing a large cloud into a small bit of rain, we compress ourselves into a body-anchored creature. Notice that, just as a small puddle of water can become a larger cloud again, so are we always a Soul, just shrunken in form.

Imagine the flow of consciousness and love between your Soul and you. Visualize it vertically (it is not actually vertical, since there is no gravity for the Soul, but for human perception it is easier to see it this way). At the top of the vertical alignment is your Soul, then lower go all the parts of your Self identity-personality (higher self, main functioning self, lower self), and on the bottom is the physical body. There is a stream of energy between them, consistent and saturated with love. This picture presents a balanced relationship between the Soul, Self and the body. A person like that would have a balanced self-worth perception. Now let us look at what most of us, regular non-perfect humans, look like. There is a gap in the vertical alignment between the Soul and the Self. We end up disconnected from the Soul's consciousness and unconditional love, and paired with the physical form. This is the initial charge on the 'original sin' issue, as if somehow by coming into a body we betrayed the perfection of the Soul.

There is no such thing as 'original sin'; it is the invention of those who knew that without self-worth people were easily controlled sheep, and exploited that fact. If you are born having a 'sin' already, you are 'no good to begin with'. This amplifies feelings of guilt for unknowingly committing the sin and shame for being sinful, which efficiently clogs the second chakra. This clogging accomplishes two things: it minimizes pleasure and self-worth, and this in turn makes a person into a servant to repay his sins. Note that the blame is placed on the physical body for the sins, not the personality of the Self. This little loophole frees up the personality for control and victimhood, while at the same time keeps the body's primal freedom-based desires in check. A perfect trap for a human, to be afraid of his power! The origins of this control mechanism are imbedded in the feelings of 'being left out by the Soul' and seeing physical form as the causative initiator of the gap.

Self worth is energy fullness in the second chakra, created by the unconditional Soul's charge continuously present in the chakra. Without this Soul's charge, worth becomes conditional. Instead of 'my worth is equal to any lesson I go through' and 'I am worthy of everything that is', it becomes 'I am not worthy of good things' and 'my worth is only a match for the bad things'. In other words, we are supposed to see our worth as a ticket to any experience, positive or negative. Worth is the sign of an explorer, the value of learning a lesson whether or not we considered that lesson good or bad from the personality perspective. But because of the energy gap in the vertical alignment, we see ourselves as separate from the glory of the Soul, which makes us small and the Soul big. We see the Soul in the position of a parent/authority/commander, giving us positive experiences as rewards and negative ones as punishments. If we experience only negative circumstances for a while, our personality, based on a conditional approach, begins to see the Self as 'not worthy of good circumstances'. A perception of a reprimand or punishment lowers self worth, further enlarging the gap. And to make this worse, we tend to go in circles: we feel the gap, project authority onto the Soul and blame the body, have 'bad' experiences as a result, then judge the Self as unworthy, which enlarges the gap.

Is there a way out of this mess? Treating yourself with respect and kindness begins to close the gap, reconnecting you with your Soul. If you see yourself as *on a mission to explore reality and report back to God*, you end up being respectful of and honoring your experiences. Your Soul/Source wants to hear a report on all that you have learned/felt/experienced, not just the things you find important from the conditional personality view. Acknowledging this teaches you to be kind to yourself, no matter what the experience. If we tune into our perception of the Soul and our ideas of the Self, we can move the focus back and forth between these parts until there is no judgment. This requires the re-framing of many concepts mentally and energetically, and leads to constructing a new understanding of the power of worthiness in the physical 3-D based world. The judgments of the Soul, Self and the body were not created overnight; they are part of a large package of data acquired over many lifetimes (from the original separation and entry into matter-based form to the karmic overlays, and into the genetic structure, which is often supported by societal systems). By reviewing and questioning your beliefs about the Soul's, Self's and the body's role in your perception of self worth, you will clear the erroneous data. Connecting to your preciousness teaches you to shine your core star into every moment without withholding or judgment. That builds a bridge over the gap, your connection to Soul worthiness.

Dilemmas of Control

Ok, everyone wants to be in control, right? But what about the idea that control is a 'bad thing', that we have to surrender instead of control? Well, if you surrender all the time, won't it mean you are not in control of your life? Is anyone ever in control or is it an illusion all together? I am sure you have wrestled with these questions before. So let's look for the answers.

Surrendering is a wonderful thing, if applied properly. It is supposed to represent an openness of the ego-personality to the Soul's guidance. When we surrender that way, we surrender to our own Soul, not to circumstances. This does not mean that we are not responsible anymore. But, more often than not, surrender is applied inappropriately. This means that the basis for surrender was not a desire to have the fullest experience possible, but a fear of responsibility. The ego-personality does not want to be responsible for difficult circumstances, and so it relinquishes its control to the Soul. This is a negative surrender, and it is actually based on negative control: the ego-personality attempts to control uncomfortable experiences by rejecting its responsibility for them. Silly, really...

There is positive control, or control *with life,* and negative control, or control *over life.* These distinctions of 'with' and 'over' are very important; they answer the question: 'are we ever in control?'. Can we control what is happening, control reality? In other words, can we *override* it? By the law of this universe, that is not possible. The personality can never have control over reality, and any attempts to do so always lead to failure. That failure to control the environment is the origin of the perception of personal powerlessness. But it is prudent to note that in truth, powerlessness did not happen because we set out to do something and failed, but because out of fear we gave up our power, projecting it onto circumstances. We got scared of life and wanted to override it, assuming that it would make us feel safer. The unenlightened ego says, 'I am in control!', while actually it fears uncomfortable lessons. By fearing the Soul's lessons the ego gives them power over itself, then reacts to the feeling of powerlessness with a renewed desire for control. This is where positive surrender becomes handy.

In the negative control situation, there is prejudice/bias among the energy levels and/or chakras. One of the levels/chakras is favored by the ego-personality over others that do not fit into its image of power. The favorite level/chakra overrides all the others. This internal dictatorship makes it seem like the ego-personality controls the 'non-fitting' levels/chakras, but in reality the ego-personality itself is controlled by fear.

Lucy is a corporate executive on the fast track to an international position. She is beautiful and focused on her career. She does not allow herself any distractions, including personal relationships. Lucy is not a hermit; she has sex occasionally and definitely seems to know how to have a good time. Many are jealous of her confidence and she seems to be in full control. Lucy's fourth chakra on the back (active will) on her mental level is the strongest in her energy field and it overrides all the others, including her crown and her second chakra. Lucy suppresses her emotions, fears and intuition so she can achieve her goals, which she sees as 'being powerful and in control'. In reality she never allows anyone to come close to her; she is afraid of intimacy. Lucy fears that her feelings will betray her, make her feel embarrassed, ashamed or weak, and so her ego-personality is vigilant to prevent that. Even though Lucy seems to have a good time in life, in truth she is terrified and always tense, never relaxed. Externally she seems to be successful, powerful and focused, while internally she attempts to override the 'uncomfortability' of life by controlling her reactions to it.

Fred is a spiritual person, he sees Christ as one of the ascended masters on Earth and believes that there is only one God. Fred prays 'for the good of all' and meditates a lot on the 'light of god', giving spiritual practice an important place in his life. He wears light colored, comfortable clothing, speaks softly and is never angry. He volunteers his time in the town's library. Many people see him as an evolved, even enlightened man. His friends can always count on his reassuring word and serenity. Fred seems to be in full control of his darker feelings and thoughts, in union with his Soul. His belief in a 'good God' is an example to many around him. Fred's crown chakra on the conceptual level spins backwards and overrides everything else. His beliefs about good and evil are lopsided and fear-based. Fred has not processed his karmic fears about the dark side of life, he judges darkness and believes it has no place in a 'good god' universe. Even though Fred is angry about the existence of negativity, he suppressed his own dark feelings. He attempts to be good all the time and to live in the Light. The unenlightened ego overrides the real lessons/data, replacing it with this illusion in an attempt to protect itself from the fear/pain. In reality, Fred is controlled by his fear of evil.

Now that we know how a negative control strategy looks, what about a positive one? Positive control is not what most people imagine when they think 'control'. First of all, positive control is an awareness of all the energy levels and what is happening in them. Not just the positive stuff, but *everything*. And not only when actively processing or meditating, but all the time. For example, tune into yourself right now. What is happening in your body? Is it comfortable and relaxed? What about the etheric level, are you tired or charged? What is happening emotionally and astrally, what are you feeling? Is your mental level confused or clear? Are you in alignment with your truth, do you sense that what you are reading is true to you or not? Are you able to stay unconditional or are you judging? Conceptually, do you feel you 'get it' or are you trying to 'leave'? This multi-level awareness is essential. Do this type of a check-up often to stay on track.

The other component of positive control is an ability to make balanced decisions. That means using your free will to choose, but not from an unenlightened ego agenda. When we choose from the whole of our identity, the Soul's curiosity is the driving force, not fear. The Soul's drive unifies the needs and desires of all the levels/chakras, acting as one balanced voice. This control *with* life is a natural form of processing, a benefit to learning and a responsible expression of Soul power. If one is exercising positive control, one does not try to avoid life, but experiences it fully. The resulting translation of the event, comprehension of the lesson, and use of active will, speed up personal evolution.

Let's return to negative control for a moment. We know what it looks like, but how does it happen? How can you recognize it and prevent it? The dynamics of control *over* life are complex, but they always follow the same scenario. To understand them we have to look at one of the basic principles of life in this Universe—change. Without change we cannot evolve. The Self has to be able to change in order to proceed with its Mission Alpha. If the Self is rigid, it cannot fuse with the consciousness of matter and instead gets stuck in its misunderstandings about reality. A rigid Self will create life after life based on past experiences. Sound familiar? We have to stay moldable to be in the flow of life, be open to experiences and the learning of new lessons. In the negative control scenario the Self is fixed, rigid; it stops the life flow, which creates an energy pocket of sorts. Imagine there is a 'river of life' and the Self is one of the fishes in it. If the Self is moldable, it can swim happily with the river. But if the Self is fixed, it tries to swim upstream. This 'against the flow of life' move makes a bubble around the Self, sealing it in its own reality. The 'inside the bubble' reality is an image, an illusory perception of life that is completely self created and has nothing to do with the actual reality of life. The Self now exists separately from life. But Universal rules cannot be overridden; the Universe contains everything and everyone and is, simply put, bigger than us and, hence, it has the last word. Since the fixed and separated Self cannot override Universal rules, it enthusiastically ignores and dismisses them. The 'fixed idea' becomes a 'new rule' or a whole set of them. The action of dismissal of Universal rules and the creation of the 'new rule' cuts off Universal support and the 'fixed' Self is alone. Like a fish swimming upstream that decided that it is in the air, not in water, it is pretty much on its own, and water cannot help it anymore. Being alone, cut off from the Universal life force, the Self creates a perception of danger. This is an important step in negative control: there is always a perceived, but usually not real, danger. When we are held by life, we feel safe; when there is a separation from the essential life force, we feel in danger. Since everything is life and the 'fish' is still in the river even if it imagines it isn't, the danger is an illusion. But it sure feels real to the isolated Self! And so the unenlightened ego-Self builds defenses against the danger, trying to protect itself from the pain of isolation.

But what does it really defend against? In its illusion, it sees the outside of the bubble as dangerous, and so it defends against the life force! It's like a fish being held by water but that imagines it is in the air and sees the water as an enemy (since it is not the air), but all the while it needs that water to survive.

Perfectionism is an extreme form of negative control. In perfectionism one rule overrides all the other rules: 'I have to be thin/loving/smart/pleasing' or, pretty much, 'I have to be right'. That one rule takes over all the levels/chakras, completely blocking the inflow of information from external reality. In the totality of isolation perfection is unattainable, and yet extremely desirable to the Self. This unattainable desire makes a person even more rigid, further emphasizing the isolation. Fanatical beliefs/behavior is a type of perfectionism, when one idea is revered above all others to the point that any action supporting the main idea is justified. Human cruelty comes from this extreme form of negative control, because the fulfillment of a fanatical idea justifies any means. In cruelty, one chakra spins counterclockwise and overrides every other feeling/thought, and compassion is not possible.

What about being on the receiving end of control? How do you know if you are being controlled? There is a difference between *watching* someone demanding that you follow his rules, and you *following* his demands. Everyone has the right to their views, including their overly rigid nothing-to-do-with-reality rules. When we get angry at controlling people, we actually end up judging them, as in 'they have no right to exist'. Sound familiar? Yes, this puts us in the same position as any other person with overly rigid rules, when one chakra/level controls all others! We get triggered by someone's demands for control, and so we try to control them instead. Even though everyone can *try* to impose their personal rules on you, you also have the right to not follow them if you do not agree. So why do we end up being controlled? Anything we do always benefits us one way or another. When you are being controlled, the self-benefit is negative. We often do not want the responsibility of coming up with our own rules and deciding our own fate, so we allow someone else to dictate their rules to us instead. This solution is based on fear. Or we do not feel worthy of personal truth, projecting our authority onto someone more worthy in our eyes (like a parent, a priest etc.). The negative benefit is that we get to feel safe from our insecurities by not having to decide, act or even know our own truth! Guilt tripping is one of the most common forms of control, shaming is another. If you fall for them, it is an indication that you resist making your own choices. No one can ever control you unless you allow them to do so.

Cindy's younger brother is a bum, he is always borrowing money and never repays, buys expensive things he cannot afford and always whines about his 'misfortunes'; he is also Cindy's mom's favorite. At the family gathering Cindy's brother asks her for money again, reciting his newest 'misfortune', but she tells him 'no more', she is done with supporting his destructive behavior. Cindy's mother overhears her answer and says: 'not all of us make as much money as you, how could you refuse your own brother! Can't you see he is struggling?! Shame on you!' Cindy immediately feels horrible for her decision and writes her annoying brother a check, just to avoid disappointing her mother, while inside she secretly hates her brother for ever asking. Cindy allowed her mother's rule ('you have to sacrifice what you have for the good of the family') to control her behavior. As a child Cindy projected her authority onto her mother ('she knows better'), and because her self-worth was low, she never claimed it back. As an adult, Cindy found that the process of restoring her worthiness was harder then succumbing to her mother's control. Cindy did not want the responsibility of a choice and her own truth. What is the moral of this story? Right, notice the fear of responsibility and claim your authority anyway. You always know what your truth is, remembering that you have the *right* to it might help you stand in it, rendering guilt tripping, shaming and other forms of control obsolete.

So we know that control can be beneficial, as in being consciously aware and making a choice to do something (like driving a car), while non-beneficial control is a form of defense. How do you know when you are being controlling? Here is a step by step breakdown for nega-tive control, so you can use your conscious awareness to notice it:

1- Recognize what happened (our mental level labels the event). To recognize what is really happening, you want to see that label in connection with you, not the other. That is often difficult. Self-referenced

157

labels can be: 'I feel hurt because of what she said to me', or 'I am angry because this is not working and I have to re-do it again', and so on. 'They have no right to do that!' is not a self-referencing label; a true label here would be something like 'I feel angry about their actions' or 'I judge their behavior because it makes me feel bad to witness it' etcetera. Always be honest with yourself.

2- React to the information you received (the label) to avoid pain. There is no free will in that action, the control occurs as a means to avoid uncomfortability (like 'I will tell them how to do it because I know better', or 'I will make it perfect!' etc.). Free will can only exist if there are options to choose from. If the choice is to avoid pain, it is no choice at all, it is a reaction. In this situation there are no options, no conscious action but an unconscious reaction to avoid pain.

Here are the steps for a <u>positive control</u> scenario:

1- Consciously label the event, self-referencing it ('I got hurt', I feel anger', 'I am embarrassed' etc.). Do not lie to yourself, a false label here is self-sabotage.

2- Apply curiosity! Curiosity is an amazing ingredient, because it can immediately align any event with Soul's purpose. It will look something like this: 'Why did I get hurt? What in me hurts in connection to this event?', or 'My anger is bigger than warranted, I wonder why I got so angry?', or 'What feeling in connection with this event made me feel so embarrassed/guilty after I felt it?' etcetera. There is no judgment in this step, only witnessing and investigating.

3- Apply choice. Notice that step #3 did not even exist in the negative control scenario. But if you have applied curiosity to the mental label, you now have options: to continue the engagement with the aggravating factor, to separate from it, to process the emotion associated with the event, to suppress it etcetera. There is no right or wrong choice, any choice here is already an exercise in free will, which leads to awareness or positive control *with* life. You did not run away from the uncomfortable circumstance, but you might choose to disengage, that is a free will choice. For example, your friend tells you that you 'never do anything right' and 'this is how you should do it'. You feel annoyed by it, maybe hurt by her low confidence in you. If you break up the friendship because she is annoying, you will be in negative control. If you, on the other hand, examine why you attract this type of behavior, why you get triggered by it, why you consider her a friend and so on, then you can choose to stay in the friendship or get out. Or perhaps something in between, like talking to her about your feelings and asking her to watch how she relates to you, then you both can learn. In negative control no learning can happen, there is only an avoidance of pain based on not wanting the responsibility of conscious choosing.

Authenticity and the Three Keys to Human Happiness

Human nature is based on three main pairs of desires, making it six desires in total. Acknowledgement of these desires is personal authenticity. We often judge and fight them due to faulty karmic/genetic/social programming, sending the Self on the path of fearful avoidance, away from personal truth. Acceptance of these basic desires leads to a balanced Self, while twisting away from real desire only amounts to an inauthentic fear based reaction to life. In each pair the desires are opposite in nature. The basic human desires, necessary for happiness, are opposite? No wonder we often feel insane! Nevertheless it is true, they are opposite and have to be balanced in order for us to feel whole. Balancing of opposites in each pair is the key to human happiness: three pairs, three keys. This is the perpetual condition of a human—imperfect. If you learn to recognize/balance these three keys and make sure that you satisfy these desires one way or another for every action, happiness and power will follow!

In the first pair, one is the desire for predictability, certainty and comfort, and the other, its opposite, is for diversity and variety. Predictability is a root chakra based component, it is important for safety, it gives us a sense of control in life. Being certain is necessary for survival (anyone can go insane with worry if there is no predictability to their environment—food, shelter, rest etc.). And planning is simply impossible without predictability. But too much certainty is also not a good idea—we get stale and bored if our environment is too predictable. The opposite desire, variety, gives us a sense of challenge, movement, creativity. How can one ever be creative, if everything can be predicted and is already done? You probably have guessed by now which chakra correlates to this component: the second. It allows the abundance of unpredictability to flow, creating an endless kaleidoscope of new possibilities and challenging us to face the unexpected. But too much variety is also not fun—the chaos of complete uncertainty makes us freak out. Life feels out of control, hence we panic. Balancing certainty and variety is one of the keys to human happiness.

The second pair begins with a desire for uniqueness, for individuality and the significance of Self. Knowing that you are different from everyone else gives you a sense of purpose. It is that personal importance that makes us feel special. A desire to separate is a third chakra component. If we go into too much significance though, it becomes arrogance and judgment, and since separation dominates we place the Self above others. The opposite of the desire for uniqueness is a human desire to be like everyone else, to connect and to feel one with all life. It allows us to feel that we are a part of something greater, that we belong to our environment. The heart chakra is responsible for that component. It helps us to connect to ourselves, to other people and to merge with the Universe. And I am sure you can already imagine what too much of this connectedness will do: being lost in another person, unable to self-differentiate, being unseen and meek, over-giving, unable to act on one's own accord and, hence, used/controlled/manipulated by others with a stronger sense of uniqueness. So to be healthy, this desire for connection has to be balanced with a desire to disconnect and stand alone in uniqueness—the second key to human happiness.

The third pair is the desire to receive/take and the opposite is the desire to serve/give. The first desire is about evolution. Everyone has a drive to evolve encoded into their system at incarnation, but sometimes it is hard to notice under all that fear we place on top of it. Evolution is personal growth done through receiving energy, processing and learning from it; it has to do with the life force flowing into the Self. All the chakras are responsible for evolution. The desire to serve, to give back something, makes us feel useful. We contribute to our environment by releasing processed life force, giving out what we have learned. The combination of chakras involved in the expression of this desire is based on the particularities of each person. When a person is overly focused on serving/giving, s/he misses most of the personal evolution because the focus is not on the Self. It's the same with someone who is trying to build personal purpose not through unique significance from the second key, but on how much they 'serve people/planet'. Balancing taking and giving, self-growth and personal contribution, is the third key to human happiness.

Now that you know these keys, how do you use them? Look at something you love to do and something you hate to do. Let's say you love to talk on the phone with your friends and you hate paying bills. Chances are that for talking all three keys are present, while for paying bills your desires are not satisfied. Here is the breakdown for talking on the phone that perhaps matches what you would come up with:

1st key: you feel secure that your friend will be interested in what you are saying and support you (predictability) and you are always interested in finding out news from your friend (variety).

2nd key: you feel significant in being able to tell your story to a friend (uniqueness) and you enjoy the understanding your friend exhibits about your story (connectedness).

3rd key: you learn from hearing yourself talk and paying attention to your friend's reaction (evolution) and you just made your friend's day by entertaining them with your story and listening to theirs (contribution).

Now let's look at the bill paying scenario:

1st key: you do not feel secure because you feel you are losing money every time you pay a bill (not enough predictability, but way too much uncertainty).

2nd key: you feel lost and scared about money slipping through your fingers, feel alone and not supported (too much separation and not enough connectedness).

3rd key: you feel like a victim of that bill and get angry or feel despair about the situation (no evolution and reaction instead of positive contribution).

So every time we enjoy something, it is because the three keys are balanced, and when we resist the experience, the keys are off. Let's say you have to make a decision about staying in a relationship or leaving.

You can look at the layout of the three keys for each action and see which one is more authentic. Or you know you should exercise but can't seem to do it. Looking at how exercising breaks up into the keys will help you to see where you have your main resistance. Then you can perhaps change that imbalanced point, realigning the three keys, so exercising can become easy. In other words, find a way to satisfy all six desires and you will *want* to exercise, because your system will associate it with pleasure, not pain. This is a form of personal reprogramming to be in better alignment with your truth, supporting authentic expression.

Passion for Life and the Anatomy of Fear

In modern culture we often associate the word passion with sexual desire. But passion is much bigger than that, it is vibrant desire for life itself, it is the intensity of interaction with reality. The outer world is the mirror for the inner world. We mistakenly view the outer world as reality, when it is simply a projection of our internal reality. This confusion distorts passion, forcing it to focus on an external mirror. Instead of feeling the intensity of direct interaction with reality we get scared of its projections.

Pain, pleasure and fear are intimately connected. Universally there are two opposites at play, and pain and pleasure is one of the ways to perceive them. Humans generally do not like pain and want pleasure. Because of it we assume that pain is bad and we have to get away from it into pleasure. The human third chakra (identity) often includes personal assumptions that if we are doing everything right, there should be no pain. This is pretty consistent with most people. On the pleasure subject there are many more views, depending on upbringing, genetics, karma etcetera. Some people overdo pleasure, making it their life's focus (which actually ends up being an avoidance of real life, which has pain in it); others guilt themselves away from pleasure as if it is a plague that will kill them.

If we look at very large conceptual understanding of pain and pleasure, they are like two opposites of the same energy, two different ways to experience the same thing. Everything is unconditionality; pain is one extreme of perception, pleasure is another. The alchemical understanding of the number two is the representation of this dichotomy: it is like a line, infinitely going in two opposite directions, two 'ends' of the same. So if we see reality as a line, like a train track, then one destination is pain, and the opposite destination is pleasure. Our consciousness is designed to ride on this track one way, stop, back the other way, stop, again in the opposite direction, and so on. It is an effortless sliding of conscious awareness along the universal continuum, pulsing with power through its excited exploration.

Fear eats passion. It further distorts reality and sucks the life force out of our systems, which disconnects us from guidance. Without the support of guidance we feel lost and even more scared. Fear undermines our aliveness and disassembles our daring to be whole. Looking at fear as a gauge for knowing our capacity to hold the vibrations of love and power shifts our customary repulsion of its frequency to an embracement of its information. This allows fear to become a teacher. When we are able to perceive true reality, we can hold the charge of personal power and allow the current of universal unconditional love to flow freely through us. But when our perception is acquired from the mirror, it is distorted. This means the internal container of the Self is also off and our capacity for relating to love and internal generation of power is minimized.

Energy directed against the flow of life causes friction and is disharmony. We are meant to slide unobstructed between the comfortable/known/pleasurable and the uncomfortable/unknown/painful. But when we step out of internal reality and view the one in the mirror instead, we create friction in that sliding, which eventually slows it down to a stop. This friction is fear. Fear is like an amnesiac—forgetting that it is a life force, it is a semi-dead energy refusing to slide (aliveness of passion for life).

Can fear be used to our advantage? Can we take the fear apart to read its message/purpose? Inside every specific fear is a pathway of the return to its origin. To make it simpler, there are only five types of fear, all other small fears arise from these:

1. fear of individualization (origin: pain of being in form; the root chakra)
2. fear of not-enoughness of the Self (origin: pain of abandonment; the second chakra)

3. fear of loss of the Self, of death of the Self, of being controlled/used (origin: pain of judgment/victimhood/separation from the Source; the third and fifth chakras)

4. fear of trusting (origin: pain of betrayal; the heart and sixth chakras)

5. fear of imperfection (origin: pain of reality of imperfection; the crown and vertical flow).

The knowledge of what each particular fear is and the ability to reverse its effect upon the personality/body is what we consider power. Following the pathway of fear to its origin takes power away from the fear and gives it back to us. As fear is dismantled, the bound-up energy inside it stirs, percolates, rises and releases. That power anchored in the body is confidence and clarity, achieved by the laser of courage cutting though the smokescreen of fear. Passion arises out of these. From this perspective passion is a combination frequency of faster-vibrational inspiration and slower-vibrational support and sustenance. In passion for life, Idea, Will and Matter unite, birthing a Creation, which leads to further evolution. This is a way of by-passing the stuckness of fear. Not defending against feeling the painful origin of fear allows our perception to clear its distorted filters of the mirrors, and to recover from this messy confusion and fear-based passionless reactions to life. The benefit is the 'usual': money, sex, power, love, authority and, oh yeah, spiritual freedom.

Sexual Energy and Internal Lovers

Sexual energy is a dynamic interplay between two opposites. It is not the act of sex, but a vibrant charge. There are only two requirements for sexual charge to exist: polarities and the exchange of energy between them. By exchanging polarized energy we create a third component, the product of the exchange; it is the origin of the trinity. (Yes, sexual energy is the origin of the trinity concept!) Sexual energy is very powerful, the original polarized elements are changed forever by every exchange. For the physical body it adds vitality and vigor; for the emotional part of us it supports attractiveness and self-love; spiritually it gives us existential completeness. When our sexual energy is free and flowing, the universe is our playground. Unfortunately people often think of sexual energy as something non-spiritual, most of religious fear-based rules are to blame for that. In truth, *Soul governs sexual energy.* Sexuality cannot be controlled externally. Religious agendas were designed to suppress the 'non-spiritual', to control the physical body. Assuming that the sexual charge comes from the body itself, it was deemed unholy, dirty, sinful and destructive. Attempting to suppress and control sexual energy is like trying to put a cork into a bottle of champagne while shaking it. Physical matter is not the origin of sexual desires, but an echo of them. Soul is the one who shouts it! How does the Soul connect to sexuality? To answer that we have to look at how the Universe/Source evolves. To evolve, something new has to be created, right? And how can the Source that is already everything, create something new? By exchanging energy internally, creating an infinite number of new combinations, exploring Itself. Sexual energy is the means by which the Source evolves!

All the judgments and the attempts to suppress/'turn off' sexuality are rooted in our fear of evolution. Our unenlightened ego at the same time desires and fears to 'be god'. When the imbalanced desire wins, we try to use sexuality as a means of power and control over others. When fear wins, we punish ourselves and other people for having sexual charge with often the fanatical faith that the destruction of it will lead to more connection with god. In reality, though, if sexual energy is turned off, we die. Sometimes the physical body will actually stop working, resulting in physical death, other times our aliveness dies and we go on as a survival machine, not a live, vibrant being. Because sexual energy is supported by the Soul, it is also a means to regeneration. The physical body can live much longer and healthier if it has sexual charge. Have you noticed how after having sex you feel more alive and younger? If sexual energy flows through you all the time the same way as if you just had sex, you will regenerate your body back to youthful health. But how does one maintain this level of sexual charge? Obviously no one can just have sex all the time, but luckily it is not necessary. Since we are dealing with energy, sexual charge is also generated by energy, not a physical action. Internal sexual charge is maintained by virtual sex between the internal lovers.

Eh? Who are the internal lovers? The electric/structural and magnetic/fluid charges within us can be perceived as two distinct personalities. Communication between them (preferably ecstatic virtual sex) is essential for the graceful flow of evolution. The main relationship is always to the Self, it is the balanced happy marriage of internal male/structure and female/fluid. The consciousness range of this internal marriage determines the intensity of sexual charge. It is different for every person and it changes as we evolve. This is why it is so important to get more awareness about your internal electric and magnetic energies. A steady increase in the range of consciousness allows for more dynamic aliveness in our external relationships and awakens more passion and potency for the Self.

Everyone has both male and female sides to their personality, but sometimes one dominates so much that the other is almost unseen. Recognizing the internal male and female is the first step for the correct use of their powers. When we use incorrect polarity for a particular action, we go into imbalance, which further activates our fears and blocks associated with them. Examples of male/electric tasks might be calculating a budget, reading and applying instructions, studying, summarizing, taking notes, making reports and balancing your checkbook. Examples of female/magnetic activities are creative decorating, having fun, abstract painting and listening to a friend. This has nothing to do with the physical females or males, obviously a woman can study and a man can listen too, we are talking about energy types here.

When we apply incorrect polarity to a specific task there are consequences. So how do you recognize incorrect use? If the internal female is doing a male task, you feel overwhelmed, fearful/panicky, confused and even depressed. When the internal male attempts to do a female task, you get stressed, mechanical/dull, rigid, block creativity and lack spontaneity. So before balancing the checkbook, you better become electric (focus on numbers/lines/structures) so you do not get freaked out, and when preparing to spend an evening with friends, get magnetic (smooth/slow/wavy) so you do not end up the only person not relaxed enough to have fun!

Now look at the relationship of your internal lovers, are they at least friends or do they not communicate? If so it is time to take your

166

internal lovers to 'marriage counseling'! How do we help these internal polarities to have a happy marriage? There are three steps that each has to take and they are not easy, but if we allow ourselves to make these adjustments, balance will follow. The male polarity cannot exist without the female one, even though it often thinks it can. On the planet in the last thousand years of human consciousness the electric/male qualities have been overcharged and the magnetic/female undercharged, so the main direction for corrections is for the male side to get off its arrogance and honor the female side, while the female side itself needs to stop pretending that it is weak out of fear of aggression/abuse from the male.

The internal male polarity has to:

1. finally let go of trying to control the female (allow chaos/imperfection to exist);
2. learn to trust her (acknowledge her unique powers);
3. learn to give her space (honor her slow speed and illogical knowing).

The internal female polarity has to:

1. believe in her power (let go of the victim mentality and stand as the male's equal);
2. learn to trust the male (see his strength as safety and the comfort of a boundary);
3. become undefended (allow life to pass through her unfiltered, honor feelings).

The exchange of balanced energies leads to an explosion—an orgasm. Orgasm is not only a physical phenomenon in fact it is not physical at all. What we experience as a physical orgasm is again an echo of the energy one, generated by the Soul's desire that the body reflects. A defining electric male and an amplifying magnetic female engaging in dynamic energy exchange, generate so much power, that it explodes. This explosion is an inter-dimensional portal between the non-physical reality and the physical one. Through that portal pure creative power from the Soul enters matter (orgasms facilitate the fulfillment of your Mission Alpha!). In other words, if we make sure our internal polarities are healthy and 'in love', their interaction opens a portal for creative power. That power can be used by our personality for anything from physical healing and energy awareness to generating more confidence or material wealth.

Emotional Pain

Most people are afraid of emotional pain, some will try to avoid it at all costs. So why do we have this pain? Is it something we did that makes it happen? Is it our fault, and if we were doing everything right would we not have it? Every experience is a teaching from the Soul, but it is up to us to learn the lesson. Out of a kaleidoscope of possibilities we choose one direction, one lesson. Sometimes it is a short-cut to a greater understanding, other times it is a fear-based decision that will make the learning harder. But either way if a choice supports the learning, it will take us *out* of the known and comfortable. This means we will have to make an adjustment as we enter new territory. This adjustment is what we, humans, perceive as emotional pain. Is there a way to avoid it? No. Not only is there no way to by-pass it, it will actually be detrimental to avoid it, because then we will never get out into the unknown, never learn. But there are different kinds of pain. In the balanced way (yes, there is such a thing as balanced pain!) the pain is an adjustment, a simple uncomfortability. In the imbalanced way we get stuck in pain. Instead of allowing it to go through us as we adjust, we try to resist it, to fight it, prolonging the uncomfortability. Our personality translates that imbalanced pain on the emotional level as fear, anger, anxiety, worry, depression, insecurity etcetera. All of these are perceptions of imbalanced human pain. We choose a few of these as favorites depending on our incarnational lessons. Our higher Self scans for a needed event in all the possibilities, and the one it finally chooses we end up experiencing through the tint of the favorite emotional pain. Our perception during the event changes the outcome. If you are able to let the emotions flow (instead of squishing them) and stay unconditional (non-judgmental), the emotional pain goes into a balanced state and is experienced only as an uncomfortable adjustment to the lesson.

So far we have looked at a very broad conceptual explanation of pain. Now let's disassemble the concept into more human components.

Fear, anger, anxiety, worry, depression and insecurity are emotional opportunities to gain wisdom. If we see these 'favorites' as entry points into the Soul lesson's meaning, we can realign the experience in such a way that it rebalances pain. A literal interpretation of events does not help here (i.e., 'I feel scared because of the meeting' or 'I am angry because he did not call me again'); expanding beyond it into a spherical 'big picture' does. Fear is a refusal to circulate energy, like a smoke-screen preventing us from experiencing the unfiltered life flow. Anger is energy splashing out and not being contained. Anxiety is overly electrical, jagged resistance. Worry is overly magnetic circling resistance. Depression is a stagnation of energy on the fluid levels. Insecurity is a state of internal collapse. So if you are in anxiety, instead of looking at a literal reason (such as, 'I have to pay attention to everything because I am preparing to travel') you can look at anxiety's spherical message. The entry point will be the knowledge that you are overly electric at the moment and in resistance to life, which your emotional level experiences as pain (perhaps something like 'I am trying to control travel by putting too much energy into my electric circuits, but travel is unpredictable and magnetic and I have difficulty trusting and feeling safe in the magnetic energy').

Decoding emotional pain is essential for not getting stuck in it. Just like any other event, if we do not get it, it keeps happening, because the Soul's message is not comprehended. Habit and negative comfort are two types of stuckness that keep us emotionally mired. Looking deeply at our chronic, most common types of emotional pain can reveal why we are stuck, and show us our refusal to become wise. Why would anyone refuse to become wise? Because wisdom comes with responsibility; it is a balance of knowledge and experience. But every new experience is achieved only by a move into the unpredictable, the unknown, which might be very uncomfortable. And so the avoidance of this uncomfortability completes the circle, we resist the experience, cannot receive the lesson, get chronically stuck in the emotional pain, which forces us to resist it even more. To break this cycle, look at the main reasons for your stuckness. Habit is a repeated astral story that sends the entire energy field into autopilot with no conscious awareness. This means no self-responsibility. Unconsciousness is familiar and can feel comfortable because we are lulled into a false sense of security by not having to challenge destructive programming. Negative comfort is an emotional form of giving up the attempts to figure life out, to comprehend and resolve the issue. Of course it is also a form of irresponsibility for the Self based on the intent to prove our rightness in our assumption that 'life sucks'. It is quite incredible how we humans with such righteousness fight for our irresponsibility! In doing so we demand compassion for our pain, while at the same time we are completely unwilling to attempt any changes/solutions. This demand never brings true compassion, only pity. While pity might not be equal to compassion, it still feels comforting, amplifying the negative pleasure we take from recurring emotional pain.

What are the strategies for getting clear from stuckness? For dealing with emotional pain in a balanced way? Step one is always energy realignment, so start with bringing more charge into your root chakra and the back of the heart chakra. These two chakras are a great support in allowing awareness on what is 'off' in our pain; without energy in these chakras we often get swallowed by negative pain, that is, we get stuck. Second step, decode your pain. This means honing into what kind of emotional pain you are having, then getting out of the literal interpretation of the reason for that pain and looking at the 'big picture' (as we did with the example of anxiety before travel). Once you are aware of the spherical reason for your pain, look at the stuckness. Are you in a habitual astral story that sends you on autopilot? (For example, 'I have anxiety because every time I travel something goes wrong, I just know it will happen so I have to always make sure...' etc.) Are you in negative comfort about your pain, refusing to stay conscious and look for solutions or different points of view? (Such as, 'I told you, agents always screw up and you can never trust the taxi driver either, or the maids in the hotel, it just sucks that I have to always watch out for their messing up, I wish I could not have anxiety about it, but I have to!'—i.e., asking for compassion, while in negative pleasure about the anxiety.) When you realize that you are in a habit or in negative comfort, it is easier to correct them. For habit correction, acknowledge that you were defining yourself with an astral story and look for another, more responsible self-definition (instead of 'I have anxiety about travel,

I am a person who is afraid of unpredictability and tends to expect the worst, and so tries to control events', say something like 'I am a person who is attempting to allow unpredictability to exist and trust that something positive can come out of it'). For negative comfort correction, acknowledge (without judgment!) that you were negatively enjoying your painful experience, using your emotional pain as proof of your rightness. Then challenge yourself to be wrong about the 'life sucks' belief. One of the ways to do that is to ask yourself 'who would I be without this pain?' The answer will lead you to the correction (instead of 'People are bad and if I do not pay an insane amount of attention to their actions, they will screw me!', to something like 'I do not have to feel screwed if something goes wrong while I travel, I can see it as a challenge, an opening for something new and wonderful or self-created teaching'). Repeating these steps, 1) amplify energy in the root and heart in the back, 2) decode the pain's message, 3) find and correct the stuckness, every time you feel emotional pain, this will guide you to a more balanced way of dealing with uncomfortability and to an easier evolution.

Courage

Wouldn't we all like to have more courage? Unfortunately our often romanticized, exaggerated ideas about what courage is tend to prevent us from actually expressing it. So what is courage? When you think of it, probably the armored knights come to mind, or perhaps a mountain-climbing-type survival, or maybe James Bond's coolness in the face of danger etcetera. All these examples are images, pictures we use to explain courage. These images are so extreme and risky that they freeze us up instead of supporting our courage. When we try to be courageous by a strategy of 'I can do it too!' it succeeds more in self-guilt-tripping rather than in an amplification of courage! It is not possible to enter courage from embarrassment that you have more fear than some driven hero ('What's wrong with you?! Go stand up for yourself, be strong, have some courage!). Courage is not the same as risk. Risk can be calculated or blind, but either way is it a sharp jump forward into something, it is an active charge through the smokescreen of fear. Courage is a state of being, not a reaction to fear.

The components of the courage state are energetic and biochemical. Thought patterns and beliefs, colored frequencies, foods and internal chemistry have to combine in our bodies in precise ways to make courage happen. We have to have both energetic and biochemical components for courage to occur. In other words, 'just thinking right' without being in your body isn't going to make you any more courageous. The energetic components of courage are a well-charged heart chakra, second chakra and root chakra. Courage is a combination of active will, heart feeling, amount of life force and quality of its application, anchored and balanced. It is not a single frequency, but a composite. The biochemical components are our hormonal 'messengers': thymusin, testosterone, estrogen and progesterone, adrenalin, epinephrine. Notice that due to their often opposite function, these hormones have to be balanced. Huge amounts of testosterone or adrenaline are not going to result in courage, as is usually assumed.

Now that we know what courage is, how do we support that state inside us? Courage can be a constant state, or an event for your system. But there are definitely some things we can do 'for' courage and 'against' courage. An internal knowledge like 'I am' or 'I am a spark of the divine' is a programming for courage, while a belief such as 'I am powerless' or 'I am lost' is against courage. Thoughts of the 'I can...' type lead into courage and the 'I cannot...', away from it. Of course victim-type beliefs ('it happened to me') destroy courage, while creator beliefs ('I made this happen') support it. If one is in the victim mode, he can only imitate courage by guilt-tripping himself into it. The colors red, orange and blue support the state of courage. Remember, every color is an energy vibration, it can be amplified by tuning into it, focusing on it, being around it and even wearing it. So if you are going to a meeting where you know you will have to be courageous in bringing up something people will not want to hear, wear a red suit/tie or a bright blue shirt, it will help your body to have the proper hormonal combination for courage. Colors like gray, white, gold or silver disperse the energy and so they do not support the state of courage. Focusing your attention on your physical heart pumping allows you to be present in your blood, which activates the root and the second chakras and generally supports courage. Eating protein, sea salt, root vegetables, onions, carrots, radishes, and paprika allows courage to happen, while pasta, wheat in general, carbohydrates and alcohol minimize our ability for courage (they do amplify the ability to risk blindly though, because they numb the fear).

So you know all the components of courage and also what you can do to support it in your body, you only have to remember one more thing: courage is balance. When we are stressed, angry or vacant from the body, there is no balance and courage is not possible. If you are stressed and nervous, at best you might end up guilting your way into an imitation of what you believe courage is. If you are angry, instead of courageous you will be risking, plowing your way forward using anger as fuel. This is not courage. And if you are not present to the situation, not in your body or root chakra, you will be *directing* courage instead of *being* courageous. Since balance is the key element here, if you are attempting courage and find yourself upset, stressed, angry or not present, rebalance yourself first. Breathe in and out a couple of times, re-center and anchor, bring the energy into the root, second chakra and the heart. Look for the ways you minimize or even destroy your courage, because if you do not feel courageous, you are blocking it somehow. We are *designed* to be courageous, it is a natural state of being for a balanced human.

Relationships and Sexual Attraction

The main relationship is always with your Soul, and all other relationships come out of that one. As my guides say, 'If they do not, you're screwed'. Pretty much the clarity and intensity of the connection with the Soul determines what all the other relationships in our life will look like. When we disregard this Soul relationship and put all our attention into human-to-human relationships instead, we generally create a painful mess. There is a Russian saying that puts it quite eloquently: 'The lower you fly, the more painfully you'll get caught'. Our 'higher flying' is the Soul connection, the 'vertical relationship' always has to come before the horizontal one. This is the mystic meaning of the equal-sided cross: the vertical line is the body-personality-Soul relationship, the horizontal is the personality-to-other-personalities connection. But since the last Fall of Consciousness, we, unenlightened humans, made the horizontal line much longer, prolonging the state of our unconscious, painful mess. And putting in an hour and a half in church on holidays is not a way to connect to your Soul, neither is an hour and a half of meditation every day. The 'vertical' relationship is based on seeing our life through the eyes of the Soul. Being able to see the magic beyond the mundane, the truth and divine wisdom beyond the circumstantial evidence of pain, these are the insights that strengthen the vertical connection. If any other relationship is seen through the Soul's insight, we receive the wisdom and bring the Self into balance. Sexual attraction in the vertical connection is built on the relationship of the 'internal lovers'—the electric and magnetic inside us, which bring us into unity.

For the physical 'horizontal' attraction we have to be present in the body. It is absolutely required for chemistry to occur. What is this magic thing we call 'body chemistry'? Is it something that we have no control over but also no way to understand? Each human has a particular combination of elemental energies that comprise his/her body. This might coincide with your astrological star chart or it might not—the body's elements are not always the same as the personality elemental energies. If your body is thin/tall/small boned, it is based on the element of air; smooth/lumpy/soft tissue represents mostly water; heavy/wide boned and with high endurance is the earth element based body, and the wide shoulders/heavy top or an hour-glass figure is usually fire. Since we all have the four elements, but in varying amounts, we each have a unique elemental formula. This elemental formula plays a crucial role in sexual chemistry. We are encoded from birth to respond to a particular combination of elements in another person's body, which relates to our own formula. The closer this compatibility, the stronger is the attraction. Our personal elemental formula is proportionally compatible with theirs but not identical or opposite. The main element in your formula has to be significantly present in the partner's formula for commonality. Also the opposite of your main element must exist for excitement. What is opposite to what? Air is opposite of earth, fire is opposite of water. Here is the formula for a balanced relationship with healthy sexual chemistry:

commonality + excitement = chemistry

This applies not only to the physical body makeup but also to the personality. If your formula's main element is water, your partner needs to have fire with some water. If your partner is mostly water it might make you safer, but if there is no fire, you will feel bored. Or if you are mainly an earth type, your partner has to have some earth and air. Too much air and you will not be able to relate, too much earth and stability might turn into stubborn boredom.

We human beings tend to resist the element we need; it is not just psychological resistance, but also physical/elemental. If you are mostly water, you need fire in a partner, but if you are afraid of the element of fire, you will try to avoid what is beneficial for you. Let's say that instead of fire, you compensate by going into air, trying to balance your water with air. You will then psychologically and energetically be attracted to the air type person, but there will be no physical chemistry because the formulas don't match. We often run into this: we like the person, want to be with them because of their personality, but sexually we are more like siblings, not lovers. Or the other way around, we have a huge sexual 'body attraction' to someone who is not good for us on the personality level at all. This messiness happens because we resist our own formula and try to hide behind the assumed one. And if the partner is doing the same, then it is a real mess! All of this is due to the judgment of sexual energy and the body in general, and out of that the avoidance to learn our true nature in this incarnation. The elemental formula changes with each incarnation, and it is up to us to discover and relate to what we've got. When we resist what we have and instead try to be something we are not, we use imagery or memories. Imagery is what is taught to us by parents, in school, in the movies etcetera. Memories are other lifetime overlays. All of this always boils down to not wanting to be who we are. When we do not want to be the Self, we borrow from genetic, social or other lifetime files.

Marcella's system is mostly fire, she has a curvy body and a vibrant personality. She really wants to be spiritual, to feel higher energies. But she is afraid of her fire, sees it as 'not spiritual'; it makes her feel out of control and often angry. She rejects fire and substitutes it with air, which she believes to be 'more spiritual'. She unconsciously activates the energy file from one of her lifetimes as a nun, when she was mostly air element, and uses this template of the air-body/personality for herself now. By the design of this incarnation, Marcella needs to balance her fire with water element, the opposite to fire. But because she pretends to be air, she attempts to balance herself with the earth instead. Marcella is also looking for a beautiful relationship. But she runs into the same problem every time: the men she falls for head over heels are fiery types that her personality rejects as non-trustworthy, and the men she ends up trusting are very airy, men who over time feel blank to her, for whom she feels no sexual desire at all. Marcella believes there is something wrong with her, that she cannot get attracted to a nice guy, and so she tries harder. Because of Marcella's rejection of her main element, the fire, she ends up being drawn to it more than necessary, and the men she falls for end up being overly fiery with no water. Water is the sensitivity Marcella craves, but cannot get. The men she ends up going for are matching her aspired element, air, but since air is not her main element, she can never be satisfied. When her natural fire comes up, she will either scare these men with her intensity or feel completely disconnected from them, as if they are not there. Air type people might not register well for a fiery person, because air is so diffuse. If Marcella trusts her own element of fire, she can begin to find ways of going more into the water, balancing her fire. That will attract to her men of a water type with a healthy amount of fire, or men of fire but with some water. This combination will create not only sexual chemistry, but a balanced relationship for Marcella.

The way to approach an imbalanced relationship is to review what is off in your own elemental balance first, and preferably your partner can do the same. Honestly review your elemental deficiencies and over-abundances. In the example of Marcella she was over-abundant in the fire element because of the deficiency of the water element, and she tried to suppress it by amplifying air. Find out what your main element is and then how you relate to it. Do you fight it and hide from it, emotionally or mentally preferring some other one? Look at the reasons you end up not choosing your main element as the preferred one, they can tell you a lot about your imbalances. Once you know your main element, look at its opposite—this is usually the element we need to work with in this current lifetime. Correcting your internal relationship brings you balance. If you are already in a committed relationship, you can amplify the chemistry by making sure that once in a while, especially for flirting and sex, you have the same and the opposite element combo. If you are water with some fire and your partner is the earth with some air, it does not mean that you have to break up if there are other types of connections. You can make chemistry happen if you accommodate each other. Sometimes both of you can go into water-fire, other times into earth-air, and it can jumpstart your attraction. Willingness to adjust is the most important element here!

When we think of the sexual energy in a relationship, we tend to assume it is only a physical attraction. Remember, in the sub-chapter on Sexual Energy and Internal Lovers we looked at sexual energy in a much broader sense? Well, we can take it further and review what the sexual attraction looks like on the different levels of the energy field.

On the etheric level sexual attraction feels like a subtle bounce between your and someone else's boundary. As if you are a blue bubble and they are a blue bubble, and you bounce towards them, touch their boundary and then pull away, or vice versa. We are consciously able to perceive this. Examples are knowing when someone is looking at us, or being very actively aware of this guy's elbow near your own, or feeling the hair on your skin stand because someone is tuning into you.

On the emotional level it is all about the subtle balance between pleasure and pain. Because this level is filled with fluid energy, sexual attraction is perceived differently based on the main element. For the earth element it feels like the balance of safety vs. fear ('I feel so comfortable with him' or 'He scares me!'—either one can work). For the air element it is stimulation vs. avoidance ('I feel so excited about her!' or 'I just hope she won't see me here'). For the fire element the balance is between curiosity and hatred ('I just *love* this guy and *really* want to get to know him' or 'I hate him!'—both are signs of sexual attraction). For the water element it is melting or over-merging ('We feel like one' or 'I feel her so much, I can't find myself!').

On the mental level sexual attraction is intelligence, compatibility of ideas and speed of thinking. You know how it feels to be fascinated with someone who is speaking highly intelligently and thinking fast, especially if s/he agrees with you on the topic. This intellectual charge is like a lightning strike between two people.

The astral level is fluid, so the storylines are again divided between the elements. Opposite stories both amplify attraction, only one is positive and one is negative. For the earth type the astral sexual story is 'Stand by me' with the fear of 'What if s/he abandons me?' The air element's astral story is 'Interact with me', with 'What if s/he ignores me?' underneath. For the fire element the story is 'Notice me' with the fear of 'What if s/he won't notice/recognize me?' The water type's astral story is 'Take me' with 'What if s/he uses me?' under it.

On the fifth energy level of truth, sexuality is trust and honor, mutual respect. Being allies in something, a project/feeling/life, is a component of the sexual attraction on that level. Seeing another or being seen as a hero, someone to aspire to be, creates an alignment in people's fields. When we consider someone our hero, we have sexual attraction with them on the truth level. That might seem strange—what if you consider your dad a hero? Are you now attracted to him sexually? No, not in 'that way', but since sexuality is a dynamic aliveness of two opposites, this attraction means that between you and your dad, something gets charged because of the activity of the electric and magnetic forces. It definitely does not mean you 'want to have sex with him', but instead that you want to interact on the truth level with him.

Unconditional level sexual attraction is based on the Soul recognition of each other. This recognition differs depending on the main element. For the earth type the Soul recognition with someone creates a freedom to be/exist unconditionally. The air type experiences Soul recognition as sexual inspiration and uplift, a muse. For the fire element the recognition of the Soul with someone brings unique special-ness. The water type person sees Soul recognition as commonality/sameness.

On the conceptual level sexual energy is experience of existential completeness. This type of sexual attraction allows us to feel completely open to life, being able to play freely and be anything we choose without limits.

It is very rare to find a partner with whom the sexual attraction exists on all the levels of the energy field. But by knowing the differences between how each attraction feels we can have more awareness of what we do have with our partner and learn to enhance it. Some of the levels you might find to be more important for your personality than others, so the sexual charge on these levels will be crucial for a balanced happy relationship, while other components can be a bonus.

Focused Presence

Being an individual that lives inside the Whole is a component of our Mission Alpha. If we over-individualize, we become arrogant. If we go too far into the Whole of the Universe, we get lost and diffused/confused. When we do not fight or over-emphasize either component, we link our genetic codes with our stellar codes. This type of a 'linked' human cannot be defined by a family line, race, gender, nationality, profession or sexual orientation, only by Soul essence. The individuality of our identity is linked with personal space/time, while the totality of the Whole is linked with shared space/time. The balanced bridge between them is presence. If we are not present in our life, the identity and the Whole inside us are at war, in competition. That competition is exactly the reason that sometimes we go too far into the Whole, other times too far into the arrogance of individuality. In truth the more present we are, the more we can individualize, which allows us to perceive more Whole (i.e., increase our range of consciousness).

Why aren't we present in every moment? When we get triggered into fear, our system translates that as being in danger. We then defend by going out of presence, either pushing against space/time or running away from space/time. Each person has an individual pattern of defense, usually a combination of pushing and running based on the particularity of a trigger.

The focus of awareness is a balanced limitation of the range. If you focus on one flower, but not on the rest of the field, you are in beneficial limitation—the field does not exist in your range of awareness, only the flower does. There are two kinds of focus: electric/structural focus and magnetic/fluid focus. Electric focus is a point, like a thought, an idea, a spark; it is what you see when you look straight at the flower, for example. Magnetic focus is 'backwards', it is a whirlpool, an area, a zone, it is what you see when you are not looking at anything, yet actively perceiving, an 'unfocused' focus. With the balanced type of limitation, focus is balanced because it is not fixed. The changeability of the focus allows modifications in perception.

There is also a negative type of a limitation based on too strong a focus (fixed). Negative stories, false definitions of our reality, constrict our internal space, limiting the range of our perception. When we get overly focused on our definitions, we do not allow other points of view, other perceptions of reality. These overly defined stories also can be structural/mental or fluid/emotional, based on the type of focus. Typical examples of the mental type of negative definitions of reality are 'I have to be right to have value', I won't succeed unless I work very hard' or, 'Everything is pointless anyway'. Guess what are examples of the emotional type of negative definition—'I feel powerless and need to be rescued', 'I am always lost/confused' or 'Nobody will ever see me'. Which type of focus, structural or fluid, is the one you overuse? What is your own personal negative story? Looking at these negative stories will help you to take the power back from them, which in turn will open the limitations you set up in your perception.

If you find yourself stuck in the past or the future, you are missing the desire to be in the present. This desire is a pull towards a point of the moment, present, past or future. The present exists on all the levels of perception, but it anchors in the body, because the body is in linear time. In other words the present cannot be conceptual, it has to be visceral, body based. Look at your personal, unique reasons why the desire for the future or review of the past is stronger than the desire for the present moment. These reasons are the clues for your absence from the present. We cannot change the present if we are not in it! If you do not like where you are in your life, escaping the situation into the past or the future is not going do a thing for making the present better. The change always has to begin with the present, then the past can support it and the future can guide it.

Marty is a high school team quarterback, he is loved by the whole school, girls fall for him and guys consider him a hero. He wins many trophies for the team and the coach and teachers are very proud of him. He relishes in the glory and thinks he is better than most. He is embarrassed to be seen with unpopular kids for the fear that their presence might tarnish his image. But he is very present in every moment in his successful life. Marty goes to college, where he also plays for the team and is a star, and he is liked and admired. Until one day when Marty makes a bad choice: drinking too much and driving, he smashes his car through a fence into someone's house in the middle of the night, luckily avoiding people, but killing a dog and breaking both of his own legs. The people of the town do not like Marty anymore, the dog gets a lavish funeral and Marty is booted out of college before he even comes out of the hospital. After a long medical and legal ordeal Marty goes back to his home town, but he cannot play anymore because of his injury. Now Marty is 40 years old and an alcoholic. He lives in a small apartment he rents with the money he gets from a stocking job at the warehouse and he drinks a lot. His reality is overly defined with the fluid/emotional type of limitation: 'Everyone's abandoned me', 'They were mean to me' and 'They do not see me' etcetera. Marty is not in the present anymore, he is living in the past, rerunning in his mind the old glory days while he drinks. His desire for the past is stronger than his desire for the present. If Marty can realize that and refocus on the present, he will be able to emotionally face his mistakes and failures, and he can learn not to be a victim of them anymore. He can take the power back from the negative events and reshape his life with wisdom, opening up the limitations and being present again in every moment.

Presence is an electro-magnetic phenomenon; it can be structural or fluid, depending of the type of focus. We all know the feeling of being jittery, jumpy and unsettled, perhaps with anxiety. This is the picture of too much electric charge focused improperly, a consequence of not enough energy in the root chakra. The electric energy does not flow through the vertical tube, but loops back upon itself, creating friction with no outlet. The active electric energy keeps charging itself as it loops, 'eating self'. A balanced electric presence is based on the proper focus of electric charge. If the electric energy can flow through the root chakra, it becomes an invigorating movement of electrons through the vertical tube, which then distributes this charge to the whole system, including the physical body. This gives direction and destination to the electric energy, and they are absolutely required for its health. A clear boundary, thought, self understanding etcetera, are not possible without electric direction and destination. If you feel that thinking has become hard, as though you have to work at it, or that you are picking up 'stuff' from other people, going into anxiety and jitters, your electric charge is off. Look for the absence of direction and/or destination for your focus. Move energy into your root and then circulate it up and down the vertical tube. Define from where and to where you are going ('I am changing this closet's disorder into order' or 'I am helping my kid's homework to go from the undone/confusing to completed/clear' etc.). This will realign the electrons in your system and clear up the imbalance, stabilizing the electric type of presence.

I am sure you are also familiar with the opposite state—overwhelm, an undefined 'soup' of feelings and overly emotional confusion. This is the picture of too much magnetic charge, improperly focused. In this scenario we identify too much with the Whole, abandoning the identity of Self. Simple tasks become overly amplified (like opening a closet door and feeling everything in that closet, unable to choose or re-organize); moments become exaggerated. The correction to this situation is based on a proper focus of magnetic energy. A balanced magnetic presence is a smooth peace. Allowing the magnetic charge to be a supportive underlying cushion, sustenance that nourishes us, a raw material supply for anything we choose, leads to a peaceful state of balanced magnetic presence.

Receptivity

Receptivity is an essential component of evolution. We can receive life force in small doses as a life-support, or in a large dose as an initiation into something new (which incidentally is not 'white robes and incense ceremony', the typical spiritual imagery for initiation). To go through this initiation type of receiving we have to work with the images that block our entry. Images are our false projections about what we think reality is; they are illusions and distortions. In order to clean up these illusory image blocks, we have to find, open and process them. Then the trapped-in-the-block power returns to our core and we become more whole.

Every being has to be fed by the life force. If we refuse to receive life force, we stagnate and eventually cease to exist. But what we receive is not always pleasant, and this ultimately becomes our excuse for our rejection of it. One of the main misconceptions about life force is that it is supposed to feel good. In its purest form it is neutral, which actually does not feel good or bad, it just is. But when we receive life force, it comes with all sorts of modifications, some of which feel just fantastic, while others do not. Illusory images about reality trap the life force, distorting it. When we attempt to process the image block, we usually assume that as soon as we set on the path of processing, we will feel good, or at least better. That is not an unconditional receptivity. Why? Because if feeling good/blissful is proof of successful image clearing, we limit the possibilities. We need to be curious about what is really present, only then can we receive reality. Otherwise we receive more of the image and get further confused and trapped in illusion. The process of going through the block never feels good; it is a hard, sometimes painful, thing to do. But if we stick to receiving 'what is' (i.e., uncomfortability, pain, pressure etc.), we eventually arrive at pure life force, which, after the block's pollution, feels very good. Notice that it is not the circumstance or the understanding that feels good, but the life force itself. In other words, you can process a block and feel the grief and recognition of some learning, gain wisdom, but this wisdom might still be difficult to experience—truth is often unexpected and hard to accept. Yet it comes with the relief of an unobstructed flow of the life force, which does feel very good.

One of the great exercises in receiving is receiving openness. If we can stay open, we perceive reality without filters. This is how we were originally designed, before we got scared and shocked, and got stuck in genetic and karmic illusion. Receiving life without filtering it is like breathing pure Source energy, pure life force, all the time. The more you can do it, the easier it is to clean up your genetic and karmic mess, getting closer to your Soul's reality. You can practice this unfiltered openness through meditation. In meditation one focuses his/her awareness on a particular vibration/thing/place. In this case the focus is on expansion of awareness unilaterally, which can help you enter an altered state of perception and change the frequency of your brainwaves. This means that more reality can be perceived. Reality is always there, even if we have difficulty finding it! When we enter expanded consciousness like that, we have to go through mini-voids as we are expanding further. These mini-voids are like tiny abysses between the levels of consciousness and they do not always feel comfortable. To do this properly you have to make sure you are not after 'feeling good only', because then as soon as you enter a level that does feel good, you will just hang there, stopping the expansion. The first 'feeling good' level is usually not reality, but an illusion, something that is familiar and comfortable. Since this is an exercise in openness, allow yourself to flow through the mini-voids in your expansion, to some extent alternating comfortable and uncomfortable. When we receive, we have to open up and let go, trust with no expectation. This is a great way to practice unfiltered receptivity.

CHAPTER 4
Mastery

CHAPTER 4

Design Your Self

The flow of universal energy is penetrating all aspects of our being with more and more persistence every day. This persistent memo the Universe sends us about our true origins is here to facilitate our awakening. Connecting to that universal flow does not only help each one of us personally, but brings about human planetary evolution. In order to connect to this flow, we must be able to recognize and let go of traumas and shock held energetically and cellularly. These blocks are 'backward' flows of energy caught in a memory pattern that holds judgment against itself, and this pattern has become the definition for our reality.

Norma's trauma is from another lifetime when she was laughed at and ostracized by a crowd after she spoke her mind, which led to her leaving the tribe and eventually dying alone. This unprocessed shock and pain turned the flow of the life force backwards. The uncomprehended experience got stuck in Norma's energy memory files. In the present life she has an issue with speaking her truth to groups of people for the irrational fear that their not liking what she is saying might kill her. This present issue is a result of the unprocessed trauma defining her current perception of reality. If Norma can find the trauma (without necessarily having to find the lifetime story) and clear it from its defining position (making it a possibility, not a definition), she can speak her truth without fear of dying. How can Norma find this trauma? She will need to tune into the actual emotion paralleling speaking out. Is it fear? What kind of fear? What does she think/feel will happen if...? Digging like that into the traumatic feeling leads to the original fear/pain, which might be a remembrance of a present life childhood traumatic event or, as in Norma's case, another lifetime fear of being 'kicked out and abandoned to die'. As adults in the present we are more equipped to deal with past trauma; just noticing what the actual issue is instead of running on autopilot will help detangle the trauma's role, making it an option for reality, not its definition. Going back to the beginning of the issue while amplifying heart energy reduces the shock of the original trauma and brings compassion to the Self. Open your heart chakra and intentionally focus on the initial trauma that you have found. Allow the energy of heart love to flow into the pain, expanding inside of it. Continue after the shock vibration softens.

Since this persistent universal flow is a wakeup call, as it enters our humanity it can intensify survival fears, emotional vulnerabilities, and powerlessness. Note that I did not say *create* these, but *intensify* them, because these issues were already there to begin with and because awakening means 'awakening to the traumas and shocks first, power later', not just power and pleasantries. Wrestling with these personal struggles is an act of courageous exploration into our internal unknown. We cannot become an awakened Self without the desire to *be* the Self. We cannot become aware and powerful without going through all the powerlessness. To some extent powerlessness is necessary to show us what power is, because we learn through comparison in duality. It is naïve to assume that when you welcome the universal flow you will suddenly leave behind all your troubles and 'everything will be ok'. When people fanatically pray to God and then feel the high of it that makes everything ok, it is not real. Fanatical praying or meditation practices actually are ways of avoiding opening to the life flow, and the high never lasts because it is from closeness to an illusion, not God. Fanatical behavior is rigidity incarnate; it is a fixed energy pattern with zero openness, so the reality of life, the life force itself, cannot enter.

Truly free universal energy feels great, but when it first enters us, it of course will hit all the blocks we have, smashing them open. Don't you think that might be uncomfortable? Right, it usually is an uncomfortable process, because you have to reevaluate your views on reality, and your ideas and beliefs. But do not despair, it is not an agony! Every time you feel the intensity of your fear, you also gain more tolerance to it, and when you process the pain, you gain knowledge and experience, which end in wisdom and power. And so with each block the clearing becomes easier, even if the blocks themselves are painful. This is the reward for doing processing work! The blocks are not necessarily any less traumatic or painful, but they do not suck us in, do not scare us as much any longer, and do not define our reality, hence they are just uncomfortable. The wisdom is well worth it!

Receiving universal energy is easier if we know what it will do. By preparing our energy field for the release of distorted patterns, we avoid or minimize painful symptoms that often accompany release, such as headache, back pain, and mild forms of instability like not remembering who you are. By training our consciousness to enter the block willingly, we can experience less painful and debilitating symptoms. We don't have to re-experience the full impact of the initiating trauma or wait for the block release to hit our bodies like a freight train. Softening our resistance to the release process will accelerate our awareness and call down our power. As illusion pours out of our blocked patterns, we heal the separation from Soul and the ensuing relief anchors the body to the rest of the energy system.

Soul, interested in third dimensional human learning, creates many forms that we experience as physical lifetimes. The design of each lifetime is a Soul Contract or 'plan for learning'. Soul chooses the range of circumstances, decides on the direction of learning and the type of karma to attempt to clear in a given lifetime. Our personality has free will within the range of the Soul Contract. In other words, Soul pre-chooses the possibilities, like which humans are going to be our parents, so that our learning is optimized by them giving us specific genes and the environment to form our personality (the optimal time period and place of birth, the social trends etc.). We, the personality, then make decisions inside these circumstances. For example, where to move; what job to get; who to be with; whether or not to have children, or follow parental, genetic or social rules etcetera—these are actions of our free will.

There is an underlying key to each Soul design; every lifetime has a particular pattern that tints the whole life (it's like looking through a blue lens this life, red another life). This key is essential to our safety and satisfaction, which are the functions of the lower two chakras. If we do not approach our life with the proper key, it 'will not open', and instead we will have to struggle to open it. Most of the struggles we have in our lives have to do with trying to pick the lock or smash through the door using the exhilaration of accomplishments. Neither approaches are comfortable—in the first one you always feel in trouble/guilty/shamed, and in the second one you cannot permit yourself to ever stop, and are forced to keep doing/going like an Energizer Bunny™.

The lifetime key tints the Soul's intent and through it our personality filters incoming messages. How do you identify your key? Well, you look for a bright colored tag...... First we have to look at how we divide reality. Internal reality has access to the Soul and to external reality. Internal reality is the energy world of our personality anchored in a perception vehicle—the body; internal reality is the self-centered reference point. External reality is everything else. The focus of the personality is the interpretation of reality. What does that mean? You can look at the internal world as the Self and the external as a mirror, and learning about yourself happens through the interpretation of what you see in the mirror. This is a well known concept, but what most people forget, is that if we focus entirely externally, we cannot have a conscious relationship with internal reality or the Soul, and so we end up being trapped in the mirror. The mirror is always an illusion. It is like watching a movie, but then forgetting that you are in the audience, and instead the movie is happening to you, scaring you or pleasuring you. In other words, you are trapped in the illusion of the mirror. But the point here is not to break the mirror, but to remember that your Self is looking into it. The mirrors are there for the purpose of learning, we just have to remember that we perceive pleasure or pain or fear from the *reflections* of the Self. Every moment is a message for the personality to decode the intent of the Soul (the lesson). A key is a perceptual distortion of the mirror, a particular one for each lifetime. Like concave or convex mirrors that distort the reflection, we warp our mirrors with beliefs like 'Life is hard', or 'Life is confusing, I will never understand it', or 'It isn't happening fast enough', or 'There is too much pain in the world', or 'I won't be included', or 'Life will hurt me', or 'People are irresponsible, in the end it is up to me to do it all' etcetera. Knowing your prevailing distortion (the key) helps you to see the true reality more clearly in the mirror (by accounting for the distortion). So if your key is 'Life is hard', next time you run into a problem, see how this key tints your reality in hardship. By noticing this you will end up separating the hardship from the reality itself, which is the whole point here. If you account for the distortion, you can see the reality without it.

When we believe the prevailing distortion, we create our Self and our life from the default settings, which are karma, genetics, social patterns etcetera. A default-created Self/life is complex, this complexity is then mistakenly taken for self-importance. If our key becomes a Self/ life definition (instead of simply opening our perception into reality), we will not feel safe or satisfied, hence the illusory self-importance becomes necessary for survival. A perfect example: instead of prioritizing we tend to go for countless tries to get organized. We get so overwhelmed with attempts to organize our life, our house, our desk, but it never happens, or if it does, it never sticks. That is because we define our reality with a key, hence following the default settings. In this case, no matter what your personal key is, the default setting is the social idea that 'organized' means 'in control'. You do not get organized to be in control, but to be *free!* Free to focus your priorities so you can create the life you choose. If you know your key, you scrap the default social idea and go for the reality—prioritizing in accordance with your Self truth/goals and, as a consequence, being free from 'having to control to be safe/feel good'.

In the third dimension we learn through looking in the mirror, and there are three main ways of how we interface with reality: share, receive, create. And they have to be balanced in order to design a balanced Self and a satisfying life. Sharing is giving what you already have, expressing yourself; in the negative it is self-sacrifice. Receiving is taking what life sends your way, allowing reality to support and educate you;

in the negative it is grabbing without consideration, not trusting life to give to us so we go after what we want too much, attempting to take it for ourselves. Creating is making something new, your own unique path, unique Self; in the negative it is a rigid focus on accomplishment, with no rest or pause. Look at any difficult situation in your life: it is only difficult because these three components are not in balance. Maybe you are over-focused on what you are creating and the effect it gives, forgetting to receive the lesson? Or perhaps you are over-giving? If you can correct the imbalance, you will correct the problem.

To keep the 'share', 'receive' and 'create' components balanced one has to listen to life's flow. Listening to the flow means going with life's rhythm, not trying to override it, slow it down or speed it up. The Universal energy that penetrates us has its own intensity and speed, and it is up to us to flow with it, or not. Since we have free will here, we do not have to follow the Universal flow of life, but it sure helps as far as making life easier! Our defiance in sticking to our override often results in more karma, because the friction created by the override process is extremely painful and hard to deal with. Following Universal rhythms is based on the vision of our agendas and the amount of the energy available for it. If the amount is smaller than the vision, then the vision needs to be reduced. Minimizing the vision is not a weakness or a failure, but an act of kindness to the Self. If you wanted to exercise for two hours on your day off, but you were feeling sick all day, your vision of exercise is too big, and scaling it down to maybe 15 minutes of walking is kindness. On the other hand, if the amount of energy exceeds the vision, the vision has to be amplified to match it. When a person sits around doing nothing and is bored, there is a lot of energy and no use for it. Finding a purpose (cleaning the house or doing the dishes) gives direction to the energy, which leads to more and more vision, because the stuckness is done. If bored, any direction will do. It is better to move the energy the 'wrong' way, than to not move at all. We often think 'oh, this task is too unimportant' or 'that is not going to make me feel good so why bother'. Well, we need to bother exactly for the reason that action leads to change. If you do not enjoy being bored, you need the change; the 'wrong' direction/action can be corrected as soon as you recognize it is not working, but at least there is movement. This movement, by the way, does not mean 'an Energizer Bunny,™ type, I am not advocating over-electricity here! If you are sitting bored at work, your 'action' can be to take a deep breath. If you are stuck in the line at the bank and getting more and more upset by the minute, tune into your vertical flow, meditate on the blue sphere of light moving up and down your spine, you do not need to fix yourself into a lotus position in the bank to tune into blue! Any change of activity or inactivity will support getting out of the stuckness, which leads to more vision for where you want to be going.

Another important ingredient for keeping the 'share', 'receive' and 'create' components balanced is patience. Without it we miss out on the full picture. If you are in a situation where you feel you have done everything you can and it is still not changed, and you cannot leave it, then there must be something you are not seeing, otherwise there would be no lesson in the situation and it would have changed. If it is still there, there is some unlearned lesson. Having patience helps us to find this final unlearned piece of the lesson, bringing us the awareness of more levels of the design.

Because patience is based on unconditionality, it creates an open space for all the information to come in, opening up possibilities. This might be useful not only for balancing the three main ways of interacting with reality, but for finding out more about your Self. In one of our workshops, Isabelle and I taught a technique called the *Big Now*, which opens up dormant abilities, supports multidimensional learning, and helps your personality to absorb what your Soul has already learned. It is like having the key to a secret library where all your Soul's memory files are stored! Here is how it works: Focus on your crown chakra, spin it clockwise, breathe energy into it slowly until you feel as if you have a large bowl on the top of your head. You can sit straight or stand straight, or even lie down if it helps you to relax and focus. Hold your intent for a specific ability you choose to receive from your Soul. I suggest not to go into too much extremes here, like 'defying the laws of gravity' or 'manifesting from the thin air'. Instead, stick to something more applicable to your life, and be prepared to get the *appropriate* portion of it for your present life, which might or might not be the whole picture you had intended for (e.g., 'being able to predict the future like an oracle' might translate into having a clearer intuition etc.) As you tune into the specific ability you want to receive from the memory files of your Soul, you may experience it as a picture, a story, a feeling or a frequency. Hold your intent on this picture/color/story/feeling with patience, just relax into it as if you have all the time in the world, wait until you feel/see/experience a shimmering energy down the back of your head. It will eventually happen, but it might take a while when you try it the first couple of times. When I do it now, it feels almost instantaneous: as soon as I see what I am looking for and drop into patience, I get the shimmering silver flow. But I know it might take people 15 minutes at first—it gets faster with practice. The shimmering energy might be a sensation/feeling for you, if you are not a color-oriented person. If you do perceive through color frequencies, your shimmer might be any color, from whitish to a rainbow, mine just happens to always be silver. Let that shimmering energy move down your spine to your tail bone and hold it there until your whole spine feels filled with it. Now take a deep breath into your spine and breathe out into the energy field (it looks like taking all the shimmers and blowing them in all directions so they fill your whole aura). Do it a couple of times until your feel your whole field shimmering. You are done! Watch for the ability you have intended to begin showing up. You can repeat the Big Now for a particular ability every day if your want to, but do not try to intend for a different ability that often, it will only overload your system. It is a powerful exercise, so use it wisely.

Personal Codes

Personal codes are the necessary programs for functioning in life. We cannot live without them. Just as you wouldn't be able to type even a letter in your computer if you did not have a word processing program of some sort, you wouldn't be able to experience anything if you did not have your codes. Every single being has its codes, but while a fish might only have one or two codes, a dog maybe twenty to forty codes, a human can have hundreds of them. Personal codes determine our interaction with the Self, the Soul and others. If each person is like a clump of clay, originally a neutral one, then each individual is imprinted with a unique and personal stamp, making each of us into a clump of different clay, imprinted with personal codes/programs. Some of them come from other lifetimes, from karmic learned and unlearned patterns and from Soul's curiosity for learning. Others come from our parents, partially from genetics and partially from the characters of the people raising us. We always have to deal with genetic patterns one way or the other; the character patterns we can choose to copy or resist. The other personal codes form later in life from societal patterns of behavior, these are learned values which we might follow or fight.

It is beneficial to know your codes, because then your can recognize the programming, know what you are dealing with, and why. You are no longer a victim of the situation, but a co-creator of it. In animals codes are instincts, like migrating paths or mating times. In humans codes are predispositions to behavior. When you know your own codes, you can modify the non-beneficial ones.

All codes are anchored in the third chakra on the front. In fact, this is what makes them codes vs. any other belief or thinking pattern. They are operational programs, the base programming behind beliefs and thought patterns. The third chakra is the focal point for the identity because it holds all these base operational programs. Even though you might have the same codes for something as another person, you will have a different combination of them. Everyone's combination of codes is unique. Often our difficulties in relating to other people are there because of the differences in codes.

Jen and Samantha are best girlfriends. Jen tells Samantha everything, how she likes something or hates it, she is kind of dramatic and open with the expression of her emotions. Jen also expresses freely when she feels upset or hurt by something Samantha said or did, but Jen lets go of the pain easily enough. Jen's code for interaction is that if you love and respect your friend, you should tell her everything, good or bad, and this keeps the relationship clear. Samantha gets hurt a lot by Jen's free expression, because Samantha's code says that if you love and respect your fried, you will not dump on them all this emotional stuff, and you surely won't tell them one moment that you don't like them, next that you do. Because of this code Samantha does not share her negative emotions with Jen. Jen takes this as 'Samantha must not trust me enough or consider me a close friend that she does not tell me things'. See the problem here? Both women are trying to respect each other, but they are doing it in accordance with different codes for 'good behavior'. What can they do? If they talk about it and recognize the difference, they can make attempts to accommodate each other a little and also to not get their feelings hurt when they do not see the behavior they want.

How do you find out what are your personal codes for life? Many codes guide our existence, but some major ones are definitely worth knowing. We will look at nine of them here: power, love, sexuality, spirituality, responsibility, honor, self-expression, responsibility and wealth. These pretty much cover all the areas of life. If you know your codes for these nine areas, you gain positive control. If you like the code you find, great! If not, then keep tracing it to find out what is the code's origin. Is it a parental code you have adopted? Is it genetic? Is it some social rule you raised into code status? If none of these apply, then it is karmic code. Considering that we all had so many incarnations, energetically we have codes pretty much for everything, all stored inside our memory files. In any particular life we choose to make some of these memory-filed codes active, while most remain dormant. And of course we gain some new codes every lifetime from genetics and parental and social values.

If you do not like the code you have discovered, there are two things you have to do. First, find out where it came from, second, ask yourself why you do not like it. This helps you to find a reason for *why you chose to activate this code.* That reason is a key to deactivating it. Here is an example:

Ingrid's code for love is 'it will never happen' and she does not like that code. She goes through a two-step process to figure out where this code came from and why she does not like it. Let's say it came from her mother, discouraged by her marriage to Ingrid's father, and Ingrid does not like it because it makes her feel defeated. Now why did she choose to have that code active so far? Maybe because unconsciously she thinks she is supposed to listen/trust her mother? Maybe, because of what was going on between her parents when she was growing up, Ingrid took her mother's position because this 'disappointed' attitude seemed to hurt less? Maybe expecting defeat felt less scary then attempting a courageous try? Getting all these answers will help Ingrid see the reason for the activation of the code. But since she does not like it anymore, she must be a different person now from the one who chose to activate this code.

This is a very important piece; it allows us to change our codes! If you go through this process of figuring it out, just like Ingrid, you find out the reasons for your code and, if you do not like it anymore, this means these reasons do not apply any longer, that is, you are now a different individual from the one who made the code active. If that is so, find which code you would like to have instead. This new code is usually a modification of the older one, sometimes it is the opposite. Find the reasons supporting the new code and really pay attention to them when the situations triggering it arise. In other words, you have now installed a new program on your 'computer', but you still have the old one in there; every time you need one of these programs it is your choice which one you activate. You have to be aware of the desire to activate the program, so you can choose correctly. If you are not aware, you will automatically choose the old one. This takes practice, but with awareness, you can change it—then the old code goes dormant and the new code you have installed activates permanently.

Looking back at Ingrid's example, she might find that she wants her new code for love to be 'possible' or 'curious', something not too threatening, but allowing. In her relationships with friends and po-tential boyfriends she can practice paying attention to the love code: every time she expects her girlfriend to not care or a guy to not call her, she can consciously say to herself 'now, that is my old love code, but I choose the new one this time—'I know she cares about me and she will listen to me, if she cannot do it now it does not mean she does not love me' and 'he might just surprise me and call, because what went on between us last night felt true'. This new attitude will activate the new code, which might be 'love is possible'. The new code might actually change the outcome of the event, and for sure it will make Ingrid's life feel better.

So let's find out: What are your main nine codes? Tune into your third chakra on the front, just relax and bring your awareness there. Breathe into it, expanding the flow through it until it feels open and the energy is actively moving. Then tune into <u>power.</u> What does it mean for you? How do you go into it? How do you recognize it in another? Use these questions while tuning into the topic of power and paying attention to your third chakra. Maybe your code for power is 'danger', or 'an ability to get what you want', or perhaps 'the ability to control life', or maybe something more dramatic like 'super-human powers', or it equals to the 'Soul's divinity incarnate'. Be honest, there is only you and it does you no good to lie to yourself by pretending your code is prettier than it actually is. Write down what you have for power; out of these small answers your operational program for power is constructed. Notice, do you like your code? Are you ashamed or disgusted by it? If so, then go through a two-step process (ask: 'Where is it from?' and 'Why do I not like it?'), find the reason you have kept this program active, choose a different one and practice, practice, practice using it.

How about a code for <u>love?</u> Remember to stay in your third chakra as you are looking for the code—if you are just thinking about it, you will not find the code, but perhaps a belief, a feeling or a thought pattern. A code is an underlying program and you can find it only in the third chakra. It is not what you think about something, it is what your perception of that something is, no thinking involved. Is your love code a 'love has to be forever'? Or maybe 'love in everything and always'? Or similar to Ingrid's 'love does not exist', 'love will never happen to me', etcetera?

Re-tune into your third chakra and ask what your code for <u>sexuality</u> is. Something like 'unknown', 'blissful', 'scary', 'dirty', 'free', or 'hidden', or maybe a 'union'? Find your own code and notice your reaction to it: are you shocked to see what it actually is? Finding out what you really believe about something might not be pleasant, but especially with the codes people often have a shock when they find out what they were operating their life on. If you do not like it, you know what to do.

Now take a breath, relax, maybe look out of the window for a moment to pause. Then tune into your third chakra again, breathe into it and open the flow there. Look for a <u>spirituality</u> code. What does it mean to you? When do you feel spiritual? Who are spiritual people? Can it be something like 'selfless', 'white light', 'poor', or maybe 'not here, out there somewhere'? Or perhaps it is 'boundary-less' or 'presence'? Find it, be honest. Then modify it if you do not like it any longer.

Next, keeping your awareness in the third chakra, tune into <u>responsibility,</u> what is your code for it? Is it 'misery', or 'loyalty', or 'burden'? Or perhaps it is 'duty'? Responsibility is often a very confusing subject for people, because we are taught such conflicting rules about it. You might actually find that you have more than one code for responsibility and that they are almost opposite! This is because you might carry an active code from other lifetimes that is very different from the one your parents taught you or the one you got genetically in this life. If you find that there are two or more codes and you like one, but not the others, just keep amplifying through practice the code you like. This will make it stronger and it can override the other codes.

Staying in your third chakra tune into <u>honor</u>, how does it ring? How does it look and feel? Maybe you will 'see' your code as a 'shiny knight on a horse'? This is a very popular, romanticized social code for honor, in its common meaning it has absolutely no power, but in a more idealistic way it does hold the concept of honor (even though that honor has nothing to do with medieval knights). But dig deeper, what else is there? Perhaps your honor code is 'cold and non-sexual' or maybe 'over-responsible and hard'? Maybe it is 'allow' and 'witness'? Or can it be 'scary' and 'guilt ridden and difficult'? Maybe even something like 'vengeance', that is often a karmic code from other lives that sometimes stays active, making a person's life rotate around revenge (with family, lovers, law suits, business partners etc.). If it is changed, the person finally becomes free of the need for revenge and is able to forgive, learn and let go of the pain.

Take another breath, stand up and walk around the room or stretch, remember that you are not only your brain, but that there is a body attached to it! Then tune into your third chakra again, breathe into it and notice the flow of energy, it is pure life force moving in there. Focus on your <u>self-expression</u> code, how do you see it? Perhaps something like 'in order for it to have value others have to see it', or 'freedom', maybe even 'torture'. That is a very important code, because it operates our ability to interact with external reality, without it we are unknown and alone. The expression of Self does not need to be related to other people (like the style of clothes you wear or how you tell a joke); it can, of course, but it is ultimately based inside. How do you express your Self? By breathing shallowly or deeply? By accepting external energies or defending against the world? Answers to these types of questions will lead you to a deeper understanding of self-expression. If you do not like the code you have for it, you know how to change it.

Now reconnect with your third chakra, breathe and relax. Look for the code for intimacy. It can be anything from 'danger' to 'a sphere of light', it is unique to you. You might only see intimacy as sex, which means that intimacy is available to you only during sex with a partner and without a partner (or sex) you do not know how to experience intimacy. Be honest with what you find, this is the only way to change it.

To finish, look at the last one of the nine codes, your code for wealth. Make sure you are in your third chakra when you are looking for it, so you do not pull out a thought pattern or emotional reaction instead of a code. Tune in, do not read further, look inside yourself, what do you get? If you find that your wealth code seems to generate a picture of a gold coin pile or a fat pack of dollar bills, your view on wealth is fused with money, which robs you of full-scale living as a child of this Universe. Wealth is not just money; in a much broader sense it is an interaction with life, experience of life. Dig deeper, what else is in your code for wealth? Maybe it is 'gratitude', or 'luxury', or something like 'hurting others'? If your code is negative, it might be preventing you from experiencing wealth, including the financial type.

Knowing your main codes you can now reprogram your entire way of interacting with life, with your Self and even with your Soul—that is an incredible power! But remember that it takes lots of awareness, practice and patience to change a code, so do not expect it to modify itself just because you would like it to be different. Now that you have these very powerful tools, this information that was taught to the initiates in Egyptian mystery schools, and in India, China, and many other places, use them wisely.

Imprint Your Self with Power

To reach full empowerment we must be consciously aware of victim patterns and look for any hidden ones as well. As we vibrate to higher frequencies of consciousness, the ego can become very fearful of enlightenment and try to sabotage the body-Soul fusion of our awakening. The ego only has a reference point for experience that it has known or lived in the past. What we are evolving into does not necessarily make sense to the ego, only to us as the Higher Self. Ever felt like you know something clearly from one side of your consciousness but at the same time that the other side is steeped in fear, anger, revenge or some other negative pattern? That is because the ego holds on to the old patterns based on the past, while the Higher Self is promoting evolution of 'taking the higher road'. The reason the ego is addicted to old patterns is that it tries to win. How do you win if the rules are constantly changing on you? So to eliminate this problem the ego cements the rules, usually from childhood when it was formed, and then attempts to win by them. This is the only way the ego knows how to stay in power and maintain its worth. True worth, as you know, is based on being a part of the Universe, not on how often your ego wins. The Higher Self is partnered with the Soul, it is Soul's 'way in' to our personality. The ego and the Soul have different agendas. The Soul wants to experience reality and has no judgment, only curiosity (true power); the ego wants to feel powerful by 'winning' (false power).

How do you recognize if you are operating on the ego's desire for false power? You are in a victim mode, you feel trapped, you have no conscious choice—that is it. If you look at this in a vertical way, the Soul is at the top and the physical body at the bottom, and in between under the Soul is the Higher Self, then the ego, then the Lower Self. See how it is all supposed to connect? The Soul talks to the Higher Self, which is already a part of our personality. The Higher Self sees the big picture, it is generous, open, curious etcetera. From the bottom, the physical body is the densest, it communicates with the most scared part of us, the Lower Self, which is also a part of the personality. The ego kind of hangs in between, it is supposed to be a neutral bridge between the scared/confused side and the wise side of us—that is a balanced ego. But how many people do you know with a neutral ego? Right, not that many, if any. Most of us have our ego making an alliance either with the Higher Self or the Lower Self so that it is no longer neutral.

You might see the ego's alliance with the Higher Self as a good thing, but it is not. Why? Because it separates the scared Lower Self with the physical body even further from the 'I am-ness' of the personality, and this separation suppresses the darker side of the Self and generates abuse of the body. In that alignment a person is not aware of or does not claim with responsibility their darker side; their unconscious fears, pains, cruelty, jealousy etcetera stay unconscious, but not inactive, which is very dangerous. This person might act on his/her Lower Self without even knowing it and then deny it, because their personality does not accept this part of the self as Self. The reasons for the ego's alliance with the Higher Self are based on the feeling of being endangered. This feeling comes from the orphaned Lower Self. The arrogant ego attempts to escape the perceived weakness of the Lower Self by pretending that the Lower Self does not exist, only the Higher Self does ('I am not afraid!' said a kid, while his knees were shaking; 'I am not being emotional!' yelled a man, while sweating profusely...)

If the ego is allied with the Lower Self, it alienates the Soul and the Higher Self, pushing them 'out' of the personality so that they cease to be a component of it. The person gets trapped in the Lower Self illusion. All fear-based patterns are attempts of the Lower Self to be safe, and these patterns always lead to codependency and eventual entrapment. If the ego takes the Lower Self attempts at getting safety seriously, it makes it equal to power; in other words the ego's goal becomes 'winning safety'. This goal of safety by winning is the victim mode. In this alignment the ego believes it will feel powerful only if nothing can harm it, it is at odds with the Universe and attempts to protect itself, defend itself. The person does not see the world and the Self as one, instead it seems that the world is 'doing something to the person', and that there is a war (i.e., no safety). The ego wants power for the wrong reasons if it is aligned with a scared Lower Self. In a time of peace a person might want power as evolution, as learning and improving, and then it is power balanced with life. But in a time of war the person's idea of power will be 'to protect myself' or 'to win over my enemies' (only in this case the enemy is the whole Universe! Who do you think will win?! No wonder the ego feels so small! Unfortunately it only makes it fight harder...)

Soul 'agenda' is true power, pure evolution by experience. The ego always feels threatened until it becomes one with the Soul. This is a very important piece of information to remember: the ego *always* feels threatened by Soul power entering the personality. When you connect more consciously to your Higher Self and make it a part of your identity, Soul's energy can flow in freely. This energy-consciousness hits your ego and it freaks out! You end up activating all your fears of not being safe (in social situations, in relationships, at work, in spiritual exploration, etc.). If you believe these fears, the ego 'wins'; that is, it wages a war against the Higher Self and ultimately the Soul in an attempt to remain powerful in its position. How might this look in a real life situation? You feel like you always struggle with money, so you investigate it and discover your beliefs in scarcity etcetera, you choose to focus on abundance and change your relationship to money. So far so good, you have expanded your personality to incorporate a higher concept and Soul's energy begins to flood your field. But then your ego freaks out and you start to doubt your choice: 'I was very frugal before and didn't save much, but still something, at least I felt safe, now that I try to trust and believe in abundance, I spend more, but not much is coming in, so I better go back to my old saving methods or I will be poorer than before I began this!' (the ego felt in power by struggling in frugal saving, and it got scared that that power would be taken away). Or you were exploring higher states of consciousness in meditation, usually this did not work very well, but one day you decided to trust and open up to the Universe, experience whatever comes not just in meditation but all the time, and it worked, you started to have vivid dreams, perhaps 'hear' voices, have stronger intuition. But instead of feeling exhilarated you got terrified: 'I do not know what I am doing! I am going crazy! Maybe I have a tumor in my brain! I will be possessed! I will end up picking up 'bad energy' from people!' and so on. Your ego got scared because its position of 'I am powerful by knowing my reality' got challenged. If you truly trust and open up, you will end up expanding your definition of reality and your ego will be proven 'wrong' in its narrow-mindedness of safety. The ego finds this threatening and makes war with your Soul.

Remember we established that the ego only knows by looking back in time, reading the already recorded files of your personal history. Through recognizing a frequency by past referencing the ego can figure out if something is good for it or not. Unfortunately this method also leaves us with no free will choice; instead it is a preprogrammed response. So what is the point of all of this? The point is that if you *know* that your ego will feel threatened when Soul's energy begins to pour into it through the Higher Self, you can anticipate and compensate for it. All the problems occur when we *believe* ego's fear, when we agree that we are not safe. The Higher Self knows that we are always safe, unconditionally. The ego makes this safety conditional by aligning with the Lower Self or by rejecting/abandoning it. When you choose to respect and love the scared Lower Self and to receive and trust the larger concepts of the Higher Self, your ego will freak out. But when this freak-out happens, be a witness to it, not a participant, this will neutralize the ego. In other words, when you recognize the frequency of the ego's fear (always based on comparing the present with the past), by-pass the past-referencing by becoming a witness to the experience; go into *'I Am Evolving'*. The ego is a bridge, it is designed to be neutral, but it forgot its design. Allow your conscious awareness to remind your ego of its innate ability to be a neutral bridge by witnessing its freak out. ('I am suddenly doubting everything in my life, must be my ego freaking out...this means that more of my Soul is coming in! I Am Evolving!...' instead of 'I am doubting everything in my life, I must be screwing up somehow, I better fix this or it will all go wrong!')

One of the ways to stabilize yourself during the ego freak-out is by balancing your vertical flow. This is a little exercise for 'I Am Evolving' that you can do anywhere, from your calm meditation space to a busy line at the register in the supermarket. As you already know, just saying something does not work. Even though words are powerful tools, they still have to be used by 'someone'; that is, you have to be aligned and centered to have your words be registered by your system, otherwise they just stay on the mental level and nothing happens. 'I Am Evolving' cleanses, relaxes tension, clears stress and allows more energy movement through the field. Focus on the vertical tube in the center of your energy field/body, you can be standing, sitting or lying down, just keep your back straight. Now simultaneously draw the energy into/down through the crown chakra and into/up through the root chakra on the in-breath. Allow the energies to mix in your heart chakra and on the out-breath release the energy through the front and back aspects of the heart chakra, while saying (inside or out loud) 'I Am Evolving'. If colors help you, you can use white for the crown energy and red for the root energy, exhaling rose through the heart; or to have less things to pay attention to, just use blue for everything, inhale and exhale blue. Choose the one that resonates with you more and do this exercise every time your ego gets into a freak-out, self-doubt mode.

Intend and Manifest

Manifestation is a realized intention. In other words, it is an anchored intent in the field, which then can be mirrored in external reality. Manifestation does not mean materialization. A lot of times what we intend can manifest, but not materialize, that is, the intention can create a desired change in the energy field, but if a person was not anchored in the body, this change would not materialize in the physical. We often discard our successes in manifestation because they did not have a physical effect. This is not a beneficial course of action, because it teaches our system not to trust our power, which only misaligns us with the Soul. Manifestation occurs in the energy field. If the field changes, it in turn changes external reality (which is a mirror of internal reality).

Simon has cancer of the prostate. His intent is to cure it energetically, to make it disappear, instead of using conventional medical treatment. He gives himself a month. Simon focuses on this intention full-heartedly for a month. During this month he becomes more aware of his suppressed feelings and self-judgments, and how he pushes himself overly hard all the time. He notices how his behavior changes, he becomes softer, smoother, kinder to himself, less rushed and judgmental. As the month comes to an end, he does another check up of his prostate—the cancer is still there. Simon feels he has failed, he did not cure the cancer, his intention did not work. By adopting this attitude

Simon ends up in emotional collapse, which pushes out the support of his Soul. This will probably reactivate all the old energy patterns and perhaps make the cancer worse. If Simon had recognized that he did manifest his intention, even though it was not able to materialize in his physical body, he would have supported his body's dealing with cancer, instead of making it harder for himself. He manifested his intention by clearing the energy patterns in his aura that created and supported his physical cancer, but he still might need a physical solution to the cancer itself (alkalizing, vitamins, stress-reduction, or more drastic approaches).

Recognition of the conscious intent-manifestation, no matter how small, is a form of support of our developing trust of the Soul. And, believe me, we need all the support we can get! It is hard enough to challenge the ego, the old patterns, never mind the emotional pains and fears. If we do not acknowledge our progress, the ego (addicted to winning) feels that we are losing. This makes it much harder to follow through with changes. So instead of going against the ego, make friends with it by helping it see how you are 'winning' in your attempts to change, even if that change is internal (in attitude, feelings, beliefs) and not yet physical.

Another thing necessary for manifestation is a *sustained* intention. This means that if something does not show up right away it is not an excuse to let go of the intention. We are conditioned for immediate gratification and if what we intend does not occur, we assume we have failed and move on. Following this path we end up creating many unfinished patterns in the energy field, which only clog it up. Sustained intention requires trust in the overall design. If you know that 'all this' is an illusion and that you are a creator of your life, then everything (everything!!) is possible. That allows your intention to stay potent and focused, un-interfered with. But when we lack that trust, intention becomes conditional on the manifestation, which is a recipe for the failure of that manifestation. Just as faith is only faith because there is no proof of what you believe and if there is proof it is no longer faith, so the possibility of manifestation goes significantly down if its intent to manifest is dependent on that very manifestation! We sabotage our own intent, dooming manifestation to failure, when we wait for manifestation as proof in order to keep the intent going.

To intend is a choice. You can choose to intend for a particular duration in linear time, or program your intent to 'always' mode (in spherical time, or at least until the rest of this lifetime). There are many variations. Your intent to manifest health when you are recovering from an emotional upset and a physical cold might be programmed for a straight three days, or a week, while your intent for self respect might be set on automatic as an 'always intent' for the rest of your life. Programming your intention means making a conscious choice to keep a particular configuration of energy potently vibrating throughout your system for a certain time. This means that intent cannot work if too many parts of you disagree with it. An example of this is a person trying to quit smoking. If she is intending to quit smoking because she mentally thinks it is good for her, but her emotions do not agree with it, the intent becomes a wish. And a wish is a form of desire, not intent. The difference is that anything in the category of desire is fluid and affects the emotional and astral levels only, while an intent holds in alignment and vibrates through the structural levels first, then the fluid ones, covering the whole system.

Commitment to a choice of holding a particular configuration in the field 'no matter what' makes intent a very powerful tool. When we take away the 'no matter what' part of the agreement, the intent loses its power. You can prolong the duration of your intent, set up check points. If you want to manifest a job and you hold your intent for that job to come in, but nothing is happening, it is not beneficial to start doubting 'does this mean it is not the right time for me to get another job?' What you want to do it set a check point, maybe two of three of them: keep the intent for a month, then reevaluate, then again for another month, etcetera. If you do not get your intent manifested after three check points, there must be something in the way: either you are not fully committed to the change (need to look for negative intents) or it was the wrong reason for the change (out of avoidance, not evolution) or the timing for it is wrong (you were ahead of yourself, not patient). These three are the main reasons for a failed manifestation. If you were intending for something for a while and it did not manifest, look at the list of three necessaries (commitment, reasons for change, timing) and find which one is blocking your manifestation. Knowing the reason for the blockage gives you the needed tools to fix it.

No one chakra is responsible for manifestation, all chakras are necessary for it. The energy of intent sets the whole field in a particular configuration, like a still drawing hanging three-dimensionally in space. It is not what is yet, but what it is becoming. All the chakras respond to this configuration of intent and clear/modify the energy flowing through them. This is why when we intend for something big, we often have changes happening in us, triggering emotional and mental blocks. It is the intent working its way through the chakras as it is manifesting level by level, frequency by frequency.

Even though all the chakras are involved in manifestation, an intent is held in place by two of them: the root and the throat. Anchored in the root chakra is a type of power that when combined with the expression capacity of the throat chakra can create what we command. But this will only work if the throat and the root chakras are clear and in agreement, they have to be aligned. This is the power of the word spoken in resonance with a grounded body, a very important component of manifestation through intention. We manifest all the time, but not always through a conscious intent. You manifest bread on your table, a fight with a partner or a near-miss car accident, but usually by unconscious intents. We have many unconscious intents; these are often conflicting and when they manifest we do not see them as our creations, even though they are. What we are learning here is how to manifest through a conscious intent, make happen what you want to have happen. The root and throat chakras are essential for this process. So before you set your intentions, make sure these two chakras are clear, that is, that you are in your body and that you are not afraid to make known what you choose!

There is a specific action you can take to attract needed opportunities—it is the setting of a *Beacon*. Energetically we have to make our intent visible to the Universe (and its inhabitants) if we want to maximize manifestation. This is how you set the Beacon. First relax, breathe, become calm and comfortable, with a straight back (laying, sitting or standing). Charge your vertical tube by first drawing the energy of the

Earth up through your root to your crown chakra. Then let the energy flow from your crown down to your root. Focus your intention on whatever you choose to attract. Tune into the ninth chakra, about a foot above your head, like a silvery bowl (or an egg) floating over you. Breathe into it the energy from your vertical tube and radiate your intention through the ninth chakra, then let it spread out spherically. Sit in this large sphere for a while, just breathing while your intent pattern is resonating through it. Then take a deep breath and slowly refocus on the root chakra, back to your body. You have set your Beacon. Once it is set, there is no need to keep resetting it; this constitutes mistrust in your ability. You can check up on it once in a while or infuse it with new energy by tuning into it as you change. If for some reason you choose to deactivate your Beacon (it was set for a particular business that you are not involved in anymore, but still get many requests for, etc.), you can do it by following all the steps for setting it up, but in the end when you return to your root chakra, pull in the ninth chakra energy with you into the root and then the Earth. This will 'recycle' your Beacon. The technique of setting a Beacon was used in the Egyptian mystery schools and is a powerful tool for manifestation, do not abuse it. You do not want 200 Beacons floating around you for every little thing, it creates confusion and an energy drain. But the good news is that you do not have to dismantle all your outdated Beacons. Some you can modify if they still apply, but most, once they are not applicable anymore, dissolve on their own. You have to 'recycle' into the Earth only the ones which are not needed but for some reason did not dissolve and stayed active, which is pretty rare anyway. So enjoy your shiny new Beacons!

Confidence

Everyone wants more confidence, but we often have a false idea about its meaning. Our egos give confidence qualities it does not have, such as 'if I am confident, I am not scared', or 'if I am confident, I knowledgeable', or 'if I am confident, people will respect/fear me' etcetera. All these misconceptions are the ego's power struggles, with confidence being used as a fix-everything solution. But confidence as an energy pattern is a totally different thing. The skill of present moment conscious awareness is experienced as confidence. In other words, if you are present and conscious of what you are present to, the resulting experience is confidence. This is not ego-confidence as power, it is a Soul-body union power reflected in the personality. That true confidence is what makes you feel 'in the right place and in the right time'; it resonates in synchronicity with the Universe and your place in it. Because you are always on the path, even if you are not aware of it or are intent on taking the backward route, when you are consciously present the confidence of this alignment with your Soul, your path, your current position and so on, feels very powerful.

Being present means witnessing/experiencing everything inside of you and outside of you in this moment. And not just the comfortable, pretty things. This is the hard part and the reason so many people do not feel confident: we are conditioned to avoid 'ugly' personal traits, uncomfortable situations, pains, difficulties, undesired components of the personality and the like. How can you be present to what really is if you only want to see/experience the desired part of it? This avoidance of reality creates a psychic splitting inside the Self, when only the nice/pretty/good part is accepted as the Self, while the 'ugly' components are projected out onto other people, institutions, circumstances etcetera and rejected. As the Self splits, its confidence deteriorates.

Energetically, during the psychic split we release many negative thought-forms into the planetary astral level. Thought-forms are energy 'blobs' that exist on the astral level, they are mostly human-created (some pets can make them too, but not the negative ones) and consist of a combination of mental and astral energy: thought + feeling = thought-form. Because thought-forms are imprinted by the mental level, they are able to become what they believe themselves to be (if it 'thinks' it is mean, its mental charge will make it act mean etc.). Because of the feeling imprint, they have a desire to fulfill. Unfortunately, most of the thought-forms on the planetary astral level are destructive and contributing to pollution, because they are unconsciously created. People who we project our negativity onto are bombarded by these thought-forms. They can choose to take them into their field or not, but either way they are stuck dealing with them. Since many of us protect ourselves from these renegade thought-forms by rejecting our own negativity ('I would have been more responsible with my thought-forms, I would have never done that!'—that in itself is a projected out thought-form), we end up further polluting our astral space. The seriously polluted astral space makes people look for confidence elsewhere, not inside themselves. Taking responsibility for your own negative thought-forms not only stops your contribution to planetary pollution, but also takes your imprint off the already released thought-forms, 'deflating' their influence. Learning to use clear, non-judgmental thought aligned with the conscious intent of the Soul or higher Self creates constructive thought-forms with beneficial desires. Releasing these positive desire thought-forms into the astral space actually helps you create what you choose in your life with confidence.

Step one in restoring confidence is mending the psychic split of the Self. It is done through practicing non-judgment. Look at what you find infuriating in life or in other people, then find these very traits in you—fear of these traits creates judgment and you project them out onto external world. Knowing what they are returns the power to you, allowing an act of free will: to choose to accept them, or not.

Step two in restoring confidence is root chakra work and presence. The energy of alignment of the vertical flow, anchored into the root chakra, is confidence. The root chakra allows you to feel internal safety, to fully experience 'here'. Being grounded enough opens an ability to listen. Sounds easy, right? We all listen all the time. But do we really listen to what is present? Most of the time we are hearing whatever we can past-reference, and judge the rest. The ability to fully listen is a rare natural gift, but it can and should be developed. Listening first is applicable to the Self, then to others. We have to fully listen to the Self in order to know what we are experiencing. If we are not in that listening-witness mode, we will assume things, play and pretend about our experiences and miss out on Soul messages and support. Without true listening we cannot receive the experiences of the Self and we try to filter them: 'I like this experience, so this is really happening' and 'I do not like this experience, so I am not going to be aware of having it'. We trick ourselves all the time in believing we are experiencing one thing, while actually we are experiencing something else, and much more of it than we think. Adding energy into your root chakra helps you to stop the trickery and listen bravely to the reality of the Self, which naturally leads to the experience of confidence. Confidence is based on the *reality* of the Self, not on the 'play-pretend'.

The vertical flow physically happens through the spine, so posture is very important in confidence. If you slouch and look like a question mark, you cannot possibly feel confident! Notice how, no matter how scared or upset you are, if you straighten and lift your head up, you will feel at least a little more confident. That is because the energy can flow more freely through the spine if you stand straight. To maximize this effect, do it consciously, really focus on how your body stands or sits. It helps to imagine as if there is a hook on the top of your head and you, like a toy skeleton, are hanging from it. It stretches your spine and makes more space between the vertebras, releasing any pressure. In the energy field the vertical tube on the etheric level has to be charged for confidence. A blue frequency flows freely up and down the vertical tube in the middle of your body/field, radiating into all the grids. Pumping this blue charge fuels alignment and natural confidence follows.

Time

There are two types of time: linear time that we all are used to, and spherical time. We all live in both of them simultaneously here in the third dimension of consciousness, usually without special focus on spherical time, so we experience only the linear one. We can learn to perceive both of them by switching the focus of perception between them. Once you are familiar with both perceptions, you can experience both times' simultaneousness consciously. This is the magical key for the freedom of creation, with it anything is possible, the Universe becomes a playground.

Everything that ever existed *always* exists. Everything that will ever exist *already* exists. Nothing disappears once it is out of its linear moment. This is the biggest secret kept hidden by priests and priestesses who are able to expand their consciousness to connect to both times simultaneously. That is why any lifetime you 'had' you are still having; it is happening, but not to you, since you have moved on. I know this is confusing, that is because our brain is trained to perceive linear time and we naturally have difficulty with spherical time. Lives are simultaneous, but due to our linear perception of time we tend to see our *other* lifetimes as past or future lives in reference to the present one. Any person you know who died might have already reincarnated and has a different life, but at the same time they are always what they were to you, how you knew them, a part of them lives at the same time as they are living their other life. This might be of some comfort for those of you who lost loved ones and suffered greatly from that separation. The person you loved still exists, just as they were, in spherical time. That is how the idea of 'heaven' (someplace where we all go where nothing changes and we always are with our loved ones) came into existence. There is no heaven quite like that, that one is a fabrication, but it is built on a distorted truth. The original concept is that the loved ones are 'there' in existence; you can connect to them in your meditations, through your intuition or dreams. The Soul has other incarnations it focuses on, but they all are ongoing. We see our own as the most important one only because we are centered in the limitation of its perceptions.

The Soul of a person who died has a different body and personality in linear timeline (they have reincarnated by now), but at the same time that Soul is connected to the person that was. What this means is that a Soul is not a localized phenomenon. We tend to think that our Soul is *ours,* as if it is a 'thing' that is attached to us. Soul cannot be localized; it is the essence of God in us, continuously creating us into being. Since Soul exists outside of linear time, it experiences everything at once. Our Soul simultaneously connects to millions of its incarnations, some in the third dimension, like you on Earth, some in other dimensions. Knowing this secret of time expands your range of options. You still have only one body, so you cannot become some other projection of your Soul, but you can gain partial access to the information from these other personalities. Imagine what can you learn from a part of you that is an angel, or a star, or a little bug on some other planet?

Linear time does not just 'float' in spherical time, but exists as many timelines. Timelines are linear time directions with a particular range of possible events. The Soul has an incarnation in a specific region of these timelines. If you imagine that trillions of universal timelines have numbers on them, each particular incarnation covers a certain range of them, like from 20 to 80 or from 5,780,970 to 5,785,000. Ok, to simplify this for our human brain, the Soul chooses its playground by determining the range of possibilities for each lifetime, then creates a form (in our case physical) in one of these timelines (it is an anchor timeline). This form now has the option to exist in the anchor timeline and never leave it, or to switch to any of the other available timelines. Why and how would we switch timelines? We do not switch to a different timeline every time we make a choice. But when a person comes to sort of crossroads in life, when a choice does not just determine an outcome of a current event, but changes the whole direction of a life, a person might switch to another timeline. Depending on the choice, s/he can end up confirming the original choice of experiences in the present timeline, or choosing a very different range of experiences from some other available timeline. We can learn in any timeline, so there is no goal to jump to some other 'better timeline'. Some lead to a more direct learning, which tends to require more courage and responsibility, others to a more relaxed learning curve with less 'scary' experiences. Either one is ok, depending on what suits your personality, or how scared your ego is, etcetera. Sometimes when you switch a timeline, you do not even notice it at first, but then suddenly you find out that you cannot relate to certain people in your life anymore, they are still there, but you do not seem to have any connection, as if the line was cut. Or you do not find something important, that used to be central in your life just recently. These are indications that you are in a different timeline.

Timelines are not the same as 'parallel universes'; that is a different phenomenon. A parallel universe is a place where your incarnation exists with different possibilities, its own range of timelines and so on. This phenomenon is based on everything, no matter which dimension, being anchored in the first dimension. Inside that anchor a splitting occurs, similar to a reflection being broken into thousand pieces by a room filled with mirrors at different angles. That is because each electron as it travels arrives at a place where we can pinpoint it by billons of different paths—the 'broken mirrors'. That splits the whole system from the first dimension, making everything double, triple, quadruple etcetera, in all the other dimensions, and so parallel universes are born. There are many of them and they are unique from the first dimension all the way up into the thirteenth, which is what differentiates them from timelines. Timelines are differentiated from each other by only one small circumstance; a parallel universe is a whole universe of options.

In order to create or locate any form, thought-form, emotional energy 'blob' form, or matter-form, both perceptions of time are needed. Linear time is a step-by-step advancement into vision and is mostly electrical, identity based, speed- and goal-oriented; it is the past-present-future we are familiar with. Spherical time is everything at once; is mostly magnetic where no identity is necessary; has no movement, speed or direction, no goal/destination; it is always the *now*. The beauty in being able to consciously connect to both times is that in linear time we experience what already happened or is happening, while in spherical time we can experience what hasn't happened yet linearly/physically. This is the means of predicting future. No one can really predict the future because we have free will and are constantly inventing our future. But one can predict a timeline probability. In other words, if you are able to connect to spherical time while you are tuned into your present timeline, you can 'read' what will happen in that timeline that did not occur yet in linear time. This is a possibility, not a set future, because one can always switch a timeline due to their choices. And it is dangerous thing to do if one does not know what s/he is doing and has many unresolved issues about the outcome. That is how fortune tellers do it, they tune into where you are and what you want to happen, or what you are afraid of happening, and tell you that. It is not necessarily a timeline reading, but it is similar, since the result is an explanation of 'what will happen' based on what is there now (your desires and your fears). The danger here is in solidifying the line. By stating what 'will happen' that linear future is set in a much more solid way than it would have been otherwise, which makes it harder for a recipient of this information to change the outcome.

Rebecca is afraid that a free trip she can receive as an incentive at her job might be given to someone else. She really wants that free trip because she thinks it will make her feel important, make her position stand out in the company, and she will not have to feel unsure anymore. But she is unsure. And so Rebecca goes to a fortune teller, who reads her future. The woman hears Rebecca's questions about the upcoming trip and tunes into what is happening. She feels Rebecca's fear about the trip slipping away, and the fear of some co-worker woman who Rebecca is competitive with getting to go on the trip instead of her. The fortune teller tells Rebecca that 'there is a mean woman who will take the trip away from her'. Rebecca leaves the reading with a more conscious fear about her co-worker getting the incentive trip. A few days later, Rebecca is told that the co-worker woman is awarded the trip, not her. Did the fortune teller read the timeline and tell the future? Chances are that what she read was Rebecca's fears and the outcome based on these fears not being resolved. Rebecca created her reality of not going on the trip and 'losing' to a co-worker because she internally already decided it is so—she already decided that she is weak and unsure and desperately needs the trip to prove she is ok, and that the co-worker woman is strong and 'mean'. The reading made these fears conscious, but also solidified them, making them the most probable reality. Rebecca was told she will not get the trip, that the other woman is 'stronger'. That is not a reality but Rebecca's fear. That fear created the outcome, but was not 'the future'. It was the possibility (the most likely one since Rebecca did not work with her fear) that became the future *because* it was predicted.

But what about really reading a timeline? Is it even possible? Yes, it is, but a reading is not like a prediction, instead there are probabilities, some more, others less, likely. To read a timeline, tune into where you are now and the events of your life that led you to the present situation. This aligns your consciousness with the timeline you are in. Then take a deep breath and expand your awareness to the eighth level, that is, just outside of the usual bubble of your energy boundary. It might look to you similar to a spider web, with many threads going in different directions. Or it might feel like something swooshes fast past you here and there. Or just like a lot of open space. Stay connected to that place, tune into the circumstance of your present timeline and let it unfold further. Try not to will it either way, allow it to happen. It will show you not what will happen, but what might happen.

There can be different scenarios, different endings to the same story, these are different timelines. Notice your emotional charge on them. If you really want something or are very afraid of something, that scenario will have these feelings attached to it, and will feel different from the more neutral scenarios. Practice with some things you do not have much charge on ('will you end up going to lunch in a particular place of not?') and the ones you do ('will this new guy/girl call/like me?'). Notice how it feels, what is the difference between them? You might have an easier time reading the timeline you are in (which is the most probable scenario) if you do not have an emotional charge on it. As you practice this, you will learn to put aside the emotional desire/fear, hence clarifying the timeline.

This exercise shows you the timeline you are in. If you do not like it, it does not mean you have to switch to another timeline, just that you might have to make choices that are different from the most obvious ones. In the case of Rebecca, she was in the timeline of not getting her trip, but if she had realized she had so much of her worry and self-worth attached to getting the trip, she could have resolved that, which might have resulted in her getting the trip at work after all. It still would have been the same timeline. If, on the other hand, Rebecca had decided that the whole job was not for her, and that she does not want other people's opinions to shape her worth, and had not only let go of the need to go on that trip but quit the job too, that would have been another timeline!

In order to create anything in linear time we need to apply spherical time. If you want to manifest through intention, by holding your intent in spherical time you end up shaping/sculpting linear time, facilitating your creation. There were special techniques in ancient schools for stretching time, to make the moment last. When someone was severely injured, for example, a priestess/priest could stretch linear time, giving this person a chance to make it until help arrived. When people had to go away from loved ones for a long time (e.g., for years at a time in caravans), they would stretch the linear moments of when they were home, creating more fulfillment and satisfaction in their long-distance relationship. This stretching is done by holding the linear present moment, but placing most of your awareness into the spherical time. Elongating the timeline, a 'stretching' of perception, occurs. If you want to save time, the best thing to do is to be in the present moment. If you really focus on what is happening without distractions, you will use less time to do it. This also requires strategy, perhaps grouping similar activities together or alternating creative and mundane tasks etcetera.

Our perception of time is determined by the pulsing rate/speed of conduction of nervous system impulses. When neurons fire fast, we feel exhilarated. When nerve impulses are sluggish, time seems to stagnate or stand still. Emotional wounds and our defenses from their pain affect our perception of time. A controlling person perceives only future time, running after a goal. A person who spends lots of time floating out of the body perceives time mostly as spherical, because outside of form (the linear definition) there is 'everything' (the spherical definition). A self-punishing person perceives time as stagnant, swamp-like, polluted or dead. An overly needy person perceives that there is not enough time. A person who is generally rigid or stiff sees time as mechanical and inevitable.

Recognize yourself in any of these typical perceptions of time? Depending on your main wounding pain and how you deal with it, you will fall into one of these categories. Sometimes we hurt from different wounds, so time perception might alternate. Instead of being frustrated with time, look at the wound you are experiencing (this is usually unconscious). If you feel that everything is boring and mechanical, instead of trying to make the situation less boring, look at the rigidity in your system and relax more. Or if you notice that you are wired and almost high on time speeding up, but your body can barely handle it, you are too far ahead of yourself; refocus on the present moment (like the texture of the chair you are sitting in) and bring yourself back. This will slow down the speedy impulses in your nervous system, helping the physical body to feel safe. If you are running at two hundred miles per hour and freaking out, you are trying to fulfill some emotional need by getting everything done (which will never be done because there is not enough time). Take a breath, remind yourself that the earth will still be turning if you did not finish everything on your to-do list, and give yourself emotionally whatever you were trying to get by attempting to do everything. If you are stuck ('my life isn't going anywhere') and time is just circling over and over the same place (as if you were sitting in a doctor's office and staring at the clock with every minute perceived equal to eternity), you are in self-punishment. Look at the reasons you are punishing yourself; resolving them changes your perception of time. If you cannot keep track and tend to usually be late, chances are you are out of your body, floating in 'everything' time. Paying attention to what you are avoiding by floating will get you back into your body and connect you more to linear time. In case you are wondering why you would want to connect to linear time if the spherical one feels so good, re-read previous paragraphs—to create/manifest 'here' we need *both* times.

Alchemical Acquisition and Material Wealth Through Emotional Money

Alchemy is an essential component of wealth acquisition. Nothing in this universe is made from scratch, we recycle different energies again and again, stretching or compressing some, diffusing or densifying others. In other words, everything is already in existence, but our focus changes its consistency, its form, even its consciousness. This is especially true for manifesting in matter: we employ the atomic domain, shaping it with our intent into material forms. Intent, internal balance of emotions and thoughts and the physical body have to be aligned for alchemy to touch physicality. We cannot manifest anything (energetically or physically) without alchemy. What this universe is made of, what already exists, we cannot own. It is an illusion to think that you can own frequency (including matter). But although we are not able to own it, we can claim it with the attraction of our identity. Attracting frequencies through the means of your identity creates your own mini-universe. We are always completely responsible for our own universe. This means that if you do not want to be an individual identity or do not want responsibility, you will have difficulty attracting energy into your mini-universe, that is, you will struggle with creating through alchemy.

Alchemy is the process of changing one frequency into another. When you transmute negative feeling into positive (like anger into compassion) you perform energy alchemy. When you buy the food you wanted, you alchemize desire into form. Alchemy requires mastery of the elements you are working with. If you are not very aware or tolerant of your feelings, it will be difficult for you to transmute them. Especially with matter, since we have not mastered matter yet, we cannot materialize intent into it (like make the gold cube you are envisioning show up in your hand physically). The more mastery you have of a particular frequency, the easier it is to perform alchemy using it.

To utilize alchemy in your life, certain operational programs have to be present on your conceptual level. The <u>capacity for change</u> is one if them. To be able to change we have to stay moldable in our beliefs, thoughts, feelings etcetera. Change itself is a concept, if it is mis-wired somehow due to fears, karma or pain, we become too rigid on the conceptual level. We stick to what we know, unable to allow other, unknown energy combinations in, which stunts the alchemy process.

Another necessary for the alchemy program is the <u>capacity to have</u>. It is the concept of 'permission to claim'. If we do not give ourselves this internal permission, we cannot claim frequencies with our identity, which in turn blocks alchemy. In order to activate a capacity to have, you have to perceive the Self as your own authority. When we project our authority onto other people, we look for them to give us permission. Because it is the external permission of a projected authority, it does not register on the Self, and alchemy does not work. Everything that we have (energy and things) is an extension of our identity, so the stronger your identity, the more permission you can give yourself, further increasing your capacity to have.

The third requirement for the alchemy program is a <u>capacity to hold</u>. It is the concept of retainership, without which we cannot contain alchemy. Seems easy, right? Everyone likes to hold their creations. The tricky part is that what we hold we are fully responsible for. While that energy is in our care, we have to keep it in existence by feeding it: our own energy maintains the charge we are holding. So if you are stressed and overwhelmed, you are unable to hold. How often are we stressed? Right...

Bringing together these three capacities—to change, to have and to hold—sets up the proper alignment for the alchemy of acquisition.

An inability to manifest what we want often occurs because of the split between emotional desire and conceptual possibility. If you want something really bad, but your conceptual level does not encompass the possibility of you attracting/having it, your wish will not result in fulfilling alchemy. Or you want something, but do not really want to be responsible for it (like wanting lots of money, but not wanting to deal with investments), you might be able to acquire money, but not hold onto it. Or perhaps what you desire will require you to change, to become a different type of person, and you want the result but do not want to go through the change. No alchemy is possible there. Knowing your stumbling blocks to acquisition is the first step in clearing them. When the emotional desire and conceptual possibilities are balanced, the intent to manifest can properly anchor, resulting in active alchemy.

The conceptual possibility for alchemy depends on your personal history, not just on your upbringing, but on other lifetime patterns, karma etcetera. But becoming conscious about it can help you override some old, unnecessary components and build new, balanced beliefs. If you accept the possibility of acquiring something, this acceptance changes you. The willingness to change amplifies acquisition, so if you want something, look at how getting it will change you and see if you are okay with that change. The emotional desire for the acquisition of something cannot be based on need. If you want something because of not-enoughness of it, it will not manifest. Emotional desire has to be based on <u>excitement</u> about what you want and <u>curiosity</u> about how you are going to get it, not neediness. Just like with any manifestation or materialization, the desire for acquisition has to be <u>constant</u> over a certain period of time. You cannot wobble your desire and expect alchemy to occur! We often wobble when what we want does not happen right away—we start doubting our ability to make it happen. This doubt is what breaks the alchemy of acquisition into pieces, mutating the process in such a way that instead of the desired 'stuff', we acquire self-punishment and self-judgment. The third component of emotional desire is the energy of deserving. If you do not feel that you deserve what you desire, you cannot activate alchemy. The emotional energy of <u>deserving</u> is similar to <u>allowing</u>, because you have to allow what you desire to come to you (if you desire a great relationship, but do not feel you deserve it, the relationship will not happen because your system cannot allow it).

To summarize, there are three major components for alchemy on the conceptual level (*change, have* and *hold*) and three on the emotional level (*excitement/curiosity, constancy* and *deserving/allowing*), necessary for acquisition. If these three exist in each level and there is no split between the conceptual and emotional levels, desire pulls conceptual energy down into the emotional level and into the root chakra. This is the physical anchoring of an intent, bringing in results of alchemy into matter.

Lena wants to acquire a promotion at her job. She decides to apply her knowledge of alchemy to make it happen. Lena looks at the three conceptual components of her alchemy process. How will this promotion *change* her? She will have to work out of a different office that is further from her gym, which she likes to go to after work. She might have to stay later at work and definitely attend many meetings she does not need to go to now. Is she ok with that? Is there enough of Lena's own authority to give herself permission to *have* that promotion? Lena notices that she thinks of her father and how the news of her promotion will please him and her failure will upset him. Is she looking for his permission to have the promotion? Lena decides to try to not use the promotion as a means to prove to her father that she is capable. This helps her to amplify her internal authority and she consciously permits herself to have the promotion. Will she be able to *hold* her promotion? Lena will definitely gain more responsibilities with the promotion; can she be responsible with her responsibilities? Then Lena looks at the three components of her desire for that promotion. There is a part of her that feels she needs the promotion to prove to her father she is capable, she already found that piece. There is also a need to be safe and she feels that the extra money that the job will provide will take care of that. Lena needs to seriously look at these needs, clean them up and refocus on *excitement* about the possibility of promotion and *curiosity* about how it can happen. Even though a promotion might not come for couple of months, Lena has to make sure she holds her intention for it without wobble, which is much easier to do if needs are not attached to the desire! No doubt does not mean 'I have no doubt I will get the promotion', but more like 'I have no doubt that I truly desire this promotion and I can wait for it'. The *constancy* of Lena's intent will activate the alchemy. Lena feels she *deserves* this promotion, and so her emotional level can *allow* it. Now we wait... Tune in to find out what happens. Did Lena get her promotion? Was she able to clean up the imbalances blocking her acquisition?

One of the ways to check if your alchemical process is working, is to do this exercise (have a paper/pen ready nearby). Sit comfortably and relax, breathe deeply five times. Exercise your alchemical muscle by practicing turning one shape into another shape (imagine your field is a sphere, hold it in your consciousness, then turn it into a cube, as if you are sitting in a cube, then back to a sphere, etc.). Then focus on your vertical tube in the middle of your field and pulse energy up and down for a few minutes until it feels full and active. Envision what you desire (what you were working on manifesting) and experience it in your crown chakra on your seventh level; that is, see/feel the concept of your desire (car, relationship, job, health etc.) at the top of your head. Take a deep breath. Using your breath, pull this concept through the vertical tube down into the hip area and hold it there. You will feel more emotions about what you are envisioning. Practice holding this desired 'thing' in and around your pelvis, while processing what comes up. If your alchemy is working, you will feel an emotional resolve, excitement, curiosity, things like that. If there are blocks to your acquiring what you envisioned, you might feel fear, anger, overwhelm, neediness, being in trouble, confusion etcetera. Track what you are feeling as if there is a separate part of you feeling it, witness the emotions. Take a breath, breathe out and write down what you have experienced.

When you are intending to acquire something through alchemy, use this exercise to see how you are doing, and work with and process unresolved issues in three conceptual and three emotional components. You can also use conceptual symbols to help you. A conceptual symbol is an energy program with a particular ability. If you apply it properly, it realigns patterns in your system (like a computer plug-in for animations, which, if it is installed, allows you to play the animations). You can even connect the use of symbols to the previous exercise (which, by the way, you can do many times to check up on your progress). In the last part, when you pull your envisioned desire into the hip area and hold it there, tune into an appropriate symbol and it will charge what you are holding.

A sphere is the conceptual symbol for support, containment and abundance.

A six-pointed star is the symbol for finding personal truth, balance and for bringing into a current situation support from similar situations in other lives (using learned positive karmic lessons).

A doorway is a portal, a symbol for short-cuts and direct/speedy solutions, but beware—use of this symbol also amplifies responsibility and the speed of personal processing as a 'side-effect', so use it appropriately.

A bridge is the conceptual symbol for connection, comprehension and support in by-passing mental rigid 'need to know' ('I cannot do this because I do not know how'), it helps in 'finding a way' to do something that our mental level was in the dark about.

A labyrinth symbolizes a treasure hunt, it amplifies inspiration and curiosity.

An upside-down vortex is another powerful symbol; it looks like a bell with energy circling into it and up (similar to a root chakra). It is the support for being in matter (like when you can envision something so clearly that you can almost taste it, but it does not materialize physically, there is not enough anchor in matter). This symbol also attracts helpful circumstances (for that purpose, use it with red color frequency).

There is also something to be said about the language you can use when intending through words. I am, I have, I know, I can, I choose, I claim—these are appropriate beginnings for worded intents. When we say something like 'I want...' it does not register enough throughout the field, only on the emotional level.

When you think of money, you might imagine gold coins or dollar bills, but money is an emotional energy. It is orange in color, thick, and it is supposed to flow smoothly. Our fears and expectations break this smooth flow, making it jagged and fragmented, or stops it altogether.

The universal law of giving and receiving is 50/50: as much as you give you *will* receive. This might not seem right, because usually we do not see the 'come back' from the same source we gave to. When you truly care about something and share your heart energy, you will receive this energy back in the same amount. But that energy might be perceived differently depending on what you attract. If you are trying to simplify your life and end up giving away a huge load of stuff to friends and charities, it will not make sense for your Soul to then attract this energy back in the form of similar stuff to the things you just got rid of! But maybe you are looking for a promotion or a cheaper way to travel for your vacation. The energy of the stuff you gave away with the open heart might come to you as a recommendation for promotion or a friend's advice on how to get, almost for free, the vacation that you want.

We break this balance of 50/50 when we go into not-enoughness. This is because Universal laws are always abundance-based, it cannot be otherwise, since abundance is a way of existence for the entire Universe, while scarcity is one of our inventions, based on separation. The 50/50 law is a mutual exchange process between the frequencies. We perceive these frequencies according to our level of consciousness and participation in abundance. Not-enoughness shows up in many different ways, but if you know how you personally sabotage abundance, you can fix it.

This is how we step out of abundance and diminish our money flow:

1. Mistrust is one of the ways we step out of abundance. Not trusting the Universe/God, we tend to look for the proof first. The 50/50 law is real and will present itself again and again, but trust is an integral component of its presentation. This type of trust is connected to seeing yourself as a part of everything, not as a separate piece.

2. We also sabotage abundance by expectations based on erroneous assumptions. Expectations are always rooted in the ego's overt or covert desire to win. When we project our authority onto someone else, we become a child and make the other person a parent. Then we attempt to do right by the parent's rules and expect abundance to come as a

reward. Abundance cannot be a reward, it just is; rewards are separation-based concepts. Disappointments like 'I worked my butt off at my job, why didn't I get that raise!?', 'But I did everything right, so why did my car break down again?', 'I worked on my emotional issues, why then did I get a cold?' are good examples. Notice if you run into these a lot, and every time you do, refocus your system like this: 'My doing it 'right' has nothing to do with me receiving what I want; I did what I did with an open heart, now I receive what comes to me with an open heart'. This will help to reprogram you into abundance.

3. The energy of <u>entitlement</u> is similar to the examples we looked at, only the reward is demanded: 'I deserve this, I suffered enough for it!', or 'I donate to charities and so you have to treat me with respect!', or 'I am your relative, you have to help me!' etcetera. Everything a person with an entitlement issue has done is seen as a pre-payment, which in turn guarantees him a reward ('you owe me because of what I did'). Kind of like if you pre-pay your trip in full, you might receive a discount or other incentive. Knowing about the incentive might have been a reason for your pre-payment. If you arrive at the hotel and do not get what you believe you are supposed to get, you will be upset. Entitlement energy, if the expectation is not fulfilled, usually leads to an emotional and astral explosion. A person did not like doing what he was doing in the first place (hence building and suppressing his fire as frustration/anger) but he did it anyway for the reward, and when the reward does not happen, all the compressed fire comes out and explodes. But entitlement does not have to look so dramatic. We often play with it in much smaller ways. A demand for anything based on the pain we experienced is the most common ('I waited for 15 minutes in line, so now you will listen to me!).

4. Another common way for one to sabotage abundance is with an overly strong desire for <u>control</u>. Instead of allowing giving/receiving to work its magic, we want to predict how it will happen to us. We give, but also plan on how, when and what we think we should receive. Since our mind cannot see the entire puzzle of life, we end up actually falling out of it due to controlling tactics (a little puzzle piece that fell off the table cannot participate in the big picture anymore). The ego over-focuses on the achievement of set goals in hopes of winning control.

When you want to do everything yourself, it is also a form of control. Life does not get a chance to give you anything if you are resolved to do it all on your own. Notice if control is your issue and see how in your life it connects to disappointments with abundance. To correct it, pay attention to the moment of desire for gripping control, breathe and let go into curiosity.

5. Not feeling that you are <u>worthy</u> of receiving is another form of sabotage. You receive what you give, pretty much, so if you give out positive, you will be given positive. When we refuse to receive positive universal energies, we reject the God within. So instead of seeing abundance as something that comes to you for 'good behavior', look at it as a 'divine right'. You are not entitled to it, you *are* it; abundance is not separate from us. If the second chakra is scarce on self-love, it will have difficulty receiving other universal energies also. If you find that you do not seem to receive (the 'return button' on your 50/50 isn't working), investigate self-love issues triggered in that moment. Notice how in situations when you feel good about yourself (your second chakra is full and open) you get back from life, while when you judge yourself, life is unable to give to you. Your Soul is interested in imperfections (why, otherwise, would it put you on Earth?!), meaning that all the things you judge yourself for have value. By rejecting their value you rob yourself of self-love and with it, abundance.

6. <u>Past-referencing</u> is the most favorite human sabotage! That is because we forgot how to use our higher mind and instead base all our memory files in the physical brain. This brain of ours is not designed to deal with the intricacies of multi-dimensional life, but only with survival. Our animal side looks to past events to predict the future. Since we are so much more than just physical brain memory, the rest of us 'bleeds through'; that is, our brain receives all sorts of messages not just from physical stimuli, but from the rest of our energy field. Since lots of other lifetime files (positive and negative karma) are accessible by our field all the time, the brain receives these messages too, but cannot process/comprehend them. Sometimes it ignores them, other times it plugs them into reality as if they were physical messages, it gets confused. So if you did something and it ended badly and then you face a similar situation, your brain will read the old file and tell you 'abun-

dance is not possible here'. What if what you are facing now is similar to another life's story, even though in this life you never dealt with anything like it? If your energy field has access to that other example and your brain decides to 'plug it in' instead of rejecting it, depending on the past experience you will get 'yes' or 'no' for abundance. But because it is from another lifetime file, your ego will not know what to do with it. The message will be more like a premonition of something bad or an intuitive knowing about something good coming to you. Either way it is past-referenced, hence it is limited. So I would suggest that if you desire to manifest something through alchemy or simply wanting your 'luck to turn' in life in general, every time you begin to worry tell yourself *'Today is a new lifetime, everything is possible!'* This code frees you up from past-referencing and allows abundance to exist in your field.

7. <u>Time displacement</u> disperses abundance. If you are too far ahead of yourself, chasing some goal, you cannot receive what is in the present moment. Fear of pain propels us ahead in the hope of gaining knowledge. We tend to think that if we know what and how something will happen, we can avoid pain. The stronger the fear, the further ahead we project ourselves. This fear of pain can look like fear of disappointment, fear of embarrassment, fear of losing, fear of being laughed at, etcetera. Look for these signs in your own Self. Time displacement also works backwards. If you are afraid to face what is happening now, preferring your earlier position in life, your energy on the eighth level connects to that 'past you', energetically sending your whole Self away from the present. Notice how many people begin to act like little children, even throw tantrums, when they are faced with having to be responsible? You would think, how does this behavior affect abundance?! But it does, because not being present is a not-enoughness of the Self. Time displacements can also take other directions, like an escape into a fantasy for example. Many people do that one way or the other, with movies, books, daydreaming, sleeping a lot, over-exercising, drinking to much alcohol to numb out, over-working at the job, drugs, gambling, religious activities without having consciousness behind the events, and so on. We all do it sometimes, but for certain people these escapes turn into addictions. Getting addicted to a made-up stimulation (physical,

228

emotional, mental, astral, even spiritual) is a way to lower your abundance connection, including diminishing your money flow.

Money is an alive, real energy and above all it has to be respected. We mentally presume money can be calculated as if it is a 'thing'. Money has a spirit; she is a very bright orange fiery tiger-like creature. It can be in many places at once and it does not subscribe to our laws of physics. The Money Tigress can come to live with you or not, depending how you treat her. She can be your enemy, showing up only to devour your life force and amplify the fear, or she can be a friend that is curious about you as much as you are about her. Curiosity is the only healthy way to relate to the Money Tigress. No one can make her stay, no one can ever own her. Imagine if you had a real live tiger in your house, living with you. How would you deal with it? You might tell it nice words, but you will watch where it is all the time and watch your behavior so as not to upset or anger it, right? You would respect its nature, take care of it, perhaps study it with curiosity. Money is the same as a wild tiger living in your personal space. The Money Tigress grants you her presence. She can come often, even move in for the rest of your life, but due to her own decision, not yours. The Money Tigress commands respect, she does not tolerate familiarity, leaving immediately (which is the reason why when someone becomes arrogant through money, the money tends to disappear or the person dies). If someone is addicted to money, it is like a love affair gone bad, the energy field is ripped apart and life force leaks out.

It is not true that 'good people are supposed to get money'. People respecting the Tigress get the money. A criminal might steal millions, but what happens after the theft depends on his relationship with the Tigress. If this criminal respects her, he might end up getting away and chilling on the beach in Bahamas. If there is a problem with their relationship, he either will be caught or get away, but lose all the money. No one 'gets away' with anything, universal law does not work that way. A socially accepted 'good person' who gives/donates a lot, by universal law might be over-giving, refusing to receive due to low self-worth. She will not have a good relationship with the Money Tigress, hence attracting 'bad money circumstances'. On the other hand, a loan shark might be socially considered a 'bad person', but having respect for money, he prospers. Since universal law always wins over human laws, investigate your true reasons for difficulties with money.

Just like any other living creature the Money Tigress requires food. Our responsibility and attention to money is her food. If you ignore paying your bills, for example, you are not feeding your Money Tigress, and if she starves, she can either leave (loss of money, debt, bankruptcy) or die (dead money). The dead money energy is an inactive irrelevant to life money. In other words, money energy has to be active to be alive, so if you have money hidden but terrified to invest it or spend some of it, the energy dies, your Tigress is starving and suffering. Money is not meant to be hoarded, it then becomes irrelevant to the Soul lessons and inapplicable to the growth of your personality. Money energy is the same color as pleasure, it is meant to be enjoyed. This does not mean you have to spend everything you've got, that is another extreme devoid of respect for the Money Tigress.

If you somehow seem to always attract the money necessary for your life, but it is barely enough, always on the edge, it is a sign of mistrust of the Money Tigress. This means your relationship with her is built on the intuitive knowing that she will not completely abandon you, but belief that she will not stay either (usually a low self-worth issue). Suggested behavior here is to apply gratitude. If, when paying your bills, instead of fear that you are 'spending all your money', you are grateful for having the money to pay the bills, you attract the interest of the Money Tigress and she in turn will help you to attract more than is necessary for survival.

If your spending outweighs your available money, you create debt. An irresponsible debt is one of the highest signs of disrespect to the Tigress and she gets very angry about it. There is such a thing as a 'responsible debt'—that is the use of strategy with money. If you need a car and you buy it on credit, it is a responsible debt if it is proportional to your means. Or if you are working at your dream job, but it is in a new place, an expensive city, and your salary barely covers your rent, you might have to put your food and other basic expenses on your credit card, but it is a proper strategy if you know that this job is your ticket up and that if you only survive this year, next year you will be able to make much more money and pay off all the credit debt. Irresponsible debt is entitlement and arrogance based. If you have debt, review it to make sure you are not insulting your Money Tigress. If you find that your debt is not proportional to your means, investigate the reasons. A single mother with two kids trying to survive working two jobs might acquire debt, but it is not irresponsible debt. Even though she might not have the means to pay it off right then, she is not insulting the Tigress. If this person knows her worth and is respectful of the Tigress, money will flow to her and she will attract help. On the other hand, a family of two young adults without children living in a house they can barely afford and driving two luxury cars they cannot afford at all, have a huge amount of irresponsible debt, which insults the Tigress. Their debt is image-based, their egos were after the lifestyle for the looks of it, for prestige. Because the Money Tigress is disrespected, she will release her fire against them, creating either some volatile explosion about money or even relationship problems. If you desire more money inflow, but have not paid up something you owe, it might be preventing energy from coming in. For example, if you did not pay your taxes or a hospital bill, or return debt to a friend, your money flow might be blocked. And not having the money is not an excuse because the Money Tigress is interested in your respect, not your actual money. If you respect your commitments and face them (like set up a payment plan of $20 per month maybe?) she will help you to generate the money for it. Always be honest with the reasons you have debt, look beyond the surface things like 'I needed to go on vacations, it is not my fault I do not make enough money!'(pride), or 'Medical care should not cost so much, I don't have to pay that!' (entitlement), or 'All the kids have these new things every year, so naturally I had to get the same for my kids' (need to fit in), etcetera. Work with what you find and 'talk' to your Money Tigress. Because she is an emotional creature, reestablishing dialog builds the bridge between your emotional level and money options. *Money is shared universal pleasure and love!*

CHAPTER 5
Earth

CHAPTER 5

The Live Earth and Other Planets

E arth is not just a dead rock in space with chemicals on it to make 'life' possible. It is a living, breathing and conscious entity. Just as we human beings have a Soul, an energy field and a physical body, so too, does Earth. The host of Earth is called Gaia, Tara and many other names depending on the tradition. Gaia is a magnificent being that incarnated into the physical body of our planet, she has a Soul like all beings, an energy field, chakras, etcetera. Her energy field extends well beyond the physical planetary atmosphere. The physical body of Earth is the planet itself. As long as we are on the planet, we are connected to Earth's intention for evolution. The full expression of our life task is always interwoven with Earth's energy fields.

The energy field of Earth looks very similar to ours, only rounder and much bigger. A huge tube in the middle actively circulates energy, and this tube is connected to the north and south magnetic poles, which are the crown and the root chakras of the planet. You connect your root chakra to the planet in order to anchor your being, what does Earth connect her root chakra to? Earth's root chakra connects to the Sun's energy, since the Sun is the anchor for the system our planet lives in. The crown chakra of Earth connects to the higher frequencies of the Universe, just like our human crown chakra. The physical location of the magnetic poles is different from the physical poles themselves—magnetic poles are energy vortexes, while physical poles are positions in space. The location of the magnetic poles has changed many times in Earth's history, but their current positions are very close to the physical poles. The vertical tube inside the planet is a gigantic transmitter of energy. Through the polar chakras (crown and root) Earth sucks in cosmic energy and then radiates it out into specific levels of etheric grid-like blueprints for all life forms, into minerals, plants, animals, emotions, thought forms, archetypes and geometries. We humans receive Earth's energy as nurturance and radiate it back to her as gratitude. The planet welcomes this energy back from us and broadcasts it out into the Universe (as self expression) and into our Sun (as a record). The more efficient this flow, the more connected and grounded we are. This exchange of energy anchors our human auric system in the third dimension, allowing us the experience of belonging in our matter vehicle—the physical body. Yes, that is right, without planetary energy acceptance (nurturance) and without the reflection of gratitude (focused presence in matter) we end up feeling like we do not belong here, and suffering from a perceived separation. Earth's exchange of energy with us and with the whole Universe is designed as a support system for our matter vehicle, as a help for the health and balance of the physical body (which in turn properly aligns the rest of our energy system).

We have looked before at external reality being a mirror, helping us understand the internal reality of ourselves. Earth is one more layer of this mirror, a huge classroom for us to learn in. All of us incarnated on Earth today are the same 'us' who created the classroom! Soul energy can divide, sometimes incarnating into one form, other times into many forms at once. All the same Souls are still playing here, in the third dimensional classroom of our planet. We are our own teachers. We are our own ancient masters, the ones who created amazing civilizations and left records for ourselves to find later on the linear timeline. The planetary classroom has many books and experiments, lots of learning material, it is up to us to read a chosen book through to the end, or to keep returning every day to the same page over and over, afraid to finally turn it. We collectively set up experiments (civilizations, social trends, religious beliefs, etc.); go through them; learn;

and move on to the next one. Earth's cities, civilizations, climatic zones and weather patterns all contribute information to the understanding of our life purpose and facilitate enlightment.

The classroom we call Earth is very unique for it is based on diversity, not unification. This does not mean that we are incapable of unity of course, but that *we are evolving into unity through diversity!* We have free will here, the amazing ability to choose for ourselves if we only claim our right to it by not rejecting our power! The classroom of Earth is designed with diversity as its integral component, this is why we are not all happily playing, singing and holding hands... We all know each other, every single human on the planet is connected to every other human on the Soul level, *we all are equal.* But we agreed to 'play rough' with each other in order to experience more of reality through the mirror of circumstances; we agreed to have lifetimes of high consciousness and lifetimes of very low awareness. Even though overall Earth travels up and down Spirals of Consciousness just like the rest of the Universe, we humans have a very wide range of consciousness on the planet in any given moment. That is what makes this place seem so screwed up, since we still murder each other, still kill other living beings, destroy nature, do harm. This diversity is not some cosmic mistake, but a part of the design of our classroom. We make agreements with each other before incarnating for support in clearing particular karma and to experience something that we had not experienced before. This Earth place in the Universe is a classroom for accelerated learning—Souls learn much faster by having diverse experiences. Here we not only have diverse experiences, but also very extreme ones; the intensity of our classroom is another unique attribute of Earth. By entering this extreme intensity of diversified consciousness your Soul creates a shortcut to the recognition of reality in the mirror of circumstances, expanding its unique identity. This benefits the entire Universe, for there are millions of nonphysical energy beings witnessing our journey on Earth! We *are* the masters, we *are* the enlightened ones who placed their enlightenment aside in order to serve the rest of the Universe by bravely entering the classroom of Earth as a new student, and not as a master. We are already enlightened, already everything we think we want to become. But we never knew before how it all worked, we just *were* it.

And so we play, learn, advance and often scare ourselves to death here in our classroom in order to comprehend our already existing enlightenment!

Now let's look at the details of the classroom design so we can fully appreciate our own creation and the magnificence of Earth. Every level of the planetary energy field consists of a particular combination of energies. You can use the understanding of consciousness from these levels as an aid in self clearing and in assisting Earth in clearing and balancing herself. By studying the classroom of Earth you gain a conscious map to the exploration of yourself and knowledge of what to focus on for a particular result. In other words, you gain a shortcut through precision instead of having to search blindly.

The first, etheric level of the planet consists of the energies of minerals, plants (from the past and present), crystals and bacteria. This is a path into the mystery school of Nature. The etheric level often gets overlooked by people interested in energy; nevertheless it is a very important component to understand. Considering its proximity to the physical level, it is the slowest level of the energy field, the first planetary energy level that can be explored and used for self healing. It has a very precise practical application if used correctly. When we connect to the energy emanating from minerals, metals and crystals, we are connecting to the etheric level of the planet. Take an iron pan in your hands—you will feel much heavier and stronger. That is because the energy of iron is very grounding, it resonates with Earth's molten iron core. When you are synchronized with iron (which happens when you are simply present with something made of iron, holding it in your hands intensifies the effect) your etheric level gains strength and the root chakra tends to open up and starts taking in energy from the planet more actively. If you are dealing with a bacterial infection, you can tune into the planetary etheric level, which will help to balance the bacteria consciousness on the etheric level, allowing your physical body to recover more quickly. Certain plants are not as powerful as they once were. When we take herbal and mineral supplements, we can tune into the greenery of the planet, asking it to amplify the supplements we are taking. The etheric level of the supplements then will get more potency from the most balanced form of this plant or mineral that ever was in Earth's history.

The second, emotional planetary level supports people's and animal's emotions, and the existence of many nonphysical beings like fairies and elves. The planetary emotional level is teeming with life. We cannot see most of it with our physical eyes because the vibration is too fast for our vision to catch. But we can consciously interact with these beings and look for the results. The effects of these interactions are all around us, we just need to pay attention. If your emotional level is thin and undercharged (a person like that would feel an absence of joy in his/her life, dissatisfaction, inability to feel pleasure, depression) you can connect through the planetary second level to an animal—to mirror at you planetary energies of fulfillment, joy and pleasure. You can also employ planetary emotional level energies to help you increase feelings of abundance in your life, which in turn attract necessary opportunities, connections, circumstances and money to you. How do you do that? Connect to your own emotional level (we looked at how to do that in the first chapter) and then intend to synchronize yourself with the planetary emotional level; hold your intent and you will begin to feel 'much bigger' than yourself; this is the time to intend for abundance in your life (make sure it is not out of fear or scarcity but out of desire and curiosity). Your intent will be broadcasted through the planetary emotional level and begin to attract abundance to you. When your second chakra is not working well (you feel like you are 'not good enough', maybe you feel guilt or shame), correct this by tuning into the fullness of the planetary emotional level—Earth is always abundant! If you are a gardener or a farmer, this is the level for you to play with! Most of the second level nonphysical beings would be happy to help you grow healthy and vibrant flowers, fruits, vegetables, trees and so on. Most of these beings like different offerings, a form of a payment for their help. I found that fairies enjoy apples the most, although other fruit is fine; elves like dark chocolate, while goblins and dwarfs prefer crystals. How do you offer an apple to a fairy? Place a healthy organic apple or two either somewhere in your garden, or even on the table inside your house (nonphysical beings will come in for it, considering your intent to be an invitation) and leave it there until you notice it begins to rot (the fairies are eating the energy of an apple). Never eat these fruits, instead let them fertilize the Earth in your garden once fairies are done with it. Don't overfeed the elves, they only need very small pieces of the dark chocolate, an inch by inch square of dark chocolate will last them about two weeks. You can support a whole community of dwarfs or goblins by placing a crystal in your garden. Crystals and other stones that you might have in your possession sometimes need to be cleaned. You can place them under the sunlight for a day, moonlight for a night, wrap them in sea salt for two to three hours or just ask fairies (who do not eat crystalline energy) to assist you in clearing the crystals.

The third planetary energy level consists of the thought patterns of all the beings living on Earth, including Earth herself. When we think of something or someone, our human thoughts are projected into the third level, it is a very fast communication network not dissimilar to the Internet. This level can help with memory. Even though memory exists on all the levels, the third and the first are the most important for physical linear memory. So if you have difficulty remembering things, you can tune into the planetary third level by thinking, just repeating the words 'better memory', they will resonate with the planetary energy, amplifying your memory (I realize it sounds silly, but your intent in resonance with the planet works miracles!). Since in American culture the mental level is the strongest, we tend to relate to a lot of things through thinking, even language itself requires thinking. You can use this to your advantage, because whatever you intend for, if you repeat the thought again and again, gets encoded into the planetary third level energies, eventually attracting similar energy to you. This is why *what we think directly affects our life.* This doesn't mean we always have to think positive thoughts. Negative thoughts are also necessary since we live in a dualistic reality, but they can be used consciously or unconsciously. In order to process some buried, unconsciousness feeling (like childhood trauma for example), we have to use our mind to label these painful feelings (like 'I am not good enough' or 'I hate my mother'). This is conscious, beneficial use of the mental energy. The problems arise when we use the thoughts unconsciously. We automatically, habitually repeat phrases like 'I don't know', 'I can't do that', 'it's always my fault', etcetera. These thoughts trap you in the unconsciousness and victimization of the Self. You can learn to stay aware of these habitual thoughts, so that not only will you be able to clear up your own energy field's disempowering patterns, but you will also stop polluting the third planetary level.

The fourth planetary energy level, the astral level, is a very unusual, magical place. It is not a location per se, but a vibrational range, just like our human astral level. Because of the diversity of our classroom the planetary astral level is very extreme, it holds the energies of people's feelings—positive feelings and the feelings of all the arguments and wars. It is also densely populated by an entire community of astral nonphysical beings. The astral level is a very potent realm of intense feelings like love, passion, compassion, hatred, envy, fear. The archetypes themselves are held in the seventh level, but the feelings and images of these archetypes are supported by the astral level. In other words, the archetypes (concepts) are fed by astral energy (stories). Depending on the type of archetype (of a warrior-hero, mother-nurturer, angel-protector, demon-possessor, etc.) it will be supported by the higher or lower energies of the planetary astral level. One of the particularly intriguing 'tools' we humans stuck into our classroom is the archetype of the devil, which is constantly fed by the negative feeling energy that was disowned by people and dumped into the planetary astral level. The devil (the 'evil twin' of God consciousness) as such does not exist, it is not a being, although many nonphysical beings, some with questionable intentions, did play into the archetype. It is an image, a mass of disowned energy clumped up together and 'it' believes that it is real. Evil is our own invention, it is not an actual type of energy charge in the Universe. Some very potent astral energies are destructive, but their potency is fueled from pure Universal life force so that when we feel the Source energy behind the destruction, we label it evil (the opposite to Source). This is because we do not see the entire plan but we witness the destruction, and assume that the Source can only create and never destroy, which is a misconception.

The astral level is the level of connections. It is supposed to anchor the higher vibrations of unconditional love and translate them into frequencies (gradations) of love that are more digestible for us. But because for so long we have been irresponsible with our negative feelings, disowning them and throwing them away from us, over time the planetary astral level became clogged and very little love energy could come through. We decided we are 'only good, only light', and pushed away our 'badness and darkness'. We forgot that we are human, which is by definition imperfect, we live in a duality of good and bad, light and dark, which we will eventually transcend into Unity. The 'bad and dark' has to be honored as much as the 'good and light' and it is our responsibility to know our dark side and then act from the light side. We went through the 'dark ages of the soul', forgot who we actually are and only now have begun to remember; the planetary astral level is finally clearing up. Everything that is projected onto it is our disowned power. This power has no place in the planetary systems, it *has* to be returned to us. Earth is doing just that—she is releasing more and more of that stored energy back to us. How does that work? The planetary consciousness scans for the Soul whose incarnation generated the rejected astral energy, finds the existing representative of that Soul (you) and releases your (perhaps from other incarnations) rejected energy back to you. It might seem difficult or even cruel that we now have to receive some astral fear, or pain, or madness that our personality had nothing to do with, since the rejected energy is from the many other lifetimes our Soul had on Earth, and often not the current one. But even though it is a difficult process to go through, it is also an incredible opportunity to receive power you otherwise would have no access to! By allowing yourself to not get scared when the planetary astral energy is coming your way, you receive, process and integrate the power of other incarnations into your present Self! That is a component of an amazing design of our Earth's classroom that we all came up with a long time ago! A self-correcting system in which Earth allows us to grow at the pace we are most comfortable with, reject the energy we cannot deal with so she can store it for us, but then, when we are stronger, get everything we thought was lost given back to us to excavate our power from. The time for the return of power is *now!* We live in an incredible age and all of us are very special to be chosen to experience this event in Universal history.

But how do you receive this past-rejected energy? Notice how lately more often than not you feel frustrated or scared, or sad, for no logical reason? Or something in you gets triggered (you begin thinking about some upsetting situation from the past) without any visible circumstance that seemingly triggered the memory? It is because the astral planetary energy has come in contact with your field and, if it holds your past-rejected energy, it is synchronized with your own astral level, and so it enters and asks to be processed. Let's say, over many lifetimes, your Soul's other incarnation personalities rejected lots of astral fear. This fear energy is now returning to you. Since fear is an unenlightened energy that is made of your original power, if it is integrated and transmuted it will add to your personal power. But when it comes in contact with your field, you will feel the fear, no power yet, right? If we allow this planetary returned energy to be felt without giving it a story (like feeling the fear as an animal feels it instead of associating that fear with a phone conversation, for example) we shortcut to its integration and transmutation, adding to our power. But the returned energy often triggers in us energies similar to it (returning astral fear might trigger other unprocessed fears in your energy field). That is not a 'bad thing', because again this component of Earth's classroom design adds to our ability to shortcut through the junk straight to the core of any issue. How? One resists processing their anger, for example, hides it, suppresses it. Then one receives past-rejected astral energy, which also happens to be anger. Of course, that returning anger will trigger the current suppressed anger. If this person persists in attempts to suppress anger, he will have a difficult time and void the opportunity to integrate more Self power. On the other hand, if that person allows himself to change, to feel the anger and to figure out a different approach to that type of energy (instead of suppression), he will not only get the benefit of integrating the power of past-rejected energy, but will also clean up many karmic patterns about anger from the current lifetime ('bonus'). And do not worry, you only get what you can process, never more, that is a preset fail-safe of our classroom! In addition to this brilliant fail-safe, we have another one: we only have to deal with/process/integrate/transmute our own energy (or what your Soul dealt with in other incarnations), never someone else's. It is arrogant and sacrificial to assume that you can clean up someone else's pain or fear, because if that were possible, that action would rob them of an opportunity to learn their lesson and to receive their power.

It is very important for the evolution of humankind to learn to feel responsibly. It is not 'bad' to hate something or be afraid of something, or feel jealous, angry, cruel. We have to learn to hate well, to rage well, to fear well. There is a pure life force behind everything. For example, the scale of Fire element spinning out negatively is:

pure life force → vitality → mild annoyance →
frustration → anger → hatred → rage

Hating well or raging well means freely sliding back and forth on that scale, so that pure life force is felt behind the rage. This purifies the hatred or rage, erasing the unnecessary astral 'story' and leading straight to the lesson. That type of processing of hatred or rage is well contained, does not harm others and is self responsible. If we own our feelings, do not reject them (i.e., do not project them out due to messy stories, dumping them into the planetary astral level), we can stop being afraid of our own feelings. We can work with them, balance them in love, clear them, integrate them, transmute them into their original purity, learn what they are teaching us.

The nonphysical energy beings of the planetary astral level are very diverse. There are beings that look like animals or dragons, some have shapes unseen in nature, and there are even human looking beings (which are not 'dead people' but beings who chose to take that shape, they are not actually human). Astral beings can be friendly or not, and have good intentions or their own agenda. If you choose to interact with the planetary astral beings, look at it as if you are interacting with people: you will naturally trust some and fear others, you will look for particular signs to find out if you want to build a relationship with that person or not. Apply your human interaction skills to your communications with astral beings. Because the astral level is in duality, astral beings need to be 'paid' for their services, meaning an exchange of energy is necessary. If you make friends with a higher astral being and it helps to keep your house free of lower astral beings for example (not unlike a watch dog), you have to give it something in return (a conscious interaction with you, which is fun for the astral being, might be a good form of payment!) Remember to always honor these beings, even if you choose to not interact with them because for some reason you do not like them. There are no 'bad beings', just like there are no 'bad people', just confused, or scared, or simply unenlightened ones.

The fifth planetary energy level looks so unusual that it is difficult for our minds to imagine. There are no regular shapes as we would normally see and the planet does not have trees, mountains, animals, etcetera, but is a round grid-like structure. What is usually light planetary space is instead blue, and it is cut through by many lines of 'nothing', a transparent energy. When the planet is balanced, the blue is very bright and the lines feel alive, with energy running through a complex web of them. But since our planet has been in a polluted state for a while, the fifth level looks washed out and gray in places instead of blue, and some of the lines form very tight, nut-looking black webbing. The fifth planetary level consists of the information about the planet, its visitors, and us, humans. It is also the level of many truths: Earth's truth about her journey and our truths (each of us has a different truth, even tribes, countries have their own truths, and they are not necessarily all the same). Some of them are in alignment with the Soul's energy and actually are truths; others are in alignment with fear and only perceived to be the truth. But the perception and belief in these 'truths' can be very strong, strong enough to have wars over and to kill and die for. The fifth level does not have any feelings, only the patterns of truth, plans, information.

We can visit it to find out more about our own truth perception, what in us is aligned with the Soul and what with fear. In order to connect to the fifth level you can ask yourself to finish mini-sentences like 'women are.....', 'men are......', 'I am always....', 'I will never.......', 'life is.....', 'I hate people who....', etcetera. These truths are connected to the ego that is afraid. When we recognize that, we can start correcting our perception of truth with more Soul energy, which also aligns us to Earth's truth. For example, if your habitual way of perceiving the truth about people is, 'people are untrustworthy', you can recognize that this belief is supported by a social, fear-based truth. Then look into your own real truth, the one in alignment with your Soul, and notice what comes up to balance the other statement, perhaps something like: 'People are different'.

When you need information about something, you can tune into the fifth level for help. The planetary fifth level will then create an energy pathway for you to find the information you are looking for. For example, say you need more information on a particular product before purchasing it, but what you could find on the Web or through friends is not enough. You could tune into the planetary fifth level by expanding to the personal fifth level, finding your personal truth about the product (your opinions, what you want and why), then intending 'more info about the product' and broadcasting that intent into the planetary fifth level. This might lead to finding out that your coworker knows an expert on the product you are interested in. It attracted information because you put out a request for it. We can attract information in the form of books, people, places and experiences. I have had some of these 'the book-literally-fell-on-my-head-so-I-would-read-it' experiences myself. Also, if you are interested in receiving information about any species that ever lived on Earth, the planetary fifth level is the place. This includes not only prehistoric animals, but also ancient civilizations, tribal cultures, etcetera. You can intent to connect to the fifth planetary level in your meditation while requesting information on a particular memory of yours of culture or animals from the past. Your energy system will be downloaded not unlike a computer with the specified information. Then you can access it either by writing what comes to you in meditation, or visually if your third eye is open, or in dream states.

The sixth planetary energy level consists of the unconditional love frequency. Ideally, Earth's entire sixth level is flooded with love. But because of our previous unconscious behavior and Gaia's past journeying into the unconsciousness, Earth's sixth level has holes in it. These holes are the places where love is absent. The sixth level is a transitional step for unconditional love energy before it reaches the astral fourth level, where it gets translated into a more digestible energy for humans. Animals can take in unconditional love directly from the sixth level, while we humans have to grow up a little bit more to be able to easily do that. Because of the energy holes on the sixth level of our planet, the astral level gets less energy, hence we have fewer love vibrations for a while. Now Earth is healing herself, repairing these energy leaks. As she gets more love energy for herself, she can direct more of it for us. The nonphysical residents of the sixth level are angels that work with our planet. There are many types of angels, some work with people (the 'guardian angels'), some work with Gaia, others are visitors from other places in the Universe. Look for the information on how to connect to and work with angels in the 'energy beings' subchapter farther in the book.

The seventh planetary energy level holds concepts and archetypes. When we think linearly, we think in the third level, but when we think in non-literal conceptual terms, we use the energy of the seventh level. Concepts are an entire program, while linear thought is a small part of the program. To expand consciousness and get a higher point of view on any situation, we can tune into the seventh planetary level. Anything that occurs on the planet, including famine, wars, terrorism, has a human linear perspective based on limited consciousness, but it also has a larger system, a bigger program. When you feel horrified by current events, you can tune into the seventh level for a larger perspective, which allows you to balance the fear with love. For example, you saw a news broadcast about a recent earthquake and felt 'what a waste! So many innocent people died!' That is a linear perspective. If you expand to your own seventh energy level (the golden egg around you), and then match it to the planetary one (by holding both your own and planetary golden egg in your conscious awareness), you will see the bigger reason for the event—perhaps the planet needed to clean up arrogance and separation energy, so she created an earthquake in a highly populated area, and everyone living in the area signed up to go through the event so that other people on the planet could learn compassion and clean up separation and arrogance. Or, another example: a terrorist bomb went off in a crowded restaurant, killing the female terrorist herself and twelve other people, and your feelings were of fear, outrage and disbelief about the woman's actions. On the seventh planetary level you might find the rest of the story: the woman's brother and father were killed; her lover helped her to survive the emotional devastation but was also killed recently; she stood up for her feelings the only way she could; people who did not have an option from their Soul level to exit material reality left the restaurant just as the terrorist woman was walking in; each of the twelve killed had their own personal reason for exiting their incarnation; the entire act opened up bottled down emotions for people who witnessed it, relatives, friends, viewers, helping them to clean up unprocessed old feelings.

The seventh planetary level also is home to many nonphysical beings who work with Gaia. These are usually not our personal guides, but the ones who oversee and support planetary changes, and many are part of the team of Earth's personal guides. They also work with human evolutionary changes, facilitating our harmonious alignment with Earth and doing damage control for our destructive learning behavior (not dissimilar to when children set up to play pirates in the living room, destroying the furniture in the process). You can communicate with these beings if you are looking for answers, for the larger picture about some event on the planet or in your personal life.

The eighth planetary energy level holds time. As we talked about before, there are two types of time, linear and spherical. They coexist in our reality, even though we tend to perceive only linear time. On the eighth level time connections, intersections, distortions create an intricate web. Conscious interaction with this level can be useful when you are in need of a direction for small things like place for a vacation or business planning, or larger things like the direction of your life. When we are looking at options, we are connected to the eighth level of our energy field. If you feel like you have run out of options and are stuck, you can use the planetary eighth level to show you more possibilities. Simply intend to connect to the eighth level (through a clear mental thought) and ask: 'I do not know of any options that might work, please show me other possibilities that I might not be seeing on my own'. You will be given these options. This does not always happen consciously. Most of the time you might not 'know' anything different right there in the moment, but throughout the course of your day and dreaming at night you might come up with the 'aha!' you were looking for.

There is no such a thing as 'normal time'. There is mechanical time, which is chronological, measured by machines, and there is personal time, measured by our internal clock. If your internal clock is in tune with the flow of life force through your eighth energy level, you will never encounter a perceptional time distortion, like not enough time, or an overly slow flow of time. But if your perception of time is not based on the flow of life force, but is instead based on a made up idea of how it should be, there will be a discrepancy between the natural clock and the demanded time speed. This creates time anomalies and distortions, which can be corrected using the help of the eighth planetary level. If you are waiting for something and time is 'barely moving', it means that your personal time is off because you are processing some emotional stress. This makes your internal time feel 'off' in connection with planetary time (the flow of life force on the eighth planetary level). Tune into the eighth planetary level—you will notice that time will realign to 'normal'; you also might get the urge to do something you did not think of before, which will help you to apply the time available correctly. The 'not enough time' situation is very familiar to most of us. This occurs because of our attempt to stuff more electric energy into the natural flow of life force (which is electromagnetic). We try to ignore the balance of electric and magnetic in the flow of life, demand that our life accommodate more electric active energy and so create a time discrepancy. There is no such a thing as 'not enough time', but there is such a thing as an overly long to-do list based on an overactive mental level and emotional stress, not on the natural flow of life force. To correct the perception of not enough time, you can relax into the magnetic energy on the eighth level of your own field, then expand your awareness and connect to the planetary eighth level, holding both in your consciousness. The planetary eighth level will then rebalance the overabundant electric charge in your field and you will feel that all the time you need is available to you.

The ninth planetary energy level consists of crystalline energy and sacred geometry patterns in connection to our planet. It looks and feels like a giant snowflake around Earth, brilliant white and transparent at the same time. All balanced geometric patterns (equal-sided geometric figures) have their origin on the ninth level. Each geometric pattern consists of repetitions of a particular figure locked in a very intricate embrace, creating an amazing weave of a crystalline structure that supports the evolution of Earth and all creatures on and in it. A conceptual understanding of the seventh level is required to comprehend how geometric patterns change consciousness. Sacred geometry is one of the most natural forms of energy balancing and amplification. All of Earth's physical crystals get their energy through the sacred geometry of the ninth planetary level. Every crystal has an energy flowing through its matrices, and the purer the stone, the more it connects with the ninth planetary level and so its charge is stronger. This charge can be further amplified, which affects our physical body and energy system. If you are connected to the ninth planetary level and a crystal at the same time, you will end up clearing and charging that crystal. Why does that happen? Because when you hold a conscious bridge between yourself, a crystal and the planetary ninth level, the sacred geometry of that level and the geometry of the crystal synchronize, and that gives the crystal its power.

When you feel too 'all over the place', scattered and unable to focus, the ninth level of the planet can also help. The sacred geometric figures hold consciousness, so if you give yourself the figure of missing charge you will bring that charge into your field. For example, if you feel scared of invasion (emotional, astral or physical), your boundary is weak. Draw an imaginary circle on the floor around you and you will feel safer because it will connect 'small' you with 'big' planetary ninth level and amplify your boundary. If you feel wobbling and 'all over the place' emotionally, or feel like you are going to have a panic attack, your root chakra is limp and twisted, propelling you upwards out of your body. Draw an imaginary cube under your feet or, in case of an impending panic attack, imagine that you are in a huge strong cube and keep tracing the ridges and corners with your mind's eye. This will stabilize even the most freaked out root chakra!

These nine planetary levels have a direct influence on us humans. This third universal dimension has twelve levels, so there are also the tenth, eleventh and twelfth, but they are more Earth-to-Universe connections than Earth-to-humans. The tenth and twelfth planetary levels are similar in that they are fluid and hold lots of unconditional support for the planet. The eleventh level is like a library (you might know it by the term Akashic Records), it is an energy matrix that holds the memory for our planet and anything on and around it.

Earth has many vortexes (similar to chakras) on its surface. All vortexes explore different consciousnesses. Humans have many incarnations to do that exploration, we change bodies to change lives, but our planet doesn't change bodies for a long time because she can support many diverse consciousnesses at once. In the past, people were drawn to different areas of the planet to create new civilizations because of the energy emanating from there. These civilizations used the Earth's vortex energy in each particular location to fuel their unique expression of planetary life. Each major civilization drew upon the knowledge and quality of energy provided by the Earth vortex that it was built upon. The multiplicity of ideas, architecture, technologies, foods, religions and growth of all kinds of consciousness through past eras has brought us now to the point of challenge that calls us to unite as one global entity with many diverse experiences. Earth is ready to unify the knowledge she has received, hence we are unifying our cultures. But Earth does not erase the knowledge, she integrates it. We used to believe that when we unify, we erase cultural identity and merge the 'weaker' culture with the 'stronger' one. But now Earth is challenging us to unite without erasing anything. We can do this only by honoring each other.

Humans often tend to think that if they are drawn to a particular geographic location, it means s/he should visit or move there. That is not always true. Because every location holds a certain type of energy, experiencing this energy can help us move on to the next step of personal evolution. Why are we drawn to different places? There are two main reasons: karmic and current. A karmic reason means that we experienced something in that location in another lifetime and to resolve or integrate something from that life we have to connect to the vortex of that geographic location. A current reason means that there is an encodement on your life's contract to activate something in your consciousness by connecting to a particular location. The karmic reason does not require your physical presence in the geographic location (although depending on the strength of the draw, it might be very beneficial), but the current reason does require your physical presence. If you feel that you are either very attracted or scared by a particular location, it is usually a karmic reason. It creates a very strong astral level reaction. This means that you need to tune into that place's energy to resolve some karma. You can do that by reading books about the location, looking at pictures, traveling there for a visit or even relocating there (though a move is usually overkill). Current reasons tend to 'just appear', for example if you were traveling and somehow ended up in a place that 'just felt right', as though you could live there.

Because of the diversity of consciousnesses that different places on Earth carry, we can face a certain difficulty when choosing a place to live. In choosing places to live or visit, fuse with the energy of that place and receive information about what that environment specifically offers you. You can do this by reading about the culture in books, about its past and present; looking at pictures of the area, touring guides; and watching movies about that place. This kind of self introduction to Earth's geography alerts her to your desire to experience her in that place. She responds as a friend preparing for your arrival. This will maximize the learning you will receive from the energy vortex at the new location.

The energies of the cities and the open spaces of Earth are very different. This is because cities are built on huge energy vortexes and have very high creative energy. If there was no vortex, a city could not exist, people simply would not feel magnetized to the area and would move somewhere else. Every city had a healthy clean energy vortex in the beginning, but with time people tended to discard 'energetic junk' into all the lower levels of Earth, even penetrating the ground up to fifty yards deep! This energetic junk consists of 'over-creativity' and disowned feelings. People in a city are continuously fed by the city's vortex, which intensifies their personal journey many times over; they go much deeper into the patterns their Soul set out for them to explore, feel passion, anger, love, hate and fear much more intensely. They become unable to process this overflow of information, desires, speed and fears, and so they disown it, they push it away, defending their survival. The energetic junk then in turn creates imbalances in human and animal brains and intensifies feelings of low self esteem, cruelty, hysteria, panic and loneliness. The disowned energy kills the life force in the city, which is why so many cities eventually die—people lose interest in a life that attracts destructive circumstances, like the closing of businesses, loss of work, darker types of entertainment, etcetera. People then leave a city or town with a clogged vortex, looking for either a slower pace of life, or a new, healthier vortex in another city. Without people dumping new energetic junk into the vortex it eventually cleans up, but that can sometimes take hundreds or even thousands of years. Then people return and rebuild, and the whole process begins again. As we learn self responsibility, cities will become centers for beneficial creativity amplified by the vortexes.

Open spaces, on the other hand, have much less creative energy and usually no major vortexes. Rarely would there be an unused vortex in the wilderness, usually people end up finding it and creating pilgrimages to it or building a sacred temple of sorts. The advantage of rural spaces is that Earth is clean there all the way down, no fifty yards of discarded energy junk to experience in your root chakra!

The weather patterns of Earth are breaths of her sensory system. Earth corrects imbalances and clears energy by rearranging the flow, which on the physical level is perceived by us as storms, tornadoes, tsunamis and earthquakes. Each weather type also has a very particular effect on the human energy field and can be consciously utilized.

Thunder storms, tornadoes, electrical pre-rain ozone and rains are cleansing mechanisms for the planet. When she needs to clear something from her fluid feeling levels (emotional, astral, unconditional or even time level), she creates a storm. A fast flowing energy disperses the fluid block. Certain areas have more storms than others because they serve as release portals. The emotional planetary block might be in New York, but it will rain a lot in Wisconsin to clear it. The human energy field becomes charged by these storm patterns and fast movement of energy due to an increase of negative ions in the air—this clears the energy field. So if you feel sluggish and low on charge, come out in a rainstorm or thunderstorm, don't be afraid, instead ground the incredible power of Nature in your energy field, allow the storm to clear and charge you.

Large waves on the sea and oceans, including huge tsunamis, are resonant of a transfer of energy between the levels. There is a system of communication between different energy frequencies, and the waves serve as a sort of echo of these transfers. The energy has to be relocated constantly due to Earth's evolutional development, her processing and dealing with us and animals, new developments in cultures and the Moon pulling on the magnetic field. For the human energy field the effect is very grounding. If you do not feel present during conversations, unable to remember things, freaked out or overwhelmed, you can use the grounding effect of waves. The larger the waves, the stronger is the effect. Obviously, make sure your physical body is out of danger. The vibrations of very powerful waves like a tsunami can be felt even fifteen miles away from the shore. Proximity to the sea even on a calm day expands the human aura, damp salt air clears the energy field of frequencies that are too low to sustain life, then charges the field. When you swim, sea water clears old stagnated mucus from the aura.

Winds are incredibly powerful cleansing mechanisms. Our planet expresses her freedom through winds. Any time you want to feel true freedom in your life, stand in a windstorm. When changes need to be made to a particular energy pattern, Earth activates the winds by changing the pressure, precisely controlling intensity.

Earthquakes are a release system and pattern of growth. Earth's body is still young and she is growing, which sometimes is followed by growing pains, like volcanic eruptions. When Earth quakes her structural levels get readjusted. The effect on the human energy field is somewhat uncomfortable, because we depend on the stability of Earth's structures. To reinstate a feeling of safety you need to make sure that your root chakra is working well during the earthquake (yes, flying out of the body in terror is counterproductive!)

The sunlight is bathing Earth in life-supporting energy: it charges her field and it delivers messages from the Sun. Sunlight is an intelligence communicating with Earth. The consciousness of the center of our Universe, the Great Central Sun, communicates with many of its galaxies through the black holes in galactic centers by means of light. Not necessary visible light, but the entire spectrum of it. The light is an encoded intelligence. Just like you download upgrades to your computer from time to time, so does our Sun receives new information from the Galactic Center, which in turn got its information from the

Great Central Sun. When Earth receives the light of the Sun, she takes in all the upgrades now available from the shared pool of experience of this Universe. Sunlight and other forms of light (stellar radiation, etc.) are necessary for all life on Earth, including humans. We have to learn to receive the intelligence of the Sun through sunlight, instead of only doing it for vanity reasons (getting a killer tan!). Fifteen minutes per day of sunlight is a required minimum. If there is no sunlight because of clouds or rain, you can still tune into the Sun for at least fifteen minutes per day. To receive the intelligence of sunlight into your body you have to be in your body! It is not possible to download a program into your computer if you do not have that computer handy, right? You need the hardware to download software. So step one is always to be in the body: breathe deeply while focusing on how oxygen flows through your blood everywhere, make sure your root chakra is open and charged (either do something physical or just focus on the downward flow). Step two is to activate your etheric and conceptual levels (blue 'body double' suit and the 'golden egg'). Having these three levels aligned—the physical, etheric and conceptual—allows you to download intelligence from the Sun (by physically being under the sunlight or by tuning into it if sunlight is not available). This helps you become a conscious, participating citizen of this solar system and the Universe. Even though visual sunlight invigorates Earth's entire energy field, humans are not designed for large amount of that type of fuel. Due to the fast movement of highly charged energy our aura does get charged, but too much actual sunlight charges the first etheric level of human energy field to the point of breaking (sunburn). Sunscreen protects only the physical skin, not the etheric level.

Clouds are Earth's protective cover, one of her boundaries. The thinner ozone layer, the stratosphere and higher orbital charges are other boundaries. Overly thick clouds create a saturation of Water and Earth element in the area, which the planet uses for rebalancing the issues present. Sometimes a problem can be right in the area that later ends up being covered by cloud a mile thick. Other times a problem can be far away from the overly clouded area, but Earth chose that location for the most appropriate energy. Even though thick clouds are a planetary way of clearing, this situation is not always great for the humans in the area affected. Too many clouds slow down our energy field and we get imbalanced, tired, depressed and grumpy. When humans create a planetary imbalance (for example, by polluting a city environment), Earth might choose to change the climate in that area more permanently to a cloudy state in her attempt to cleanse. Clear sky devoid of clouds sometimes fries the area by allowing too much sunlight, which overcharges the Fire and Air elements. Earth sometimes creates these conditions intentionally to cleanse sluggishness and indecisiveness somewhere else, but usually it is a response to destructive human behavior. The absence of clouds for a long time overcharges the etheric planetary level in an area, creating a physical, destructive effect (drought) and killing life instead of nourishing it. For humans some clouds and sunlight together or evenly interchanging are the ultimate balance and charge system.

Being close to a lake also has a very positive effect on the human energy field. The energy of the lake is a pocket of calmness in the aura of Earth. It soothes and relaxes us, takes away stress and tension. Fast and active rivers have a different effect. They are pathways of energy flow in the planetary field. If there was no flowing current energetically there could be no river. If the current stops flowing, gets diverted or diminishes, so does the physical river. A fast river's energy enhances our aura, making it vibrate rhythmically and fast in a healthy, vibrant way.

Another piece of Earth's energy anatomy we haven't yet talked about is the Line of Intention, or Hara Line. It is located inside the vertical tube, just like our Intention Line is located inside our energy field in the vertical tube. It has the entire plan for Gaia's incarnation encoded in it. Pure intention is beyond emotion, feeling and reason. Pure intent can imprint physical matter when anchored all the way down in frequency through the etheric level into physicality. The 'miracles' of changing and moving physical matter require not only well anchored intent, but clarity, and a high charge of it. Every Line of Intention has to anchor somewhere on both ends. Earth's Intention Line anchors on the top into the highest Soul energy of Gaia (planetary host) and on the bottom through our Sun into the Galactic Core. By aligning our personal intent with the Intention Line of the Earth (and hence also with the Galactic Core), we are in sync with our purpose for being here on the planet in our current incarnation. The Universe and Earth in particular respond by providing exactly what we need to fulfill our purpose, our life task, our own Intention Line's plan.

Each stellar body (planets, moons, Sun) in our solar system, like Earth, is a living and breathing being in the body of a planet, moon or a star in the case of the Sun. Each of these beings has its own Intention Line, energy field, its own journey of learning to go through, and hence holds a distinct state of consciousness. All the planets have a unique influence on life on Earth, including on us. In many star systems the number of planetary bodies (beings) is much smaller. We have a large number of conscious planetary beings. For human beings, planets represent attributes of humanity. Planetary energy has to flow through our energy system for us to be healthy, balanced individuals. When we have an overabundance or a deficiency of planetary energy, it throws us out of balance, creating emotional, mental, existential and physical problems. Planets are in direct relationship with the human energy field and body, while star energy is higher in frequency and less digestible by the physical body. Because planets are in direct relationship with us, they can help when we are in hardship or pain. We can bring the appropriate planetary energy into our field/body by tuning into it, connecting to the consciousness of a particular planet. Drawing down the power of these planetary attributes into the human energy field can help in moving through a difficult situation or in processing a painful experience. This magnifies the particular planetary wisdom in our lives. In a way, it gives us a 'big brother' or a 'big sister', so we do not have to go through our problem alone.

The attribute that our Sun represents is identity. Everything has to have an identity, an 'I'. The Sun holds the identity for our star system. When we feel like we do not know who we are, during an identity crisis (which can happen many times per lifetime, often at midlife) the Sun's energy can be very healing, as the Sun can hold with us what is hard to hold alone. Our Sun acts as an anchor for our identity in a true, balanced way, with Soul energy guiding it. The Sun's energy will not resolve anything for us, we still have to do it ourselves, but it can be an anchor in stormy times. To connect to the Sun energetically you can imagine becoming the sun, entering it, or at least sit under the sunlight for a while, soak in the sunlight through your skin and your breath, allow it to penetrate every cell in your body. A deficiency of the Sun's energy shows up as insecurities, over-association with others, following someone or an idea blindly, and caring too much about what other people think, do, or say. An overabundance of the Sun's energy makes a person egocentric, overly self focused and narcissistic, uncaring and even cruel. Usually if someone has too much of the Sun's energy it is part of their Soul Contract, something they signed up for before incarnating. But one can learn to disperse this extra energy from the Sun by connecting to Earth's vibrations and to one's own heart chakra.

The closest planet to the Sun is Mercury. It has very fast moving energy that connects with the Sun and all other planets via a web of electric impulses. This web accounts for its main attribute: communication. Without the help of Mercury planets would have a harder time talking to each other. Mercury is a very active being, able to process a lot of information at once. The energy of the planet Mercury is necessary for us to have a healthy ability to communicate with external reality, and also for physical health. In the physical body all the organs, tissues, many different fluids have to 'talk to each other', be in healthy contact all the time, in order to be able to self repair or send a timely signal for help. That process of inner communication in the body can be greatly enhanced by aligning ourselves with Mercury's energy. Mercury can also help clarify and accelerate the flow of energy between many levels in our field, so the mental level can know more about the feelings or emotions, and understand what we believe is the truth. Mercury energy is a great processing aid. An overabundance of Mercury's energy makes us unable to focus because we get overloaded with information. Often, children with ADD have too much ungrounded Mercury planetary energy bouncing around their system (although it is not the only reason for ADD). When we ground this vibration, it becomes healing, not destructive. To connect to it use your intention or envision the planet itself. The energy is burgundy-red in color, with fast moving currents, sometimes color changes with speed to silvery gray or brown; it feels like a strong, dry desert wind.

The next planet out is Venus. For humans it represents the attribute of love. Since we live in duality, love is also dualistic in addition to being unconditional. Venus holds both of these types of love. There is a passionate, free, joyous and romantic love consciousness, with its poisonous, jealous and destructive counterpart, and the unity of these two—unconditional love. Venus energy is the perfect frequency for dealing with jealousy, fear and other destructive feelings in connection with love. When Venus energy enters your system, you will feel as if you were wrapped up in a warm blanket, releasing any fears and worries, melting you in pure comfort. If you are looking for a new relationship, a partner, Venus energy can be very helpful in attracting him or her. It is because Venus' vibration resonates with the second chakra, not just the heart. The second chakra opens up and becomes much more active, magnetizing sexual attention from others. It is itself not sexual energy, although it does amplify that energy in us. Thousands of years ago when people still accessed knowledge consciously, Venus energy was used as an aphrodisiac. (This planet later became associated with the Greek goddess Aphrodite, hence the word 'aphrodisiac'.) If a person has sexual issues, low libido, physical pain during sex or feelings of sexual inadequacy ('I am not sexy', 'I am ugly, disgusting, unlovable', etc.), that person is deficient in Venus's energy. In rare cases of an overabundance of Venus energy, it becomes a substitute for the Sun's vibration. In other words, sexuality, desire and the need to have constant adoration replace identity, making a person dependent on the 'pedestal' they get placed on by their lovers, through sex, affairs and intrigues. An overabundance of Venus's vibration happens only by disassociating the heart and overusing the second chakra. If this person connects more with heart energy, allowing Venus's vibration to enter there, s/he becomes balanced again.

The next planet farther out from the Sun is our Earth. In our solar system she represents compassion, amplifying this attribute for humanity. Earth's vibration is connected to two chakras: the root it enters through and the heart it opens. Her energy feels warm and nurturing and flows into our field through the root chakra. If in the middle of an argument you focus on your root chakra and welcome Earth's energy in, you will feel a wave of compassion moving through your heart,

259

which might help to resolve that argument. We cannot have too much of the Earth's energy because we are of the earth. But we do have to balance it with higher vibrations in order not to be too matter-oriented (having an 'only what I can touch is real' mentality). When we are deficient in Earth's energy, we become ungrounded, unable to be present in each moment of our life, daydreaming all the time, or are negatively selfish, unable to perceive the point of view of others, cruel and cold.

Like our Sun and Earth, our Moon also falls under the category of 'adult' planet because it has an independent being inside. For its first 500 million years it developed as a planet in its own orbit around the Sun, then chose to connect its personal journey with Gaia, becoming Earth's moon. The Moon represents intuition. Its energy looks like a white fog, and when it enters our aura it feels like a white blanket with mist-like tiny particles (not unlike carbonated water). It also has the component of nurturance, as Venus and Earth do. Allowing the Moon's energy to freely flow through your physical body will greatly amplify your intuitive abilities, connecting the previously unconnectable, revealing the previously unseen. The Moon's energy also tends to have a positive effect on the sixth chakra, the third eye. It doesn't actually open it, but it clears it. So if the chakra is opened, but we can see very little because it is clogged up with our fears and expectations, the Moon's vibration acts as a gentle cleanser, bringing more flow to the third eye chakra. When we are deficient in the Moon's energy, we become too pragmatic, too linear, even cynical. We are overabundant in the Moon's energy when we are dreamy and 'in la-la land' all the time. An overabundance of the Moon's energy doesn't go through the root chakra, so to correct the flow, we need to make sure we are grounded. Then the effect of the Moon's energy is positive, making a person more intuitive, instead of taking a person away from reality.

The next planet out is the red one, Mars. It represents attributes of strength and active force. Mars's energy can be constructive or destructive, like most things in our dualistic reality. When we procrastinate, feel indecisive or scared to make the next step, we are deficient in Mars' energy. Its energy feels as if a jet just flew very close by, it comes in very powerful waves, warm or cold; the vibration of Mars is almost palpable in the body when a wave moves through. These powerful waves rejuvenate the vertical flow in our energy field, intensifying the pumping, giving us the extra boost for action. It has a positive effect on metabolic processes in the physical body, charges the adrenals and liver, helps detoxification and enhances circulation to all the muscles in the body, including the heart. When Mars' energy is overactive in a person, s/he becomes warlike, overly temperamental, prone to sudden bursts of anger and rage. Mars' energy becomes overactive only if there is a deficiency of other planetary energies. Mars, being very active, naturally compensates for that deficiency by filling in the empty territory. To bring overactive Mars energy into balance, one must look at which other planetary energies s/he is deficient in and correct that imbalance first.

Next in order from the Sun is Jupiter. The being that inhabits Jupiter is very ancient, older than all the other planetary beings except for that of the Sun. The last incarnation of that being was a star, not a planet, so it carries a unique conscious understanding of creation. For us it represents mastery. Jupiter's energy is extremely important for our personal evolution. We use it automatically when we begin the journey of self exploration. When we are deficient in Jupiter's vibration, we end up 'lopsided' in our development, preferring one 'side of a coin' to the other, stuck in judgment and separation. How does Jupiter's energy look and feel? The vertical threads of brown, copper and gold frequency align with one's spine, amplifying the energy current inside the vertical tube and physically inside the spinal column. They can feel warm and cold at the same time, like the burning of a frozen fire. That's the expression of mastery: the balance of two opposites. But beware, too much of Jupiter's energy when one is not ready can create overly potent polarizing, expanding one's consciousness too wide. If one is not grounded enough, this can be very confusing and even lead to a loss of identity. To avoid that, simply make sure you are well grounded when connecting to Jupiter's vibration. In the physical body Jupiter's energy runs mainly through two systems: the skeletal and endocrine. Osteoporosis is an indication of a deficiency in Jupiter's energy in the lower chakras. It is often believed that osteoporosis is an inevitable consequence of aging. This is not true! So if Jupiter represents mastery and the older we get, hopefully the more masterful we get, why then do older people have osteoporosis? It's because when we get older, we tend to tune into higher vibrations more, that is, using our lower chakras less (especially the root). If one corrects this by making sure one is charging and actively using the root chakra throughout life, one ends up running Jupiter's energy through the root, and the bones remain dense, strong and healthy. There are other factors, but Jupiter's energy helps. In the endocrine system Jupiter strongly affects the pituitary gland, which then spreads the benefits throughout the body.

Saturn is the next planet from the Sun. Everyone knows about it because of its magnificent multicolored rings. Even though the planet Saturn is not really physically solid but gaseous, its energy is a very structural type. Saturn is a very saturated gaseous form, a very large ball made of heavy particles spinning at different speeds, creating vortexes, lines and rings. The experience of Saturn's energy is similar to walking into a swarm of bees or some other heavy, large insect. Saturn consists of two main systems: the particles swarming (creating a weight) and structural container charges (the armature that the particles fill up). For humanity it represents form, structure and containment. It is a great boundary enhancer. If you feel lost in others, you are deficient in Saturn's energy. Its vibration might feel like an armature around your body, a structural definition of your personal space. When you notice that someone seems to have a fortress-like boundary, overly strong and protective, like an armor that nothing can penetrate, that person has too much of Saturn's vibration. A boundary is necessary, but as a container, a self-defined space to interact with others from, not as a defense against the world. To correct this overabundance one needs more magnetic fluid energy in their system. This can be accomplished by doing something creative or pleasurable for the self, like taking a bath, smelling essential oils or taking a walk in a nice environment. When we feel too exposed, overly vulnerable and unprotected, we need Saturn's energy. If called, it usually comes in all around you, without any direction or flow, it just sits around the physical body and vibrates, you can even hear it buzzing like a high-voltage power box. In the physical body Saturn is responsible for the resiliency of cellular membranes. If they are healthy, we regenerate health quicker and age less.

The next planet out is Uranus. It has fast and zapping, brilliant white electrical charges, and represents the electric side of our nature. Uranus' energy is completely silent, yet moves at incredible speeds. If you tune into it, it feels like very fast cold wind with many lightning-like bright white charges, but it comes with no sound, so it feels as though you went deaf. One needs more Uranus energy when one feels overwhelmed, confused, depressed, fatigued, stuck or sluggishly pessimistic. It also works well breaking down overabundant fat cells, hence dispersing obesity by speeding up inner metabolic processes in the body. Its energy might be helpful in raising thyroid activity when it is too low. Uranus can be a great friend to people who are disorganized and unfocused. Uranus' zapping electrical charges focus the thoughts, giving organization and stamina a chance. If on the other hand one feels anxious, nervous, freaked out, stressed, overly tense, unable to sleep, volatile and irritable, one has too much Uranus energy. One then needs to disperse it either by movement (shaking the body like a wet dog drying himself) or by grounding the Uranus electrical 'lightning' through the root chakra. Or connect to Neptune's energy for balance.

Neptune's energy is exactly the opposite of Uranus. It has many sounds, it moves very slowly or not at all, it has warm and cold inner currents; in color it is greenish, bluish and whitish, with some gray and black. It is very clear like the water in a lake, and in parts slippery, like a pond on a humid day. Neptune's attribute is magnetic fluid energy. When one does not feel supported, feels bored, uncreative, lonely or stuck in self judgment, Neptune's vibration is low in the system. If one tunes into Neptune, its energy will flow into one's fluid levels (astral and emotional), enveloping this person as if a clear lake is all around. When we are too dissociated from life around us, too lost in our fantasies or worries, we have too much of Neptune's vibration. We can bring it into balance by focusing on vertical straight lines (anything will do: columns, sides of the doors or picture frames, railing posts), and/or connecting to Uranus as a counterweight.

The farthest outer planet is Pluto. Considering its attribute it is very comical that we humans 'decided' to officially exclude Pluto from the list of planets in our solar system! Lucky for us, the Universe does not care much about our mental decision and Pluto is not offended. Pluto is significantly different from other planets in our solar system. First, it's very small, the size of a tiny moon, it is not a large planet. Second, it has a unique orbit, not round like all the other planets, but elliptical. And its orbital plane is not the same as all the other planets. The attribute Pluto represents is deepest transformation and extreme change. Its energy is very useful when we feel stuck or depressed. It comes like a storm and swirls energy in our aura, opens closed pathways, unblocks clogged and stagnant energy. It might feel like a wind, or a tornado-like spinning. Pluto also has vacuum-like energy. It is not an actual vacuum, just empty pockets of energy, and when the pockets come in contact with our aura they tend to pull the energy in their direction, dispersing and unblocking, creating movement where there was none. If a person is always running, afraid to settle anywhere, or is so focused on the ego's 'mission' that s/he cannot enjoy the everyday pleasures of life, Pluto's energy is overabundant. To correct the overabundance we need to focus on the present moment ('I am sitting on the chair', 'I am drinking my tea', etc.); this stops the overactive, speedy flow and anchors the energy field in the location of the physical body. Pluto's energy works very well for dispersing non-beneficial patterns. Let's say you have a pattern of always being late. When you are running to meet someone and know you are already late, tune into Pluto's energy (by intention 'I choose to bring Pluto's vibration into my field now'). You might feel the swirling of its energy all around you, intent on changing the pattern of being late. Next time you have to be somewhere, it will be much harder to be late! You can do this as many times as you need. If your child (or spouse ☺) leaves his room a mess all the time, teach them to connect to Pluto's energy, sit with them and tune into it together, the room will be much cleaner soon! It works the same way for addictive physical habits like smoking and overdrinking.

The last planet of the Solar system is mystical Nibiru. It is not around all the time because it has a very long elliptical orbit that takes it very far away from the Sun and the proximity of other planets. Nibiru returns every 3,600 earth years. Nibiru is not a completely physical form; most of its consciousness anchors in the etheric level and up, not in the physical. Its attribute for humanity is power, the ability to create and follow our destiny. Nibiru's energy is high intensity red light, its colors are red and black, and it has a slightly muffled boom-ing sound, like a nuclear reactor would. It is the energy of confidence. If you are not confident, too self conscious, self minimizing and your self worth is low, you need Nibiru's energy. It might feel warm, even hot, pulsating or booming, saturated and very charged. When con-necting to it, you might feel like you are engulfed in a ball of dark red fire, while everything around you went black. That is because the astral energy level is the main calling card of Nibiru. Do not be afraid; allow the energy field and physical body to soak in this powerful fire. Then any time you need more confidence tune into the memory of how it felt in your field and body to vibrate with the red Nibiru fire—you will feel more confident instantly. This is also very useful if you are facing a challenge like telling the hard truth to your friend/parent/child/spouse, or a job interview, public speaking and so on. An overabundance of Nibiru's energy leads to a hunger for power, disconnection from reality and tunnel-vision focus on gaining power over something or someone. It becomes destructive, as it brings too much of the Fire element into a person's life, eventually burning them in power struggles. To cor-rect that, a person needs to connect to the Water element. In the next subchapter we'll talk more about how to do that. In the physical body, Nibiru's energy has a revitalizing effect, 'spiking up' the blood.

Elements

Inspiration (Air), peacefulness (Water), passion (Fire) and stabil-ity (Earth) are the products of elemental balancing in the body. Each one of the many dimensions of this Universe has its own form of con-sciousness, its own aliveness. The elements we are talking about are not chemical or physical, although all physical forms are built out of these elements; they are second dimensional consciousnesses. They can be considered beings without a localized form. Together their conscious-ness acts as building blocks for everything in any dimension above the second. Our physical body consists of elemental energy also. These four elements are required for the creation of anything, from form to con-cept, feeling, idea and so on.

The elements link us to Earth and synchronize our combined evo-lutional progress. When we know which of the four elements we are favoring and learn to identify the deficiencies and overabundances of them, we gain the conscious cooperation of the Universe. Instead of floating without knowledge, we become co-creators. There are many ways to co-create and becoming conscious of the elements is just one of them, but since elemental energy is the closest to our physical body, this way might be one of the simplest. Mastery is in the equilibration of the four elements.

If all the elements were always balanced in us, we would be healthy, grounded, strong, emotionally satisfied, mentally focused, inspired, passionate and stable. This balance does not mean that all the elements have an even twenty-five percent share, or are always in the same amounts in our system. We are living and evolving beings, so the elemental energies always change according to the situation. Sometimes we need more of the Fire element, or during processing we can bring in a lot of the Water element, or we are focusing on Earth elements, etcetera. But even though the primary focus might change often, we can stay in elemental balance by learning to recognize an imbalance and adjust the other elements. As part of our Soul Contract we have a predisposition to a particular elemental combination based on previous lessons and karmic influences. Then the genetics of our physical body bring up a habitual 'favorite' element. Awareness of these two influences is the key to self balancing. When one is calm and safe, one might have totally different dominant elements from when one is in defense. We also often use a deficiency (and sometimes an overabundance) of a particular element as an escape from dealing with some block, fear or pain. For example, if someone has too much Fire element, when challenged with an issue she might attempt to fight, adding more Fire, instead of calmly looking at the issue (by adding more Earth and Water). Or someone with lots of Earth element might become stubborn and stuck when painful issue comes up, adding more Earth, instead of adding Air and Fire and bravely facing the challenge. We also can consciously amplify a certain element to aid in the processing or clearing of energy.

When the element of <u>Air is deficient</u> one has no inspiration. We feel stuck, bored, uninterested in life, reality seems too mechanical and often pointless, and we are unable to create. Writer's block is an example of too little of the Air element in the system. It feels like there is no space for us in life (in our family, in relationships, at the job). Physically, a deficiency of the Air element shows up as poorly oxygenated blood, shallow breathing and low lung capacity, easily breakable bones, damaged cellular membranes which lead to the premature aging of organs, including the skin. To amplify the Air element, we can use the physical air, breathing deeply, and consciously (high mountain air is especially good). To do that, focus on your body and then expand your awareness to your energy boundary, a bubble about seven feet around you. Once you feel the boundary (or have a mental picture of it) keep expanding in all directions equally, you can go as far as encompassing the atmosphere of the entire planet.

A <u>deficiency of Water</u> shows up as agitation. When we feel annoyed, frustrated, coarse, unable to connect and dissatisfied, the Water element is needed. In the physical body this deficiency looks like dehydration, poor circulation, thinning and low charge in the blood, shrinking of the cellular membranes, dryness, headaches, poor distribution of nutrients, constipation, hormonal imbalance, slow or blocked lymphatic draining, and deficiency in the cytoplasm of each cell, which makes metabolic processes inefficient. To bring more of the Water element in your energy system, the simplest thing you can do is tune into physical water: drink a glass of spring water, take a shower, a bath, sit by the ocean, lake, water fountain or put your hands under water and consciously feel it. The Water element is still, so you can also sit or lay quietly, imagining that you are floating on a lake. You can envision gentle waves rocking your body as you are letting go of the tension, agitation and annoyance.

When <u>Fire is deficient</u>, we have no vitality. We feel sluggish, barely dragging ourselves through the day, with no desire but to crawl into bed. Surviving everyday life becomes the only goal. Curiosity disappears, leaving physical and emotional fatigue, indecisiveness, depression, apathy. Physically, a Fire deficiency shows up as low thyroid activity, slow metabolism, accumulation of unnecessary fat cells, constant fatigue, nagging muscle aches and pains, poor absorption of nutrients from food, low or nonexistent sexual desire, impotence, frigidity, low adrenal function and toxic liver. To amplify the Fire element you can look at actual physical fire (like a candle flame) or sit by the fireplace, soaking in the warmth and activity of it. Meditate on fire, envisioning yourself inside a red flame (a blue flame is also good, but for emotional and physical vitality red works best). You can also use pictures of flames as a conscious reminder for your energy field.

A deficiency of Earth element makes us ungrounded. We feel unstable and afraid all the time, even if nothing circumstantially occurred to make us afraid. We feel insecure in our actions, our relationships and connections, even about our own identity and place in the Universe. Feelings of suicide come from a deficiency of the Earth element. Physically, the deficiency shows up as incorrect internal rhythms and broken communication between systems and organs. Allergic reactions to food or substances in the air, all sorts of digestive system imbalances, hormone imbalances, osteoporosis and other bone problems, neural problems and infections, are all indicators. To bring more Earth element into your body and energy system, sit on the ground (or floor) and keep expanding your awareness downward, until you feel heavy. Notice the vibration of the planetary energy. Also you can bring home rocks that you found in nature, and place them around your living space on the floor (under the bed and near the chair/desk you work at are great places!).

Overabundances of the elements are also imbalances and have unsettling effects, just like deficiencies.

An overabundance of the Air element brings confusion. Feeling 'all over the place', scattered, unable to focus, to think straight, to finish what you started, all these are the indications of too much Air. Physically, it affects the nervous system, making a person jittery, unfocused, forgetful. Cellular membranes become too stretched and do not hold their shape correctly, which (just like a deficiency of Air) leads to premature aging, including of the skin, and the digestive system has too much gas and is unable to process nutrients correctly. People with too much Air element tend to be inauthentic, have many acquaintances but no real friends, their relationships seem to stay shallow and surface-like. These people are usually over-focused on what they look like, act like, what others think of them, etcetera. They have difficulty in finding themselves, because they are overly merged with others, lost in them, unclear about their own identity. To bring more depth in your life you need to 'ground' the Air element with Earth.

An <u>overabundance of the Water</u> element leads to depression. A person with too much of the Water element feels sluggish and has almost no movement in her/his energy field; the emotional level is filled with self pity, self judgment; the second chakra is stuffed with the energies of low self worth and shame; the personal will is inactive and the identity is in collapse. Such a person often takes on the energy of other people. The fluid emotional and feeling levels of the energy field get over-expanded, drawing charge away from the structural support levels. The physical indications are constant crying, bloating, excessive menstrual bleeding, poor circulation and distribution of nutrients (just like with a deficiency of Water), diarrhea, stagnant cytoplasm, swelling of the joints and lymph nodes, low serotonin levels, but high melatonin, kidney dysfunction, kidney and gallbladder stones, fibroids, even cancer. To correct the imbalance, you need to bring more Fire element in to 'dry out' the Water.

<u>Fire, when overabundant</u>, looks like anger and rage. Someone with too much Fire is unable to control his/her angry outbursts, he/she blasts the anger out, unwilling to take responsibility for it. Another indication is over-dramatization and exaggeration of everything because of the effect Fire has on the astral level of the energy field. In the physical body, an overabundance of Fire creates irregular heart beat, overactive adrenals, hormonal imbalances, all sorts of allergic reactions, skin eruptions, overactive thyroid, burning nutrients too fast, nervousness, headaches, anxiety, heartburn, ulcers, an overactive sex drive and the inability to satisfy it. The Fire element is balanced by Water.

When the element of <u>Earth is overabundant</u>, we feel too fixed. There is no movement, we are too rigid and rock-like, only the physical is considered 'real' and life has no magic. The lower structural energy levels get overcharged, sucking the life out of the fluid feeling levels. These people are trapped in their own limitations and rigidity. They have difficulty with new ideas, considering them either unnecessary ('we did this the same way for the last fifty years, why change it, it works for us') or even dangerous. These people are very literal and do not like different interpretations of reality (i.e., chances are they will not be reading this book ☺). Anything new feels like death to them. When something does change, even if it changes for the better, they grieve for the 'lost paradise' (even if it wasn't paradise at all). Physical indications are heaviness, slow digestion and distribution of nutrients, thick blood, clogged blood vessels, storage of extra fat cells, back problems and heart problems. To correct the imbalance a person like that needs to bring in more Air and Water elements. Air diffuses the solidity of Earth, while Water nourishes the feelings.

When the elements are balanced, we feel our best. When the Air element is in balance it brings expansiveness, movement, inspiration and clarity. In balance, the Water element brings peacefulness, calmness and fulfillment. Fire in its balanced form activates vitality and passion. A balanced Earth element brings stability and security.

Crystals, Stones, Structure, Consciousness

The human energy field is a complex system, influenced by and influencing the Universe on many levels. So far we've been mostly looking at the lower seven levels of the energy field. The seventh level makes the egg-shape of the aura. But each dimension has twelve levels, and our energy field extends beyond the seventh level, interacting with higher frequencies. The ninth level is structural and crystalline. This does not mean that there are physical crystals, but it is crystalline in its nature. The conscious beings who live on this level are called Crystalline Guardians. They get their name from their job: they are guardians of the crystalline energy of the physical stones and crystals. In fact, they are the consciousness of the stones. These Guardians stay in constant communication with Earth, moving her evolution along. The energetic conscious messages of the Guardians make up the language of Earth the being. This language does not have words, like ours; it is a conceptual form of communication that looks like crystalline spheres. These Guardians are not physical, but exist on the ninth level, balancing and stabilizing Earth. Long time ago the gap between the vibrational rates of the crystalline spheres and physicality was too great for human beings and we could not get much benefit from the crystalline energy. In the age of Atlantis the gap was bridged and humans were able to use focused energy from the ninth level. But then the consciousness of humanity lacked responsibility, which eventually made crystalline energy destructive to us. With responsible use, crystalline energy can be very healing.

Our physical body and everything else on the physical level mimics the crystalline structure and is supported by it. Optimal organ function depends on the crystalline matrix. We can learn to apply frequencies of particular crystals and stones to our physical and emotional bodies to facilitate healing, processing, balance.

On the ninth crystalline level the White Light of the Universe splits into seven main color rays. A color ray is not 'just the color' we see, it is a particular direction for conscious expansion. Everything in the Universe works with color rays. When Soul separates from the Source, it takes a particular color ray. This has nothing to do with the 'color of the aura'; it is an innate Soul ray, a particular frequency path our Soul took. It never changes throughout incarnations and is unseen by the usual third eye view of the auric field. Why is it important at all? Because there are ways to recognize which color ray you have as your main one, and by knowing it know what you have to focus on, to watch out for, to connect to for power and balance. In different incarnations we anchor many different color rays depending on the Soul's lessons, but always in addition to the main one. If the main color ray is abundant in the energy field, a being can utilize all other color rays more efficiently. These color rays are carried on the ninth level by the spheres of energy-consciousness, the language of the Crystalline Guardians. In the material world color rays are carried by stones and crystals. Gaia, the being inside Earth, also anchors color rays. Her main ray (it influences all life on Earth the most) is red. If you look at the previous subchapter about the attribute our planet carries for humanity, you will see they are the same. The other three abundant color rays on Earth are yellow, green and lately blue. Rare ones are orange, indigo and purple, but all three are now growing. The main color ray shapes the Soul personality, stating the powers and difficulties we face in exploration of our different identities in different incarnations.

People with a red Soul color ray draw their power from the heart, they feel comfortable with their feelings and emotions, able to feel deeply. The difficulty might be that the person's strong feelings can 'get in the way' of his/her progress. Right now on the planet the red ray is physically carried by Ruby and Garnet. Earth also has a variation of the red ray—a pink color ray. It is the same in attributes as the red, but softer. It is carried by Pink Quartz, Rhodocrosite and Rhodonite.

The other abundant color ray is yellow. People with this color anchored in their Soul draw power from spirituality, and a reminder of their connection with the Source is enough to get them out of any difficulty. The challenge is the separation, the positive judgment of the Soul realm and negative judgment on the other aspects of the personality, as if the Soul is superior to matter. This ray is carried by Citrine.

The green color ray Soul brings power to a person from inner knowledge that Source/God is everything and everywhere, here and now. They feel that they belong and are part of a large Universal plan. The difficulty for these people, is that they can get too entangled in the material world and forget the rest (feelings, Soul, etc.). The green color ray is anchored by Emerald and Green Tourmaline. Malachite also has this ray.

People with a blue Soul color ray draw their power from the mind, the intellect and logic. The challenge arises when this person uses the mind only, ignoring the body, feelings and the Soul. The blue color ray is carried by Sapphire, Lapis Lazuli and Pink Tourmaline.

The rare orange Soul ray people draw their power from vitality, excitement, sexuality and the cause-effect cycle. Because of the natural balance of positive, negative and neutral energies, these people are very creative; they can disassemble and reassemble reality in many unique ways, like a puzzle. The pitfalls are unhealthy creations due to the use of imbalanced energies. The orange ray is anchored on Earth by Carnelian and Poppy Jasper.

The now expanding Souls of indigo ray produce people who draw their power from higher intuition and inner knowing. The challenge for them is in trusting their intuition, instead of devaluing it and looking for external support. The indigo ray has for a while now been carried by Sodalite, but soon it will switch to a new main carrier—a crystalline formation called Indigolite. This crystal is a 'teenager' now, it is forming inside Earth and it is not as yet accessible en masse by humans.

People with the Soul of the purple ray are very rare on Earth; they draw their power from inner wisdom, an inner flow of understanding reality. The challenge for them is in being human: when the ego gets involved this person can become separated, alienated, or arrogant, seeing the Self above others. The purple ray was anchored on Earth for a very long time by Amethyst, but now is being switched to a gaining potency stone called Purple Fluorite. Amethyst is a male form of purple ray, but since more and more magnetic energies are needed on Earth, the new carrier, Purple Fluoride, is female. This was the reason for the carrier switch.

Now that we know about the main carriers of the color rays, how do we work with them? The basic and very practical way is to use physical stones, wear them, carry them, tune into them. But beware: in order to connect to a Crystalline Guardian a stone has to be natural, not artificial, colored or 'enhanced'. Another way is to communicate with the Guardians through their energy language—the crystalline energy spheres. The Guardian is the consciousness within the stone. At the end of this subchapter you will find a basic list of the most common stones and their qualities, so you can better choose which one you need to work with.

Choose a stone you want to work with. Sit comfortably, close your eyes and envision a sphere made of this stone about three feet above your head. These spheres already exist on the ninth level, you are just bringing one into your awareness. Let it hover there. Find a comfortable size for your system. Usually a sphere at least three inches in diameter is necessary to invite a Crystalline Guardian. You can enlarge this sphere until it feels right (usually no more then six to seven inches, but there are exceptions). You do not have to focus on the size if it is too distracting, just focus on the round shape of it. As you focus on the sphere, it will start to vibrate brightly and actively, producing a charge and connecting with your ninth chakra three feet above your head. An energetic template of the stone's crystalline matrix will connect with the structural levels of your energy field first, eventually reverberating all the way down to the physical level. The structural charge will then mold the fluid levels and connect to them. At this point you might feel a strong vibration above you, in your crown chakra, or throughout your vertical tube. That means a Crystalline Guardian is connected to your field. Here you can ask or intend to integrate the energy of the crystalline sphere. A Guardian will move the sphere closer to your body, through your vertical tube and into a place (a chakra, an organ, etc.) that needs its energy the most. The size of the sphere might become smaller, as the Guardian adjusts it. The crystalline sphere itself can be moved into the right position in the body very quickly, but its effects are slow, as it methodically releases its charge inside the system. You do not have to worry about removing it. When the crystalline energy is integrated and you are able to support it, the Guardian will come back and remove the sphere. Once you have done this exercise there is no need to repeat it; instead, if you want, connect to the sphere already inside. The better the conscious connection, the stronger will be the effects. You can do this again for another stone, but do not do more than three different stones close together in time, allow time for the crystalline energy to penetrate the field and integrate.

Ruby brings suppressed/hidden feelings into consciousness, helps to express deep feelings, assists in the release of old emotional blocks, resolves the struggle of love and power. Beware, for it can enhance the ego, you have to have a positive intent! Ruby light naturally appears in a person when one is in love or experiencing compassion. Physically, Ruby normalizes blood pressure and heals the heart.

Rhodocrosite breaks apart blocked emotional patterns, cleans feelings, rearranges and reconstructs, builds new healthy emotional patterns in accordance with your higher Self choices.

Carnelian cleanses cells, emotions, thoughts by absorbing energy 'junk', amplifies sexual desire, emphasizes self love, optimism and a positive outlook on life. It also enhances the immune system, makes lungs stronger, clears toxins, heals disharmony. The orange light of Carnelian energy anchors abundance and luxury.

Citrine gets rid of astral blocks to progress that clog astral feelings. It senses higher Self choices and focuses energy flow in those directions. It opens inner hearing, clears chakras, gives higher clarity on why things happen. The yellow light carrier by Citrine naturally shows up when we are in the higher states of pure clarity. It increases the elasticity of cells, relaxes nerves and muscles, amplifies appetite, heals digestion, cleans up skin issues.

Emerald raises slow vibrations. It stops cancer cells from growing, speeds up the regeneration of cells, heals scarring, slows down the heart beat. Emerald light is a blanket of kindness and pure comfort. When a baby is sleeping comfortably and smiling, s/he often is visited by an Emerald Guardian. Emerald also releases addictions and heals alcoholism by softening internal struggles.

Aventurine and all the variations of Gold Sand, Purple Sand and White Sand, work well with the physical body, cleansing cells of toxins and medical dyes and tossing negative vibrations out of an affected organ. Also, these stones are great support for manifestation, all are very powerful manifesters of abundance.

Sapphire balances and calms thoughts, amplifies only positive thoughts, clears chronic fear, helps to differentiate the voice of the mind from the voice of the Soul. It enhances vision, hearing, memory, the intellect, and heals migraines. Sapphire light is a necessary support during nervous breakdowns, panic attacks, nightmares, or other feelings of physical danger. Sapphire light is also regenerative, for it retunes one's physical body with its highest balanced templates.

Lapis Lazuli amplifies hidden confidence, is beneficial to Soul Contract forms of manifestation, wakes up internal freedom, amplifies inner wisdom, helps one's intent to take away conceptual and emotional limitations and (its most famous attribute) helps release old, habitual karma. Physically, Lapis stimulates the optic nerves and memory, and heals neurological imbalances.

Pink Tourmaline has a mirror quality to its consciousness, it reflects harmful physical, emotional and mental energies. Physically, it heals the female reproductive system by cleaning, charging and balancing it. Men can also connect to Pink Tourmaline, but should not wear it.

Indigolite is a 'teenager' crystal. Upon its maturity it will be able to enhance intuition and the sensation of safety. It is a direct path to Soul energy. Physically, it will be able to support the healing of epileptic and other seizures.

Diamond is an odd crystal because its matrices are not typical of the crystalline form. But it does have a very clear, potent energy. It

275

is not as rare on Earth as we are led to believe, our planet has lots of Diamond crystals inside her to stabilize her internal changes. Diamond takes the power away from fear; it enhances the positive and reflects the negative. Because Diamond has stabilizing and unifying qualities it can help out the planet when too many changes are happening, and it also helps stabilize people with multiple personalities. If Diamond energy is brought into the field of someone having an electric short circuit (seizure), the Diamond Guardian will stop that seizure almost immediately. Diamond also enhances memory.

Sodalite connects to the experiences of freedom and responsibility, helps differentiate personal goals from societal/family impositions, clears up feelings of overwhelm and reflects negative energy. Sodalite's strong blue light also acts as a charger for our etheric level, making it strong and healthy.

Amethyst wakes up inner wisdom, helps us gain awareness of low unconscious patterns by drawing in high vibrations, releases destructive negative attachments and habits, and helps us to speak without fear. Amethyst balances lower and higher, and because of this quality it helps to heal nervous system issues such as panic attacks and other freak outs. It is healing for epilepsy and schizophrenia.

Obsidian is strong at bringing one to its center. It is grounding; it clears scattering and negative karma in connection to physicality, disconnects from harmful habits, increases productivity and creative manifestation, and heals grief. Obsidian absorbs physical and emotional pain by amplifying the void consciousness. Physically, it also clears infections.

Leopard Jasper heals the nervous system and attracts needed help. Poppy Jasper heals the cardiovascular system and generates needed energy charge. Bloodstone (Green Jasper) enhances the immune system, works with white blood cells and regulates the speed of healing.

Malachite is an amazing stone, for its Guardian has a very special Soul Contract with Earth. Malachite is a living library; like a scribe it memorizes and records throughout the planet everything that Earth has experienced. For humans, it helps us to be in the present moment and also to locate any other moment in time if we choose to glide along its memory. Malachite's wisdom of the past helps to open chakras because we tend to remember more of our wisdom when connecting to this stone. Malachite brings other lifetimes into awareness. Physically, it improves circulation, heals sinusitis and wakes up cells for self healing.

Chalcedony is the Guardian of peacefulness and timelines. It opens up possibilities, clears up chronic worry and enhances dreams. It also balances and calms the nervous system and heals head injuries.

Hematite is silver in color, but red in energy charge. It is very grounding; it naturally charges the lower levels of the energy field, stabilizes and helps concentration. Physically, it works well with blood, clears and charges it, and also amplifies the immune system.

Rhodonite has an unusual Guardian, for it has two personalities. The male side helps grounding and if worked with (represented by the black blotches on the stone) it tends to plant one on the ground solidly. The female side offers perspective on emotional drama and heals broken heart (it is represented by the rosy part of the stone).

The Positive and Negative Light, Dark and the Shadow

When we think of the concept of Light, we usually imagine something nice, pretty and light-colored. Thinking of the Dark, mean, cruel and dark-colored things come to mind. This is because you are tuning into the astral level of Earth. She holds these beliefs in her memory files; we subscribe to them and end up believing as we are told. When many people play with a particular belief for a long time, the planet keeps that belief in her memory. As we evolve, we are supposed to question these beliefs, study the planetary memory files (chatting with the Malachite Guardian) and create new, more advanced consciousness understandings. But our fear of change stunts evolution, attaching us to old, often inapplicable, beliefs. In reality, the concepts of Light and Dark are much bigger, and there is a third component, the Shadow. The human understanding of a concept can go as high as the seventh energy level, but that is it, usually. Light, Dark and Shadow are multidimensional concepts originating in the twelfth dimension. The lower the dimension, the stronger is the intensity of these concepts. Considering that we are almost at the bottom of the dimensional ladder, Light, Dark and Shadow are pretty easy to distinguish here. This is a very important component of the human experiment; we incarnate into the extreme intensity of opposites, trying to understand them. We would have surely been ripped apart by the potency of Light and Dark if not for the cushioning of the Shadow.

The Light in general is conscious awareness, it is a realized energy; where there is no realized awareness there is Darkness, the unknown. The unrealized energy is not bad, it just is, without it there would be nothing to create from and nothing to understand. Inside each of us is the 'Light of conscious awareness' and the Shadow it creates on the 'Darkness of unknown'. Shadow is the concept for our 'personal unknown'. Universe/Source/God has Light (realized conscious awareness) and Dark (unrealized unconscious), while any individual identity (a nonphysical being or a physical one like a human) has Light, Dark and the Shadow.

But it gets much more complicated than that. We tend to think (again because of the old planetary files) that the Light is 'good' or positive and the Dark is 'bad' or negative. That is not entirely true. Each side has its own positive and its own negative. Relating this to the human condition, we can see four distinct categories.

- The positive Light is the creator inside us, seen through our constructive actions, our bravery and courage, resulting in further curiosity and healthy self esteem. It is the electric (male) energy interested in co-creation with life. It wants to expand its understanding of life/God for the benefit of expansion and experience of evolution.

- The negative Light is the destroyer, the prideful competitor inside our psyche looking to place itself above others, to win over life. It is also an electric (male) energy, but it is aggressive and irresponsible. This impulse generates abuse, cruelty, arrogance, hatred and war. It wants to increase its knowledge only to place itself in a more advantageous position for dominance.

- The positive Dark side for us is a stabilizing regeneration; it is the internal reservoir of support and nurturance, the 'raw material' from which the Light creates. It is a magnetic (female) energy similar to a womb, a black velvet void teeming with life. It generates humility and unconditionality. It experiences everything without prejudice, able to simultaneously hold the opposites of pleasure and pain, love and hate, courage and fear.

- The negative Dark is the manipulative part of us; it does not create from scratch as the Light does, but rearranges the pieces to match its desire. It is also a magnetic (female) energy, capable of real or false submission, devoid of love. It generates jealousy and masochistic behavior ('I want you to make me feel better, but I won't let you help me, so in the end you will be wrong either way because I will still suffer!'). It experiences life conditionally, attempting to avoid pain.

Now we can look at the Shadow. The Shadow side of the psyche is the unconscious, hidden, shunned and judged energy that has not found integration. Focused attention is the cohesive force that can hold Shadow energy to the Light of conscious awareness with the Dark unconditionality, allowing it to unify and not shatter. This unification of energies through conscious awareness is an integral component of Human Mission Alpha, it leads to personal mastery.

The Shadow is the unintegrated and hidden power given away to the unconscious. There are two types of Shadow: the Golden and the Dark. The Golden is unrealized potential, while the Dark is false power. Of course everyone wants to tap into their potential, to activate their Golden Shadow. But we can only enter the Golden Shadow by going through the Dark one.

So this is what we have as components of the universe and the human psyche:

'+'Light- creator   *Golden Shadow- unrealized potential*   '+'Dark- regenerator
'--'Light- destroyer   *Dark Shadow- false power*   '--'Dark- manipulator

The Dark Shadow is filled with rejected energy, like hatred, jealousy and terror. These are the energies of separation, energies that 'forgot' their origin in unconditional love and became twisted and warped. It is possible to enter the Dark Shadow, but without love our identity tends to believe the energies trapped there, and get either scared or lost. It takes a lot of core strength to love what we hate about ourselves. It takes even more love to discover what we don't even know we are hating and hiding. The love we bring into the Shadow creates a state of fearlessness in the energy field. This means that we become able to recognize and face the Shadow qualities within us, then enter the Shadow and vibrate in it. This vibrating helps us to move deeper on the path of self discovery.

Fearlessness is electromagnetic superconductivity in a body that has no resistance to the flow of life. Remember, that even though Shadow is a rejected energy, it still consists of life force. When we are fearless, our energy field and the physical body are allowing all life force to pass through it without judgment. Resistance forms as a result of an overly limited self definition. In other words, what we consider ourselves to be is so different from the Universal life force, that we see that life force as an enemy of sorts, resisting its presence in our being. The judgment of 'good' and 'bad' is the separation, and it only perpetuates the empowerment of the Shadow. A person who rejects the negative and tries to believe only in the positive wastes a profound opportunity to reclaim the power of the whole Self.

Since this Universe is dualistic, everything, including us, has both sides, which in balance become Unity. By striving for pleasant experiences ('good') and fearing/rejecting uncomfortable ones ('bad') we become lopsided and unable to reach Unity, hence generating a Shadow.

In American culture the Shadow has been considered 'bad' and Light considered 'good'; this is a representation of this lopsidedness. Other world cultures saw the Shadow differently, and they approached it by running towards it and diving into it, calling it forth and befriending it. This is what became the 'realm of the Hero'. The concept of a Hero is entirely based on fearlessly entering the personal darkness of the Shadow, transmuting its rejected life force, and arriving at the 'reward'—the potential and power of the Golden Shadow.

In ancient Egypt the being Anubis was an honorable representation of the Shadow. The Egyptian fascination with cats is also anchored in the understanding of the value of the Shadow in human development. Cats were seen as guardians of the underworld and powerful mystical deities, able to bridge the two opposites in this Universe. Part of the Egyptian initiation ceremony included walking on the backs of crocodiles, or diving into a pool filled with them, as a catalyst for the state of fearlessness.

In ancient Tibet, monks honored the Shadow side of reality by participating in the stillness meditation on dead bodies. Their focus would stay with the decaying physical form for days and sometimes even months, while they witnessed the process of matter dissolving and faced their fears of mortality. This brought them into a state of fearlessness, allowing them to enter into the Shadow.

In ancient Siberian traditions a shaman would consciously enter the realm of the lower astral level of Earth, knowing s/he would meet 'dark' creatures there. The skill was in not becoming defended, because that is the separation which empowers the Shadow. A shaman would enter with the power of his/her identity and undefended, which commanded respect among the lower astral entities, and he/she then proceeded to make deals with them. These deals were always sealed by the personal power of the shaman, who had to remain in the state of fearlessness in order to walk his/her path in and out of the Shadow realm.

In the pagan Russian tradition people celebrated the Shadow by setting up times to express it en masse. Villagers made large hay dolls as a representation of their internal negativity (jealousy, bickering behavior, anger, aggressiveness, untruthfulness, etc.), then at the end of that day burned them, seeing fire as a transmuting agent for the Shadow. They cleared negative energy by expressing it, not hiding it.

The Hebrew tradition has a 'wailing wall' and many other ways to show grief. Jews did not hide, shame or reject their pain. They dove deep into the experience of it, fearlessly entering their Shadow. The trick was to be able to hold the bridge between the pain and a more positive internal reality, not to get swallowed by pain (which happens when pride, entitlement or identity in general attaches itself to the idea of pain).

In India the female goddess Kali is a great representation of the Shadow power. She has an attractive body, but a mouthful of fangs; she wears a necklace of baby skulls and she dares us to look fearlessly at our own Shadows. She is the magnetic power of the positive Dark, the unconditional experiencer, able to hold pain and pleasure simultaneously. Our reaction to her nondiscernment is an indicator of the doorways into our personal Shadows.

Many Native American tribes had a similar approach to the Shadow through survival initiations. A young adult would be left alone in the wild and would have to find his/her way, becoming fearless in the process and entering his/her own Shadow. Another Native 'crash course' in Shadow-entering is 'snake medicine'. That is, a person was given poison in the form of snake venom, and as the poison was making its way though the blood, this person could either die in terror and pain, or go into fearlessness, face the poison (Shadow) and transmute it. A powerful Native shaman could do that; this is the true meaning of snake medicine. Another Native technique was a saying 'it is a good day to die'. That stated the absence of the fear of death, allowing openness to the potential in the Shadow.

When we are not accountable for our energy, we do not own our Shadow. Rejecting it, we push it away, project it outside of ourselves as if it is not us, but something separate from us. Projection of a Dark Shadow outside of the Self creates negativity. There is a 'dead zone' around our planet, which is created by this projection. Inside the 'dead zone' resides rejected energy; it is like a huge garbage dump in Earth's aura, generated by all of us. Just as with physical waste, we generate a tremendous amount of it if we are not responsible for the Self! The rejected energy in the planetary aura amplifies all sorts of negative societal patterns, supporting our beliefs in powerlessness, victimhood, poverty, war, etcetera. Lately, since the early 1990s, the process of breaking up the 'dead zone' has begun. We have to own our power! In 2001 Gaia speeded up this process, allowing the trapped energy there to return to its originators, that is, to us. Gaia scans for the Soul signature of the person who was not able to deal with the difficult circumstances and rejected pieces of the Self, disowning the Shadow energy. That person might be long gone in linear time, but his/her Shadow energy still hangs in the 'dead zone'. You will be presented with the Shadow energy that might not even be from your personality in this lifetime, but from some other life your Soul had on Earth. The Dark Shadow is a false power because it represents an attempt to be powerful without being accountable for that power. It is not the qualities themselves that are the problem, but our inability to integrate them into our identity. If you believe you are a 'nice person that never gets upset' and then you, as any human, gets angry, that anger is not owned; it is a powerful expression of life force that is rejected and sent into the Dark Shadow. It sits in the planetary 'dead zone' for many thousands of years, you are long dead by then. Now you are a different person, a reincarnation of the same Soul. Gaia finds your Soul signature on the planet's surface and sends the 'Shadow package' to you. You might think it is unfair that now you are stuck dealing with something your personality did not create, but since the Shadow holds power, this is actually an opportunity to receive power you otherwise might not have access to.

What can you do to facilitate this process of power returning? You can learn to track energy back and forth from your own Light to your Shadow and back using the third chakra as an entry point. The tracking creates an energetic grid structure for consciousness to travel on. It is an active engagement with withheld power.

For this exercise, first breathe; then tune into your vertical flow of energy, open your root and your crown chakras, breathe deeply and slowly. Make sure you are relaxed (physically and mentally). To help your mind relax, imagine what stillness would look like, or how will it feel to be a flower, something like that... You will need courageous focus. Love creates courage, so open your heart and gently move your mind's focus from stillness or a flower to the vertical flow inside your aura. The combination of energies of courage and focus creates the necessary charge to enter the Dark Shadow. But do not worry about what it will feel like, just breathe with the vertical up/down movement of energy. Find your solar plexus area, open and amplify energy in your third chakra. Tune into one positive Light quality you have (tenacity, creativity, perseverance, inventiveness, sincerity, observance, etc.) and allow your third chakra to experience it. Then, using your courage, tune into the Dark Shadow quality (something you do not want yourself to be: an angry person, jealous, mean, selfish, ungrateful, etc.) and hold that in the third chakra. Alternate between the two, it builds an energetic grid. This grid is a bridge for your awareness to enter your Shadow. You can do this exercise using many different qualities or the same ones every time (for example, if you are working on a particular issue with anger, then use anger as a Shadow anchor every time). The energy grid set up through this exercise will begin to work in your regular life—you will start to notice how hidden or rejected components of your Shadow come to your conscious awareness more and more. If you are aware of something, you can work with it and change it, reclaiming the hidden power.

The Trap of Victimhood

Victimhood is one of biggest traps humanity ever fell into. But as always, there is a reason for it. Gaia the Earth chose to experience victim consciousness. We, creatures living on her, had to 'get with the program'. Why would someone decide to become a victim? It is a very complex reality, and the Soul chooses to experience diverse situations in order to comprehend, to grow, to evolve its Light. Gaia the being wanted to learn humility—that was the first lesson she played with when she inhabited our planet. The second lesson was motherhood and everything that goes with it. We humans are products of that lesson, this is why we feel so connected to Gaia as if we were her children and she, our mother (not every planetary host feels like that). After motherhood was the lesson of victimhood. You could say that it is Gaia's personal schedule. As Gaia was experiencing victim consciousness, humans dealt with it too, but less successfully. Gaia the being pretended (successfully) that she was a victim to learn what it was like; we *believed* we were victims and so we *became* victims. The victimhood experiment for Gaia went for thousands of years, and humans experienced this programming for hundreds of thousands of generations. In 1989 Gaia ended her victim experiment, she is done. We humans, though, have had a much harder time ending it, because we became addicted to the role of the victim.

A victim is a person who forgot that s/he creates her/his reality, and so feels s/he is not responsible for what happens in her/his life. From the victim's point of view, life happens to them. Responsibility itself is pushed outwards from the person. Where will it go? You've guessed right, into the planetary energy, adding to the 'dead zone'. Even though Gaia completed her participation in the experiment, we still have to dismantle this monstrosity of rejected programming that we created. The massiveness of victim programming is the reason for the human addiction to it. It is always there and it takes a lot of self differentiation, courage and accountability to unplug from it. We have to be kind to ourselves as we learn to let it go. The planetary 'dead zone' rejected victim energy is only one component, each one of us has the victim program written inside our genetics and in our karmic patterns. It is in our genetics because every human's line comes through Gaia's victim phase. It has been in our karmic patterns for the same period of time, almost no one is free of 'victim-karma'. This is all the more reason to focus this lifetime on cleaning up victim energy, because Gaia has already let it go.

Our physiology reflects the programming of belief. We are either living authentically or being controlled by someone else's agenda. Just as viruses invade and control cellular structure, manipulating it to their advantage, victim energy slices through wholeness, rips apart clarity, seizes doubt and destroys power. When we subscribe to victim programming, it begins to alter all our perceptions and our internal reality changes to match victim mode. This then affects external reality, so our life becomes the life of a victim. Victim beliefs take over our reasoning, behavior, and lives the same way that a virus takes over physical systems.

Each chakra supports our existence in unique ways and so the victim programming manipulates us differently depending on which chakra is affected. Sometimes only a few chakras hold the victim pattern, but more commonly all of them do. Depending on how much personal processing you have done, you might stop activating some of the old victim programming you were born with and into. The idea here is to become aware of all these hidden patterns, so you do not run them automatically. Being conscious of these patterns gives you a choice in every situation: perceive yourself as a creator, or as a victim.

- In the crown chakra victim energy creates a disconnection between the personality and spirit, effectively cutting the Self apart from the Soul. The conceptual understanding of the Self becomes limited to a small box, and the ego-personality is lost without Soul uncon-ditionality and a higher point of view. When the 'driver's seat' is empty, the ego jumps in and attempts to protect the Self by win-ning safety and power. Victim energy in the crown chakra makes you a victim of your own Soul, preventing a repair of the connec-tion with it. The Self as ego is looking to please (get love) or anger (entitled to love) the Soul. (It is the behavior of a teenager with a parent: you left me, so now I will either try to make you mad or try to get your love by pleasing you).

• The sixth chakra with victim energy presents an inability to see oneself. A person cannot acknowledge who s/he really is, instead pretending to be either what s/he thinks s/he should be, or what s/he wants to be, or what s/he is afraid to be. It creates an illusion. Since we tend to base a lot of assumptions about life on what we see through the third eye, it makes sense that much of what we think of as reality is actually delusional. Instead of dealing with real life, we are stuck dealing with what we think we have in front of us, chasing what we believe we have to become or fearing nonexistent monsters.

• In the fifth chakra victimhood looks like a cork in a bottle—we cannot receive life or give to life. This leads to not being able to be truthful with your Self, which is irresponsible. We end up blam-ing others or life in general for our pain and losses. Self expression becomes thwarted by internal fears. Like pond water, the energy inside stagnates without the inflow of new stuff and exchange with the external world. Fear wins. Fear in the fifth chakra tints our perception of God, making it a projected separate authority (seen as good/bad luck, religious deity or energy guides, etc.).

• The heart chakra response to victim consciousness is also separa-tion, but in heart feelings. Victim programming creates a sense of disconnect from other people, as if you are alone. It is not the same feeling as abandonment, but is more of a coldness in the heart. People with a victimized heart can become cruel, because they cannot sympathize with others (people or animals). There is also an expectation to be hurt, which only leads to closing the heart chakra more.

* The third chakra experiences victim consciousness as lack of power. The person feels like a victim, that s/he is powerless in changing her/his Self or life. The self esteem of a person like that is really low and there is a sense of collapse in the Self. Victim programming tends to change reality to match itself, and so the person feels many limitations ('I cannot do that, I will fail'). Sometimes life becomes too hard to live and the person gives up (either emotionally or physically).

* In the second chakra victim programming kills pleasure and abundance. Suffering becomes a way of life; a person even generates a certain sense of pride from how much they have suffered. Sometimes the ego makes this into a competition: 'Look how much I have suffered! I must be very important and strong in spirit to be able to withstand so much pain!' (This is overcompensation for not feeling important.) Generally, self worth is low; a person like that expects nothing and is very grateful when something does arrive, but it is an internal trap because of the dependency on the outside world for support. Internal support of the Self is incomprehensible. These people can also solicit love, acceptance or even pity, and this behavior is usually combined with entitlement victim energy in the crown chakra. Usually second chakra victims look like very nice people who just have lots of negative stuff thrown at them by life, generally eliciting a desire to help them, support them, fix things for them. They learn to rely on this outpouring of support, almost expecting it, while upholding themselves with an idea that 'they are good people' (a victim twist on deserving).

* The victim program in the root chakra amplifies the survival fear. Living is forgotten, everything becomes about surviving. We become victims of our animal nature and separate from the higher Soul vibrations. Usually the physical body is blamed for all the

problems and either punished by avoiding physical needs/pleasures or, with the 'whatever' attitude, fully given in to/catered to. One of the material indications of the root chakra victim energy is over-planning for 'safe future' (life/health insurance, investments with extra safety procedures, etc.)

Now that you know what victim programming looks/feels like in different chakras, you can find your personal Victim. Here is an exercise to get to know your Victim. Relax, breathe deeply and focus on your feet. Then slowly expand your awareness upwards through your legs into your hips (lower pelvis area), keep breathing and stay relaxed. Find and focus on your favorite victim energy, like 'I am not appreciated', or 'I hate my job, but I am stuck with it', or 'I am too busy to be conscious', or 'How am I supposed to know what my Soul wants from me?', or 'I did not get enough love as a child', etcetera. Move that energy into your root chakra, as if it is in a well-contained ball. Hold that ball in your root and let it inform you about its reason for being. Then move the victim energy up through each chakra letting the meaning reveal itself. You might find that in some chakras there is a lot of information, while in others not much, or that you already knew/worked with/resolved it in particular places. You might ask 'how do I fix it now that I know about it?', but the very realization about what/where Victim lives gives you the conscious choice of not playing its game every time it shows up. Create your own victim map so you are in power, not your Victim!

Victim programming does not just exist in the chakras, it anchors there and affects entire energy levels. For example, third chakra victim energy might color the whole astral level with expectation of failure; root victim energy can make the entire conceptual level overly rigid. To simplify, we can place all the levels in two main categories: fluid (unconditional, astral, emotional) and structural (conceptual, truth, mental, etheric). There are imbalances in the fluid levels because too much energy is taken in, and in the structural levels because too much energy is being pushed out. These imbalances are represented in our internal landscape, affecting perceptions and behavior. Looking at the diagram below, notice which category you tend to fall into, it might be different depending on the issues (for example challenges of single parenting might send you into fluid imbalances, while dating into structural ones). Knowing how your Victim kicks your field off balance gives you one more tool to deal with it.

FLUID IMBALANCES	STRUCTURAL IMBALANCES
Collapse	Arrogance
Despair	Demand
Do it for me	Do it my way
Feeling the negative pleasure of being wounded	Feeling the negative pleasure of wounding another
Emotionally frozen	Hyper vigilant
Procrastination	Over-activity
Being overly affected by the outside world and over-worrying about your actions towards it (over-identification with others/world)	Being unaware of how the outside world affects you and not noticing how your actions affect others (not connecting to others/ isolation from the world)

When we experience an imbalanced perception/behavior, either structural or fluid, it is because somehow this acting out serves our Victim. Of course it is a negative service, because it helps the Victim to stay in power. Our positive desires are able to manifest only in the state of empowerment, so if you want to create something great (balanced relationship, fulfilling job, physical health), the Victim has got to go. Making the negative servicing of your Victim conscious is another tool for disarming it. This also diffuses the negative charge on realizing your desire. You can use a particular procedure to help you with this. Here is one of the ways:

Drop into your body and let your awareness guide you to the origination point of the imbalance you are experiencing or choose to work with. This origin point may be anywhere in your physical body or energy system. Once you have identified this location, the goal is to find the reason that this imbalance serves the Victim. Using patience and perseverance expand into the origin area and discover why this form of powerlessness exists in you. The resultant understanding is the healing.

The energy imbalances create physical symptoms. Yes, our own victimhood creates physical conditions that seem to perpetuate feelings of a victim type. Since everything is one organism, the physical symptom is an anchoring point for the victim energy in the physical level of the energy system. To heal the physical condition we need to stop supporting it by our energy programming. Remember, nothing can exist physically unless it is energetically supported. Put your hand on your body in the place that represents the physical symptom of the imbalance. Connect to the pain and move into a state of gratitude for the lesson that the body is giving you. Gratitude is the gateway for reversing the process that brought the imbalance into form in the first place.

To eradicate victim programming we need to use conceptual understanding in tandem with experiential states. Nonattachment, internal safety, excitement, curiosity and willingness are the essential attributes for the demise of victim consciousness. Non-attachment represents the conceptual understanding that all this 'reality' is an illusion and experience instead nonjudgment (no right or wrong). Internal safety is the concept of self reliance and the experience of Soul related peace. Excitement is a conceptual acceleration and experiential joy. Curiosity conceptually is open-endedness and a desire to experience. Willingness is the concept of participation and experience of courageous anticipation. Applying these principles helps you to face victim obstacles with compassion. As you use all these tools we were reviewing here, remember to not allow yourself to care about what others will think of your choices and actions, because the Victim is often supported by social patterns. To get out of your victim mode you have to be an independent Self!

Energy Beings as Guides

Who are our guides? Any being can be a guide. Connecting with an energy being can be an exhilarating experience or a scary one, depending on your perception. Energy beings have different personalities, they are not all the same type. Some have families, others many friends, yet others prefer to be alone. How do we perceive them? Each chakra receives information in a particular manner. The sense of the guide's presence is determined by which chakra is the strongest one in your system. Most people tend to want to see energy beings, but the third eye is usually not the strongest chakra. It is important to use your strongest chakra, because it will give you the clearest perception. You can use it as an entry to connection with an energy being, then build on that initial connection by exploring other chakras (start with the strongest chakra, do not jump to the third eye if it is not your regular perception center). If you do not see an energy being, it does not mean you did not have any perception of it. Because we expect to see, we assume it is the only way to 'be sure' of the guide's presence. Here is how chakras can perceive energy beings:

- Crown chakra knows there is a being, what that being is and what its message is;
- Sixth chakra receives visual information, we know how that being looks;
- Fifth chakra is hearing perception, you can hear sounds or words from a being;
- Fourth chakra is the heart feeling of a connection with an energy being;
- Third chakra gets our intuition going, you can sense intuitively a guide's presence and its message;
- Second chakra receives emotional exchange of energy with an energy being;
- Root chakra gives you kinesthetic sensations (hot, cold, something is close or far away)

One of our major misconceptions is that all guides are always angelic, beautiful, loving and blond. That is human fear talking—we feel more comfortable with an image like that, and so assume that if a being is a teacher to us, it has got to be an angel. Guides exist in many forms, some are humanoid (similar to us), but they are also insectoid, geometric, aquatic, reptilian, sound, nebulous, group-mind beings, animal guides, crystalline guides, etcetera. Because we expect an angel, seeing a huge spider, for example, might not jive well with our emotions and will not elicit trust. This is human limitation. We judge everything as a 'good thing' and a 'bad thing'. Snakes, spiders and lizards might be on your bad list, yet your personal guide might look similar to one of them. Because of our perceptual limitations and biases, guides accommodate us by interfacing through our most comfortable perceptual capacity. In other words, if you have an emotional reaction to spiders, your arachnidan guide might present itself as a beautiful human girl. It does not become a girl, just projects that picture into your third eye or other chakra. Guides will choose the easiest sense to deliver the message. A beautiful girl might elicit a trusting response due to her innocence/wisdom, so you feel more comfortable with your guide, never knowing its actual form. So your angelic guide might actually be a geometric being, or a lizard creature, or a mousy looking fur ball with a tail! Guides do this pretend-shape out of kindness to us; they are not trying to trick us, but to accommodate our lack of consciousness.

Another major misconception is that guides always know better than us. That is not true. There are high frequency angelic guides, lower frequency fairy guides, and everything in between. They, just like us, specialize in different areas.

There are personal guides, beings that connect to us from an early age and stay with us for a long time. Sometimes we have only one personal guide for our whole life, other times two or three. These beings have contracts with our Soul to be our companions and teachers. With these guides we build personal relationships, they are like lifelong friends. Personal guides usually know your Soul Contract, know what karma you came to clear and many other things about you, and so they can guide you to shortcuts in these missions. They can emotionally support you when you are suffering and rejoice with you when you are celebrating. Personal guides often give us little nudges of intuition to help us pay attention. For example, when you are driving and 'something tells you' to not go 'that way', you turn and avoid an accident—it is your guide that spoke into your third chakra and you got an intuitive sense to adjust your path. Personal guides are not here to protect us, though. Normally we do not need protection; we should be able to deal with whatever is happening in our life since it is we who choose it. But in more extreme situations, when a person is 'losing it' somehow, emotionally or mentally, for a short period of time a personal guide can create a protective shield, helping the person figure things out and stabilize inside the shield. It is not appropriate to ask for protection when you are trying to get support from your personal guide, instead ask for help in dealing with your difficulty. A personal guide is *always* there for you, you are its 'job'. This is the true meaning of 'you are never alone'. Personal guides have only one 'client' at a time, so you are its sole interest and focus, they do not take vacations and are never far from our aura (some guides literally walk behind the person or float right on top all their life). Any energy being can become a personal guide to someone, but they have to 'submit a proposal' and 'pass the test' to qualify. A personal guide has to have a wide range of experiences and more wisdom than you. This does not mean that this being will have answers to everything, but it will have a broader view. It is like having a best friend that has traveled a lot and knows tons about life, but might not know about the digestive system of a hippopotamus.

Each person always has a team of medical guides. They are professionals with medical skills. These guides are not fluffy and cuddly, they usually are deep blue in color and kind of cold in energy. They can be from many different species, but if they are signed up to be your medical team, they go through a particular process to set up the team, which temporarily (for the duration of your physical life) make them appear cold and blue. Your medical team usually has five, seven or nine beings, and they can all be the same species or different ones. They are knowledgeable about your biology, your body and energy systems, they are great energy surgeons. They are not typical healers, a personal guide can help you heal; medical team guides are there to 'fix' what needs to be fixed. This might sound odd, but they maintain us. Imagine a race car driving 200 miles per hour, then it stops and the support team runs to it, they check everything, change tires, gas it up, fix and adjust whatever needs help and the race car is back on the track. We are like race cars inside our physical bodies, and our medical team is like a support team to help us go. If you are having a physical symptom, like a toothache, your medical team will attempt to fix it: maybe numb the nerve, or restructure the enamel, perhaps activate an immune response against the infection. They will do it either way, automatically. But the block (that is, the cause) that created the toothache prevents them from completely clearing the symptom. This is why, even though the medical team works automatically all the time to maintain us, it is always a good idea to help it do its job. You can do it by intending to not interfere with their work (one of the main reasons these guides are not able to help us is our own resistance) and to consciously ask for/look for the cause of your physical symptom (this cleans up the energy block supporting the physical situation). Medical team guides are not designed to help us process energy, but they can help figure out the cause for an issue (even if the cause is an emotional block of some sort). You can also ask your personal guide to help you find out the energy block creating the physical condition so you can work with it, clearing the way for the medical team. If you feel tired, you can ask your medical team to help you recharge. When you have physical pain, you can ask them to help guide you to the tools you can use to help yourself, and also they can minimize the pain. But medical team guides will have no idea how to help you process emotions! That is not their area of expertise. Ask your personal guide for help if you feel upset, depressed, angry, etcetera, it will know how to help you, but medical team guides will have no clue. Also, do not be afraid to tell your medical team to slow down or back off. You have cold-like symptoms and you have asked your medical team to help you clear it in 24 hours. Sounds great, right? Since your medical team has no understanding of your emotions/feelings, they will see if your request is possible and if it is, will try to make it happen. Now imagine that an hour after your request is acknowledged you suddenly feel so horrible from your cold that you almost pass out and feel like you are going to die. It is because your medical team speeded up the recovery time according to your timetable, but did not account for how you might emotionally freak out from the intensity of it. This is where you tell them to please slow it down and that you are ok with 48 or even 72 hours instead of 24. They will comply and you will feel the pressure lessening. So do not always assume that they know better. They do know a huge amount of information about your system, but similar to a computer with a huge data bank, will give out the shortest, fastest solutions, which might not take into account your fears, karma or emotions. It is your responsibility to work with your medical team as a unit to help maintain your own body!

The Guardian Angel is another type of a guide. It is assumed that each of us gets a guardian angel, but that is not quite true. Usually people mistake their personal guides for angels because of the preconceived idea that it is supposed to be an angel. In reality, though, a person might have a Guardian Angel as their guide if their lifetime has a particularly difficult path, or if it is part of some complicated mission including many Souls (they all will have angels as guides). The Guardian Angel stays with a person throughout the whole lifetime. It is not any better or more important to have an angel guide, just different. Because an angel does not have lower emotions, this guide might not be able to relate to a lot of your human experiences, instead it just loves you. The Guardian Angel does not eliminate the personal guide, a person will have both. Your Guardian Angel can protect you if you are facing danger, because it is there to make sure the mission goes as planned (in your personal life or in a team of lives). Your personal guide does not care about any mission; it has no agenda but only wants to educate you on how to live more consciously. The Guardian Angel is not that interested in your consciousness, but in you 'turning the right key at the right time' for benefit of the overall picture.

Few people have Guardian Angels, but many of us have angels visiting us. They are supporters and sometimes guides that come to us in a time of great need. If you are sitting in the hospital and waiting to find out if your child will survive an operation, you might end up attracting an angel. You might feel connected to something large and powerful, beautiful and harmonious, and pray to it to help your child and you to live through this situation. This is a connection with an angel. But once the moment has passed and the compassion and love from the angel has flowed through you, the angel will leave.

Animal guides are the creatures of this planet, they have never been actual animals, but are animated animal programs that Earth holds in her memory databank. Some animal guides look like the animals we know, but many have forms we do not see anymore, because the planet holds blueprints for every animal being that ever existed on/in her surface. Through many catastrophic events like ice ages, quakes and floods, animals have been wiped out on the physical plane, but all of their blueprints are stored in the planetary consciousness. Some of these blueprints contain more consciousness than others, and they can choose to become animal guides. Each animal guide has its own set of qualities and talents depending on its character. They have distinct personalities; they can get angry or upset, happy or mischievous. Shamanic traditions see animal guides as guardians, totems, sentinels, advisors, guides, teachers. All of this might be true, depending of the personality of the animal being and the role it chooses to play. One particular thing about animal guides is that they are with you because they want to, not because of some mission, contract or agreement. An animal being might take a liking to you when you are a tiny little baby and stay near you, play with you and have fun. Then as you grow up it might leave, since the childhood play is over, or stay for the rest of your life near you because it developed a friendship. Most people have at least one animal guide in their lifetime, some people might have many. The animals who were your pets and have died do not become animal guides, only wild creatures can guide humans. A crossed-over pet might stick around for a while out of love for you and to honor the connection, but it will not become a guide. Some animal guides are very wise and these were traditionally considered guides for the lifetime. Native peoples even gave human names according to the nature of the main animal guide of each person.

There are always visitor guides, beings that are specialists in their particular area and that come to help us with an individual problem. You might be having emotional breakdowns and ask for help, and it will attract to you an energy guide that can work with your personal guide to help you clear up the fear or trauma. When it is done, your personal guide takes over and the specialist leaves. These guides can be very personable and compassionate; you might end up building a relationship with one similar to your personal guide, depending on the time and strength of the connection. But because, unlike the personal guide, they do not have a contract with your Soul, they leave when the work is completed. Sometimes they stay longer than the job because they personally like you, or leave but might end up visiting you here and there.

The energy community is always there for us, we are never abandoned, nothing is ever withheld from us. It is our own limited definition of reality that blocks their support. The Universe is a busy place, filled with many different creatures, and because we are in physical matter form, we get a lot of attention! Imagine that you are standing in an open field, alone. Now imagine that there are hundreds of thousands of people all around you walking fast, some talking or looking at you, as if you are in the middle of Times Square, but you are still standing in the field. This is an approximation of how many energy beings there are around us, paying attention to us, loving and supporting us, all the time, while physically we might be standing alone in an open field. They are always there for us, it is our job to make sure we do not block their insight, wisdom, help. Make friends with your personal guide, get to know it. Be open and curious about it. Is it male, female or something else entirely? Does it have a set shape/color or is it changeable? How long do you feel you have known it? What do you remember from your childhood moments of conscious connection with it? Talk to it, relate to it, build a more conscious connection, so that when you need help, you have this friend with you all the time. Work consciously with your medical team by intending your field to be open for their repair work during the night. When you go to bed, decide to have yourself available to your medical team for any necessary work, and it will give them better, deeper access to your body.

EPILOGUE
Pride, Power, Purpose

EPILOGUE

The internal comprehension of your pride, your power and your purpose are components of becoming a Creator of your own universe, your life. We think of pride as negative, but it is not always so. In the positive, pride is similar to dignity and internal nobility. This nobility is not based on any breeding or nationality, but on the understanding of the origins of the Self. We have looked at many aspects of the Self, all of which are Soul originated and matter anchored. It is that balanced positioning of the Self between the Soul and the matter-vehicle (the body) that creates the experience of dignity. Dignity like that cannot ever be destroyed, even if the ego of a person is being pushed down, because external circumstances have no bearing on it. Proper Self positioning looks like a well, flowing energy in the vertical tube in the middle of the energy field, with the crown and root chakras opened and charged.

This positioning gives rise to true power. That true power is Soul based, and if we keep an energy bridge between us and our Soul, Soul light shines through into our personality. That is an awesome power, it feels like being invincible, while at the same time respectful of the limitations of your playground.

Your purpose becomes clear: be aligned and present to experience your reality with responsibility, integrity and respect. We each have our own 'purposes' and sometimes it is very hard for the ego personality to know what it is. We tend to think that it is some action, something we are 'supposed to do'. There is no such thing. There is life, your life. Whatever karmic patterns you came here to resolve will guide you to particular events, scenarios. You will be supported no matter what. You can never 'screw up' in the eyes of your Soul, or your guides for that matter, they will always be there to help you. In the past, every time we forgot who we were and why we were here, when we lost awareness, we blamed matter as the cause of our lack of fulfillment. We understand ourselves through creation. Creation is birthed out of desire. Desire attracts substance, the raw material for building reality. As substance moves into material form, the original desire for that form is mirrored back at us. That awakens us to more awareness. Our human purpose is eternally merged with the acceptance of material reality, we are meant to create through intention and feeling by embracing matter. When the mechanics of Universal creation are understood, creation is complete and can be used as material for new creations. Otherwise it is a holographic matrix of unrealized creation. The essential component of creating in form is falling asleep, so that previous knowledge of creation outside of density becomes temporarily dormant. This tends to confuse the hell out of us as far as personal purpose goes. How can you know the meaning of your existence if most of your consciousness is on hold 'in the library' of the Universe someplace? Well, we/God have a great sense of humor, don't we? Putting a large part of our conscious memory on hold allows us to learn how to create by understanding the reality unique to each dimension. The crucial element of actualization of our purpose is reaching awareness/embracement of density.

There are certain principles that support our harmonious exploration of material reality. If we remember these principles and use them in moments of confusion about our identity or purpose, we have an easier time in density.

There *is* a design! That is a very important piece of knowledge. If you feel like you do not know who you are or where you are going, but remember that this whole reality is like a large puzzle and that you are supported and your actions are guided even if you do not know what they mean, it is easier to go through life.

Every **external circumstance is a message from the Soul.** This means that whatever happens is an opportunity to learn. If you are stuck in traffic and late for your appointment it is as important a message as the perception of your guide in meditation.

Every perception is *real.* You cannot bypass initial perception, it is an entry to the key for Soul design. If you worry, 'am I right? Did I really feel this?', that type of stuff, this Universal principle is perfect for you. There is no right or wrong perception. If three different people with energy abilities tune into the same problem in one other person, chances are that they will explain the situation differently based on their own translation, even though the actual information at root is the same (like 'there is something cold and sharp/metal/feels painful', and 'there is betrayal energy', and 'there is an astral knife in the back of this person'). Also, there are no facts! Anything that we perceive we tend to try to match with a fact ('did it *really* happen or did I just imagine it?') But what is a fact? It is a set proof of an event. There are some physical facts, a photograph can testify where the car was parked before it was blown up, for example. But if you asked different people where that car was parked, they might give you different answers. Are they wrong if the answer does not matching the 'fact' on the photograph? No, no one is wrong. People's perceptions are more complex than a pure record of a physical event, we see through our own lenses. Someone might fear what is in the car and say that the car was 'very close to the building', while someone else might want to unconsciously protect the owner of the car by saying that the car was 'far from the building'. Inside their systems these perceptions are real! Always start with an acknowledgement of the perception you have, instead of worrying about it matching or not matching some facts. Then you can dig into that perception and find out if there were any strong emotions in the way or if were you present, and so on. You can then compensate for the interference of this emotion and have a different perception of the event. But all these perceptions are still true to your being.

There is *no right and wrong,* only choices. The Soul learns with every action and non-action. It is our ego that wants to be right, basing what is right on what matches its expectations. From the Soul level, reality is unconditional, we are equally loved no matter what we do, it is up to us to strive for a more harmonious existence.

Everything has its *timing*. Sometimes when we try very hard to make something happen and it does not, or it is too hard to move the energy, it is because of incorrect timing. Every action of every person on this planet (and in the Universe) is timed, like a key that we are supposed to turn at a particular time. It is a very complicated program. So your acceptance of a particular job, moving to a different city or entering a relationship is going to facilitate/activate some other component somewhere else. Yes, we are all that important!

When we do not want to be the Self, we reject Soul power, and with it internal pride for being human (dignity/nobility), and purpose (meaning). We repel the Soul, depositing our memory of the true 'us' into the planetary matrix. We do not want to play the grownup game, and so we pretend to be children. The only problem with that is that we do not feel pride for who we are, but instead feel kind of unworthy and pathetic. We do not feel powerful, so we replace the true Soul power of energy alignment with the ego power of 'being right'. We lose purpose, and so we make up 'missions' for ourselves, false agendas that set our ego on proving its rightness. There are changes coming, you can probably feel how energy is accelerating, and our planet is not going to hold for us all this rejected energy much longer. It is time to grow up. This is why it is so very important to become yourself, your independent Self, so you do not base your identity on planetary social files. This is the Human Mission Alpha: be present in the moment, in the body, as the wise and passionate you.

GLOSSARY

Air – an elemental second dimensional energy; opposite of the Earth element

Alchemy – a process of changing one frequency into another, e.g., transmuting negative energy into positive

Anchor timeline – the timeline in which the Soul creates a physical form

Astral level – fourth level of the energy field of consciousness; feelings about Self in relation to something else; level of connections and personal feelings/stories; holds dream-like, mini-universes; it is fluid; Earth's astral level holds the energies of people's feelings (love, passion, compassion, hatred, envy, fear) and the stories supporting archetypes; is densely populated by astral nonphysical beings

Astral travel – separation of a person's consciousness on astral level from the lower three energy levels and from the physical body, as the consciousness sets out to explore different perceptional realities of the astral level

Authenticity, Personal – being true to what is on every energy level, an acknowledgment of the three main pairs of desires: predictability and diversity, uniqueness and sameness, receive/take and serve/give

Chakra – an energy center for interpretation of consciousness; each chakra is responsible for a particular range of frequencies; an energy vortex through which energy levels interact

Color rays – universal vibratory frequencies that shape the personality; the seven rays of Earth: red (main ray), yellow, green, blue and the rare rays indigo, orange and purple

Conceptual level – seventh level of the energy field of consciousness; it represents our belief systems and the concepts from which our lives assume significance; it is structural; thinking in conceptual terms happens on this level; Earth's seventh level holds concepts and archetypes, it is home to many nonphysical beings

Conceptual symbol – an energy program with a particular ability, e.g., a sphere is the conceptual symbol for support, containment and abundance and a doorway is the symbol for shortcuts and solutions

Courage – a combination of active will, heart feeling, amount of life force and the quality of its application, anchored and balanced; it is a composite of frequencies; it is a natural state of being

Crystalline level – earth's ninth energy level; consists of crystalline energy and sacred geometry patterns; structural; everything on the physical level including our physical body mimics the crystalline structure and is supported by it; here the White Light of the Universe splits into seven main color rays (see 'Color rays')

Crystalline Guardians – nonphysical, conscious beings living on the crystalline level; they balance and stabilize Earth; they work with planetary stones and crystals

Dark – unrealized energy; the unknown

Devil – clumped masses of our disowned energy, projected onto the astral level

Dimension – an energy range, where learning is set to particular rules; each dimension has twelve energy levels; dimension is similar to an octave and levels to separate notes; our Universe has thirteen dimensions

Earth – a conscious planet with a Soul and the intention for evolution; the being who resides inside the planetary body is called Gaia (among other names); Earth has the same type of energy levels as humans; full expression of our life task is always interwoven with Earth's energy fields

Earth – an elemental second dimensional energy; opposite of the Air element

Electric – an active expression of life force; defined, focused, separate; anchored in the energy field through structural levels and in the physical form through subatomic particles called fermions

Elements – inspiration (Air), peacefulness (Water), passion (Fire) and stability (Earth); each person has a unique combination of elements in the energy field and comprising the physical body; elements are second dimensional consciousnesses – Elementals

Emotional level – second level of the energy field of consciousness; extends two to three inches from the physical body; home of our personal emotions; fluid, flowing and ever-changing; responsible for emotional wellbeing; Earth's second level supports people's and animal's emotions and the existence of many nonphysical beings like fairies and elves

Energy field of consciousness – pathways of consciousness from the Soul to the physical body; surrounds body with interpenetrating levels; has two complementary forces, structural/electric and fluid/magnetic; is a complex system, influenced by and influencing the Universe in many ways

Energy level – a defined diapason of awareness

Etheric energy level – first level of the energy field of consciousness; closest level in vibration to the physical body; represents safety, vitality, stability, physical health; structural, mostly non-movable; Earth's etheric level consists of the energies of minerals, plants (from the past and present), crystals and bacteria

Fire – an elemental second dimensional energy; opposite of the Water element

Hara line – the Line of Intention; located inside the vertical tube of the energy field of every human, Earth, planets and stars; the human Line of Intention is encoded with the entire plan for a particular incarnation in matter

Human energy field – see 'Energy field of consciousness'

Karma – unintegrated experiences; lessons not learned; not punishment!

Life force – pure energy of the Universe, encoded with aliveness and curiosity of the Source; splits into electric and magnetic forces

Lifetime key – pattern that tints the lifetime/Soul intent; it is essential to our safety and satisfaction

Light – conscious awareness, a realized energy; related to Universe/ Source/God

Linear time – third-dimensional perception; time as we understand it, measured using events that move from one to another from past through present to future; mostly electrical, identity based (the body is here), speed- and goal-oriented; coexists with spherical time and needed with spherical time to create and manifest

Magnetic – the receptive expression of life force; undefined, unfocused, all-containing; anchored in the energy field through fluid levels and in the physical form through subatomic particles called bosons

Magnetic poles – energy vortexes of the electromagnetic field of humans and Earth, not necessarily located at the north and south poles

Mental level – third level of the energy field of consciousness; it is structural; home of our thoughts; linear thinking happens on this level; it extends up to eights inches from the physical body; Earth's mental level consists of the thought patterns of all the beings living on the planet, including Earth herself

Money – live emotional energy, aka the Money Tigress; fiery orange color, thick consistency; the energy charge and consciousness behind material money and its attraction/repulsion; it is shared universal pleasure and love

Parallel universe – a place where your incarnation exists with different possibilities, different timelines etc.; originates in a first dimensional anchor point

Passion – vibrant desire for life itself, the intensity of interaction with reality

Planetary levels – the levels of the Earth's field; there are twelve levels in this dimension, levels one through nine relate Earth to humans and ten through twelve relate Earth to the Universe

Perfectionism – an extreme form of negative control

Personal codes – necessary programs for functioning in life; they come from karmic patterns or Soul's curiosity, or from genetic or societal patterns; predispositions; humans can have hundreds of them in unique combinations; major codes include power, love, sexuality, spirituality, honor, self expression, responsibility and wealth

Present, The – visceral, body-based moment; exists on all the levels of perception, but is anchored in the physical body because the body is in linear time

Presence – a state of being present, experienced as an electromagnetic phenomenon; can be structural or fluid, depending of the type of focus

Self – an individuated component of the Soul, anchored in the physical body

Shadow – multidimensional concept along with Light and Dark; the unconscious, hidden, shunned and judged energy that has not found integration; the power given away to the unconscious; there are two types of Shadow: the Golden and the Dark; the Golden is unrealized potential, while the Dark is false power.

Soul – a spark of God; individuated component of the Source; one with the Source yet separate from it; the Soul wants to experience reality through curiosity

Soul Contract – a plan for the incarnation, agreed upon before entering form; the agreement between the Soul and other entities (planet on which incarnation is to take place, governing energy council of that system, guides, future parents, siblings and people who might participate in lessons); contains plans to clear particular karma (old lessons) and desires to explore (new lessons); does not override free will, but sets up a range of possibilities for the lifetime

Sound – an energy that is thicker then light; produced by friction

Source – all that is, God/Goddess

Spherical time – Universal time; all times at once; mostly magnetic so that an identity is not necessary; involves no movement, speed or direction, no goal/destination; is always the now; can experience what has not yet happened linearly; coexists with linear time and is needed with linear time to create and manifest

Spirals of Consciousness – cyclical state of the Universe which involves periods of upward moving consciousness (waking up) and downward moving consciousness (falling asleep); it is part of the plan of Universal evolution

Time level – eighth level of the energy field of consciousness; fluid; human time level hold personal timelines and is an access to the spherical universal time; Earth's eighth energy level holds linear and spherical time as an intricate web of time connections, intersections and distortions

Timelines – linear time directions with a particular range of possible events chosen by the Soul; differentiated from each other by single experiences

Truth level – fifth level of the energy field of consciousness; structural; holds Self perception; records everything happening to us; has consciousness of sound; Earth's truth level consists of the information about the planet, its visitors, and us, and is also the level of many truths: Earth's truth about her journey and our truths

Unconditional level – sixth level of the energy field of consciousness; energy of interconnectedness and unconditional love from the Source flows through this level; fluid; Earth's sixth level also consists of the unconditional love frequency and is a home to angelic nonphysical beings

Unconditional love – acceptance without judgment

Universe – a thirteen dimensional system of conscious exploration through preset perceptory limitations, for each one of the dimensions has its own form of consciousness

Universal Pulse – a rhythmic transmission of intelligence between our own body/energy field, our Sun, the Galactic Sun (which is the black hole region in the center of this galaxy) and the Universal Central Sun (which is the conceptual center for this Universe)

Water – an elemental second dimensional energy; opposite of the Fire element (also known as a big blue wobbly thing that mermaids live in ☺)

About Author

I was born in Russia and from my early years have been practicing consciousness expansion healing work (which in Russia is called 'wholeness-making') with people and animals. I was born with a perceptual awareness of my birth process and a memory of where I came from prior to birth. I could see and read energies that were invisible to those around me and this ability, coupled with an intense curiosity, fueled my search for spiritual answers and an ever-expanding comprehension of how life works. I came to the United States from Russia, after the collapse of the Soviet Union, and learned English, worked many jobs, graduated from art school and then continued the healing/ teaching/creative work that I had begun in Russia.

I now live in Maine with my beloved husband Adam and my cat, Gypsy. I have an energy healing practice and I teach what I know. I work on all levels of the energy field of consciousness, from the conceptual/spiritual, through the unconditional and the truth levels, into the emotional and mental levels, anchoring the modifications in the subatomic and cellular. From many years of practice I have learned to do energy surgery which is the reconstruction of patterns that are torn or broken. I am able to read timelines and other lifetimes and assist in releasing or integrating judged experiences and old karma. I teach how to assess problem areas in the energy field and move blocks out of it. My work includes covering physical and nutritional questions and finding new wholistic solutions. I have studied science, history, archeology and astronomy in Russia/U.S. and have a BFA degree from the Art Institute of Boston.

I believe that true personal mastery and peace come from welcoming Soul into our physical bodies, leading to an experience of ecstasy that is Life.

For more information about workshops please visit Energy Pulse website

www.energypulsesource.com